Islam in China and the Islamic world

Gorgias Islamic Studies

21

Gorgias Islamic Studies spans a wide range of subject areas, seeking to understand Islam as a complete cultural and religious unity. This series draws together political, socio-cultural, textual, and historical approaches from across disciplines. Containing monographs, edited collections of essays, and primary source texts in translation, this series seeks to present a comprehensive, critical, and constructive picture of this centuries- and continent-spanning religion.

Islam in China and the Islamic world

A History of Chinese Scholarship

Alimtohte Shiho

2024

Gorgias Press LLC, 954 River Road, Piscataway, NJ, 08854, USA

www.gorgiaspress.com

Copyright © 2024 by Gorgias Press LLC

All rights reserved under International and Pan-American Copyright Conventions. No part of this publication may be reproduced, stored in a retrieval system or transmitted in any form or by any means, electronic, mechanical, photocopying, recording, scanning or otherwise without the prior written permission of Gorgias Press LLC.

2024

ISBN		ISSN 2637-3998
Hardback	978-1-4632-4587-0	
eBook	978-1-4632-4588-7	

This work was supported by the "NIHU Global Area Studies Program East Eurasian Studies Project" fund.

Library of Congress Cataloging-in-Publication Data

A Cataloging-in-Publication Record is available at the Library of Congress.

Printed in the United States of America

For my Uyghur people

TABLE OF CONTENTS

Table of Contents v
Acknowledgments vii
Preface... ix
Introduction 1
Part One. People, Institutions, Journals, and Academic
    Conferences 17
Part Two. Collation and Publication of Reference Books and
    Historical Materials... 33
Part Three. Research in the Field of History............................... 43
Part Four. Research in the Field of Religion—Centered on
    Chinese Islamic Studies....................................... 75
Part Five. Research in the Field of Religion—Centered on
    World Islamic Studies... 99
Part Six. Research in the Field of Philosophy 119
Part Seven. Research in Political and Social Fields 135
Part Eight. Research in Culture and Other Fields.................... 149
Summary. Islamic Studies in China 173
Appendix 1. Summary: Chinese Islamic Studies in the West... 179
Appendix 2. Summary: Chinese Islamic Studies in Japan 197
Appendix 3. A Survey of "Uyghurs" in Nanjing—Misconduct
    and Correct Analysis... 213
Bibliography.. 221

ACKNOWLEDGMENTS

I would like to express my gratitude to the National Institutes for the Humanities (NIHU) that has provided me with research opportunities. I am immensely grateful for the research environment provided by Tohoku University of Japan, in particular the Center for Northeast Asian Studies, and the teachers and administrators of the Institute. I especially want to offer thanks to Prof. TAKAKURA Hiroki (the Center for Northeast Asian Studies, Tohoku University) and Prof. Takashi Kuroda (Graduate School of International Cultural studies, Tohoku University). Thanks are also due to the Faculty of Oriental Studies, University of Oxford, in particular, Prof. Christopher Melchert. This project would not have been completed without the faculty's help and support. Thank you very much!

I would also like to thank my wife. My research work has meant that all childcare responsibilities have fallen to her. This was not easy. I am grateful to her beyond measure.

PREFACE

The academic history of Islam in China not only refers to the academic history of Chinese scholars' research on Chinese Islam but also includes various areas of research and publications of Chinese scholars on foreign Islam and Muslims. This includes the study of Islamic classics, such as the Quran and Hadith, and the fields of history, pedagogy, philosophy, politics, society, and culture. Islam and Muslims in different regions of foreign countries have different characteristics, and the research methods respect this reality. According to my previous research, academic research with contemporary significance began at the dawn of the 20th century. With the introduction of Western learning to the East, modern academic research methods impacted the study of Islam in China. There are four imams with high academic degrees, such as Ha Decheng, Wang Jingzhai, Da Pusheng, and Ma Songtin. Chen Hanzhang, Chen Yuan, and Chuan Tongxian are a few of the non-Muslim scholars joining the ranks of Islamic researchers.

There was little research on Islam and Muslims in China before the 20th century. The period from the beginning of the 20th century to the founding of new China (1949) can be regarded as the beginning period. The period from the founding of new China through its reform and development can be regarded as the intermediate period. During this period, due to various political movements and other social reasons, China's Islamic academic history and many other fields suffered setbacks, including stagnation to varying degrees. The period from reform and development to 2000 can be regarded as a prosperous period of Islamic academic research in contemporary China with the year

2000 serving as the dividing line in the evolution of modern Islamic academic history. During the period from 2001 to now, the subject has been clarified and its research methods diversified. Many industries and scholars have actively participated in this research field using the theories and methods of religious studies, ethnology, anthropology, sociology, history, philosophy, linguistics, culture, politics, and other disciplines to systematically study the historical, political, economic, cultural, and other phenomena of Islam and Muslims, laying a foundation for the further development of China's Islamic research.

INTRODUCTION

1 THE SIGNIFICANCE, PRELIMINARY RESEARCH, AND IDEAS OF THE PROJECT

1.1 The Significance of the Topic

"Academic history" is a research field with special value and significance. It emphasizes the need to provide a comprehensive and critical reflection on the history of research from an academic perspective and is the so-called "research" of research.

Over the past half century, China has accomplished a great deal in the study of Islam and established a certain disciplinary system. In the field of contemporary Islam and Muslim studies, the concept and methods of Chinese Islamic research open an unprecedented area of study. It is regrettable that, for a long time, few scholars conducted case studies or systematically organized the academic history of Islamic studies in China. For example, in the 1980s, Bai Shouyi[1] and Ma Tong,[2] respectively, published the

---

[1] Bai Shouyi (1909–2000) was a prominent Chinese Muslim historian, thinker, social activist, and ethnologist who revolutionized recent Chinese historiography and pioneered the heavy reliance on scientific excavations and reports. Philosophically a Marxist, his studies thus take a very class-centric view and reasoning. Born a son of a Hui merchant in Kaifeng, he became learnt Arabic from his mother and aunt. His principal work is A History of Chinese Muslims, Zhonghua Book Company.

[2] Ma Tong (1927–) is one of the best-known experts in the study of Islam and Hui history in China. He used to be a professor of Lanzhou University and Northwest University for Nationalities. He is the author of A Brief History of Chinese Islamic Sects and the Menhuan System (Ningxia People's Publishing, 2000), and other academic monographs. His main

papers "Several Opinions on Hui History Work"[3] and "Review and Prospects for Islamic Studies in the Five Northwest Provinces (Regions)"[4] regarding China's attitude towards the academic history of Islamic studies abroad. Little, however, has been written on the history of Chinese scholarship on Islam.

The significance of the academic history of Islam in China cannot be ignored as such achievements should be continuously referenced and relied on by the Chinese academic community. If we can learn from existing achievements and stand on the shoulders of our predecessors, we will have a broad perspective despite being small, which will inevitably lead to a qualitative transformation in domestic research.

1.2 Previous Studies

In recent years, the above issues have attracted the attention of Chinese scholars, and there have been significant achievements in the Islamic academic history of China to sort out and reflect upon. The most outstanding are the achievements of the Chinese Academy of Social Sciences.

For example, in 2008, Zhuo Xinping edited *Thirty Years of Religion in China Studies (1979–2008)*, and in 2011, he edited *Research on Contemporary Religion in China*. The section "Islamic Studies" in the 2008 book was jointly written by Zhou Xiefan and Li Lin, who stated, "The 30 years of [Chinese] reform and development also represent a new stage of academic research on Islam in China. We take these 30 years as a base line, looking back on the past and looking forward to the future to review the

---

research is into Islam in China and Hui nationality. The research involves many fields such as ethnic religious theory and policy, and its style pays attention to macro and theoretical research on the basis of micro and empirical research.

[3] Bai Shouyi, 1984, "Opinions on the study of the history of the Hui people," Social Sciences in Ningxia, Vol. 1, pp. 8–14. (白寿彝，"有关回族史工作的几点意见，"《宁夏社会科学》, 1984 年第 1 期，pp. 8 - 14.)

[4] Ma Tong, 1987, "Review and Perspective on the Research of Islam in the Five Northwestern Provinces," Ethno-National Studies in Gansu, Vol. 2, pp. 1–5. (马通，"对西北 5 省（区）伊斯兰教研究的回顾与展望，"《甘肃民族研究》, 1987 年第 2 期，pp. 1 - 5.)

INTRODUCTION

achievements, mistakes, gains, and losses of Islamic studies in China over the past 30 years, and to sort out the development stage in its logical context, not only [to] showcase existing achievements but also to reflect on existing problems."[5] This article briefly presents the academic study of Islam and Muslims in China from 1978-2008 from several perspectives, including a century long history of Islamic research, academic seminars, Chinese Islamic research, world Islamic research, reference books, data organization and academic publications, contemporary Islamic research, recent major issues, and disciplinary construction. In the 2011 edited volume, Xiefan and Lin write that their chapter, "aims to summarize and sort out the thoughts of contemporary Chinese scholars on the academic study of religion, so as to lay a solid foundation and make religious studies more prosperous and promising in the future."[6]

In addition, researcher Li Lin has successively published papers such as "Research on Islam in China: A Review of Academic History and Previous Studies," "Issues and Reflections on Contemporary Islamic Doctrine Research in China," "Issues and Reflections on Contemporary Islamic Law Research in China - Concurrently Discussing the Two Major Academic Traditions of Islamic Law Research," and "Trial Analysis of Issues and Mainlines in Contemporary Islamic Philosophy and Thought Research in China."[7] He defined the "academic history of Islam in China" and analyzed the stages in the evolution of that academic history, referring to the total amount of academic research on

---

[5] Zhou Xiefan and Li Lin, "Islamic studies," recorded in Zhuo Xinping's *Thirty Years of Religion in China Studies (1978-2008)*, China Social Sciences Press, October 2008 edition. (周燮藩 李林, "伊斯兰教研究" 载入卓新平主编《中国宗教学 30 年（1978-2008）》, 中国社会科学出版社，2008 年 10 月版，333 - 392 页)

[6] Zhou Xiefan and Li Lin, "Islamic studies, recorded in Zhuo Xinping (edit), *Research on Contemporary Religion in China*, China Social Sciences Press, December 2011. (周燮藩 李林, "伊斯兰教研究" 载入卓新平主编《当代中国宗教学研究》, 中国社会科学出版社，2011 年 12 月)

[7] Li Lin, 2011, "Analysis of Contemporary Islamic Philosophy in China: Issues and Mainlines of Ideological Research" *World Religious Studies*, Issue 5, pp. 142–148.

Islam conducted by Chinese scholars as "Chinese Islamic research," rather than "research on Islam in China."

The modern study of Chinese Islam began at the start of the 20th century and continued for half a century. During this period, as Western learning spread to the East, modern academic disciplines and research methods were introduced into the field of Islamic studies in China. The second half of the 20th century was the stage when the discipline of contemporary Islamic studies in China was finally established, but there was a prolonged pause after the 1949 establishment of the People's Republic of China due to various political movements and other social reasons. It was not until China's reform and development that significant progress was made. From 1978 to 2000, various debates, such as the "religious culture theory," also had a certain impact on the study of Islam in China. Islamic research is no longer limited to the study of Islamic history but is viewed as a cultural phenomenon with a vast system and rich content, analyzed and studied from multiple perspectives, including ideology, systems, and material culture.

Since the beginning of the 21st century, contemporary Islamic academic research in China has gradually matured. During this period, disciplinary awareness became clear and research theories diversified. Scholars are now able to use the theories and methods of religious studies, ethnology, anthropology, sociology, history, philosophy, linguistics, culture, politics, and other disciplines to interpret and analyze the ancient books and records, historical phenomena, and practical problems of Islam. Li Lin has provided his own discourse on several aspects of the academic history of Islamic studies in China with a high level of academic proficiency.[8] However, most of his research subjects are Muslims living on the mainland, and to some extent, he has overlooked relevant academic history issues in Xinjiang and other regions.

---

[8] Li Lin, "Research on Islam in China: sorting out and preceding the academic history," *China Social Science Daily*, February 2013. (李林, "中国伊斯兰教研究：学术史梳理与前", 《中国社会科学报》, 2013 年 2 月)

INTRODUCTION 5

Islam was introduced into China from the Arab and Central Asian regions in the middle of the 7th century. Due to the different customs, social history, environment, and cultural background of various ethnic regions, two major systems of Islam and its culture were formed in relation to the dissemination, development, and evolution of Chinese ethnic groups (e.g., Hui) and Turkic ethnic groups (e.g., Uyghur). For this reason, I place special emphasis on the ethnic and regional characteristics of China's Islamic academic history.

In addition to Lin's work, important contributions to the academic history of the study of Islam in China also include Xiao Xian and Gao Zhanfu's "Summary of Islamic Studies in China in the 20th Century,"[9] Wan Yaobin's "Reflections on the Study of Islam in China in the New Century,"[10] Zhang Ju ling's "Commentary and Review on Islamic Studies of the Hui Ethnic Group in China in the Early 20th Century,"[11] Gao Zhanfu's, "Review and Commentary on the Study of the Western Islamic Church in China,"[12] Habaoyu's "Academic Research and Characteristics of Islamic Law in China,"[13] and Habaoyu's

---

[9] Xiao Xian and Gao Zhanfu, "Summary of Islamic Studies in China in the 20th Century," *Northwest Ethnic Studies*, Issue 2, 2000, pp. 26–32. (高占福，"中国 20 世纪伊斯兰教研究综述"《西北民族研究》，2000 年第 2 期，26-32 页）

[10] Wan Yaobin, "Reflections on the Study of Islam in China in the New Century," *World Religious Studies*, 2000. (宛耀宾 等，"对新世纪中国伊斯兰教研究的思考"《世界宗教研究》，2000 年）

[11] Zhang Juling, "Commentary and Review on Islamic Studies of the Hui Ethnic Group in China in the Early 20th Century," *Hui Studies*, February 2000. (张巨龄，"20 世纪初中国回族伊斯兰研究述补及评"《回族研究》，2000 年 2 月）

[12] Gao Zhanfu, "Review and Commentary on the Study of the Western Islamic Church in China," *World Religious Studies*, December 2002. (高占福，"中国伊斯兰教西道堂研究的回顾与评述"《世界宗教研究》，2002 年 12 月）

[13] Habaoyu, "Academic Research and Characteristics of Islamic Law in China," *Hui Studies*, 2007, Issue 4, pp. 113–120. (哈宝玉，"中国伊斯兰教法的学术研究及其特点"《回族研究》2007 年第 4 期，113-120 页）

"Islamic Studies in China," [14] all of which discuss various issues related to the academic history of Islamic studies in China using different perspectives and methods from different fields.

The above research situates the study of Islam and Muslims in China within the academic history of religious studies, that is, the academic history of China's five major religions, and only in the length of a chapter with the overview not fully developed. The main purpose of my research on this topic is to sort out the evolutionary history of academic research on Islam and Muslims in China comprehensively and systematically in the form of a monograph, not only sorting out existing achievements but also classifying and analyzing them.

1.3 Research Ideas and Methods

The main purpose of this research project is to summarize and analyze modern Chinese research achievements pertaining to Islam and Muslims from the perspective of academic history in order to provide a foundation for researchers seeking to engage in related fields. The second is to provide later scholars with literature on the state of Islamic studies starting with the early 20th century. Its more profound significance lies in enabling scholars to fully recognize that sorting and summarizing existing academic achievements is an indispensable part of the research process, thereby enhancing the awareness of academic history research.

1. The title of this project has been designated as "Islamic Studies," so it is not only a study of the religion of Islam but also involves the historical, philosophical, political, social, and cultural fields of Islam. The research on Islam and Muslims in China is divided into two periods around the year 2000. It is worth reminding that the research methods for Chinese speaking Muslims and Turkic speaking Muslims vary in each period. Therefore, the author tries to use flexible methods while answering questions and to systematically analyze the research

---

[14] Habaoyu, "Islamic Studies in China," *West Asia and Africa*, 2010, Issue 4, pp. 50–52. (哈宝玉，"中国的伊斯兰研究"《西亚非洲》，2010 年第 4 期，50-52 页）

INTRODUCTION 7

trends of each period and stage. This involves monographs, academic papers, survey and research reports, and other sources.

2. China has achieved fruitful results in the process of researching Islam and Muslims. These include field research reports, literature research, translation research, folk research, and more. The author does his best to collect all the works and materials relevant to the research object, to classify and summarize them, read and understand them word for word, and then analyze and synthesize them, so as to express their thoughts correctly. Given that the domestic academic community is mostly unfamiliar with the works and ideas of these scholars, I often cite heavily to avoid misunderstandings. The materials used are as first-hand as possible, and all citations are categorized according to their own understanding.

3. The study of Islam and Muslims in China is paralleled by the complex history of China itself, and there are many complex factors related to different historical periods of Islamic research and publication. The political background of research cannot be ignored, but attention should also be paid to the characteristics of academic research that are not closely related to politics, that is, analyzing and commenting from an academic perspective. In the book, I analyze research achievements and publications related to politics and academic perspectives separately, and comment on their historical significance. I also offer a critique of the materials. The criteria for criticism are first whether the ideas themselves are logical and then whether the arguments are consistent with historical facts.

4. This book provides a foundational understanding of the overarching history of the academic study of Islam and Muslims in China by presenting systematic, comprehensive, and in-depth research achieved by collecting, organizing, and analyzing sources. In my current situation, I lack the ability to creatively propose new viewpoints to be recognized by the academic community. However, I strive to comprehensively collect, organize, and analyze data, and to describe the overall characteristics of China's research on Islam.

Finally, regarding the future prospects of this topic, it is well known that in today's era, English works hold a special position in the global academic community, greatly influencing the entire world's understanding of Islam in China.[15] The study of Islam and Muslims in China by Western academic circles such as Britain, France, Russia, Germany, the United States, and Japan, can serve as an important link in building China's Islamic research and should be paid attention to by Chinese scholars. Unfortunately, apart from a few papers, no scholars have collected and organized Western research literature in this regard, and of course, no systematic exploration has been conducted. I hope to fill this gap.

2 A BRIEF INTRODUCTION TO THE HISTORY OF ISLAM IN CHINA[16]

Islam in China has a history of more than 1,300 years. Introduced in the Tang Dynasty, the religion spread through the Song, Yuan, Ming, and Qing dynasties, and has endured different stages of development.

During the Tang Dynasty (618–907), Chinese Muslims were a small minority community. Centuries later, the northwest border of the Yuan Dynasty (1271–1368) was conducive to the spread and development of Islam in China because it was in an open state. Unlike in the Tang Dynasty, Muslims were all over China in this period: "In the Yuan Dynasty, there were many people who lived in Gansu" ("元时，回回遍天下，及是居甘肃者尚多").[17] The social centers of Islam increased dramatically. In the Ming Dynasty (1368–1644), Islam finally had a relatively fixed name and was referred to using terms such as "Huihui Jiao" (回回教), "Huigui Jiaomen" (回回教门), and "Hui Jiao" (回教). During this period, Chinese followers of Islam finally had a fixed

---

[15] Zhou Chuanbin, "Stones from Other Mountains: A Review of Western Studies on Chinese Hui Islam," *Northwest Ethnic Studies*, 2005, Issue 1, pp. 97–118. (周传斌， "他山之石—西方学界对中国回族伊斯兰教的研究述评" ，《西北民族研究》，2005 年第 1 期，97–118 页)

[16] "A brief introduction to the history of Islam in China," (Alimu Tuoheti, Islam in China – A History of European and American Scholarship, Gorgias Press, 232 pages, February 2021, pp. 6–14.)

[17] 《明史 西域传》 (*The History of Ming Dynasty: Biography of the Western Regions*)

INTRODUCTION 9

social designation—"Huihui people" (回回民). This is a milestone event in the development of Islam in China.

The formation of the Muslim community in the Ming Dynasty marked the end of the stage of Islamic conversion in China. In this respect, Sha Zongping states, "At the end of the Yuan Dynasty and the beginning of the Ming Dynasty, based on the common belief and common customs of life, the Hui nationality, today's Hui nationality, was formed with Islam as the link. The formation of Hui nationality means that Islam has a solid national foundation in Northwest China, just like in Xinjiang."[18]

Thus, Muslim society emerged. In the establishment period (i.e., the Tang, Song, and Yuan dynasties), the carrier of Islam was the individual Muslim, while the carrier in the Ming period was the social community. The community also played an important role in the religion's development in the Qing Dynasty (1644–1911) during which the degree of Islam's social infiltration was more profound, leading to a marked increase in its predominance. Saliently, in the early Qing Dynasty, the localization and contextualization of Islam in China was over.

During the Ming and Qing dynasties, a group of scholars engaged in the study of Chinese Islam emerged. They wrote on Islamic doctrine and cultural thoughts in Chinese, engaging a series of practices called "Yi Ru Quan Jing" (以儒诠经 – interpreting scriptures by Confucianism), "Yuan Ru Ru Men" (援儒入回 – assisting Confucianism into Hui), "Fu Ru Yi Xing" (附儒以行 – attaching Confucianism to practice), or "Yi Ru Jie Hui" (以儒解回 – interpreting Hui by Confucianism). Their works are rich and cover a wide range of topics. According to Bai Shouyi (白寿彝), the activities of these scholars in the Ming and Qing dynasties divide into two stages: "From Wang Daiyu to Liu Zhi is a stage. Ma Dexin and Ma Lianyuan are another stage. In the first stage, Jinling (金陵) is the main place for translation and expression, and its content is either a special translation or a

---

[18] Sha Zongping, 2004, *Arab-Islamic Studies in China*, Beijing University Publishing. (沙宗平，《中国的天方学》，北京大学出版社，2004 年，p. 49.）

special description of a theoretical system. Its interests are mostly limited to religious philosophy and religious canon system."[19]

Wang Daiyu and Liu Zhi were proficient in both Islam and the traditional culture of Confucianism. They explained Islamic classics in Chinese and explained Islam in relation to traditional Confucian thought. To his end, they created several Chinese Islamic classics:

Author	Work	Summary
王岱輿 Wang Daiyu (1580–1660)	《正教真诠》 Zhengjiao Zhenquan	This is divided into two volumes. The first volume mainly discusses the problem of recognizing the Lord, and the second volume mainly discusses religious lessons and the theoretical significance of personal cultivation. This book presents a systematic theory of "Trinity," specifically, "Zhenyi, Shuyi, Tiyi," and comprehensively interprets Islamic doctrines through Confucianism, which is the beginning of "interpreting Islam with Confucianism."
	《清真大学》 Qingzhen Daxue	This is a work of religious philosophy, divided into five parts: "Outline," "Zhenyi," "Shuyi," "Tiyi," and "General Introduction." This work makes a comprehensive and in-depth explanation of the theory of "Trinity" proposed in *Zhengjiao Zhenquan*, involving ontology, epistemology, and many other aspects, with strict logical argumentation and profound content. The purpose is to use Confucianism

---

[19] Bai Shouyi, 2000, *A Brief History of Islam in China*, Ningxia People's Publishing House. (白寿彝, 《中国回教小史》, 宁夏人民出版社, 2000 年, p. 75.)

INTRODUCTION 11

		to expound Islamic doctrine, or "interpreting Islam with Confucianism."
	《希真正答》 Xizhen Zhengda	Wu Liancheng, Wang Daiyu's disciple, reorganized and compiled his works under Wang's name according to the records of his classmates. The content of his book pertains to the "life of heaven and man" and other issues. It is a popular interpretation of the relevant themes of *Zhengjiao Zhenquan*.
张中 Zhang Zhong (1584– 1670)	《四篇要道》 Sipian Yaodao	Zhang Zhong explained foreign classics to his disciples, including Shaweichong, who made notes. Four volumes exist in total. As the book is a translation of the Persian *Chahār Kitāb*, it also initiated the practice of Chinese translation of Islamic texts in the Qing Dynasty.
	《归真总义》 Guizhen Zongyi	This work is based on the contents of Ashge's lectures and other classic translations. It discusses the ways of knowing Allah and human nature, and reflects on the philosophy of Sufism characterized by poverty and asceticism.
伍遵契 Wu Zunqi (1598– 1689)	《归真要道》 Guizhen Yaodao	*Mirsad* was written by Najm al -Din Razi (d. 1256), a Persian, in the middle of the 13th century and is a famous work on religious philosophy and cultivation with obvious Sufi foundations. Wu Zunqi translates it into classical Chinese and adds brief notes to translate it into the vernacular. He made full use of his knowledge and opinions, so it extends beyond mere translation.

马注 Ma Zhu (1640–1711)	《清真指南》 Qingzhen Zhinan	This comprises ten volumes, about 200,000 words. It is rich in content, involving the history, scriptures, philosophy, laws, astronomy, legends, and other aspects of Islam, and every insight and explanation is based on Arabic classics. This book further develops the discussion of the relationship between Islam and Confucianism, asserting that the two have almost the same social role. This is one of the early works to interpret and expound Islamic doctrines in Chinese using Confucian thought. It has the same purport as Wang Liu's works and is one of the seminal works in the formation of Chinese Islamic doctrine.
刘智 Liu Zhi (1662–1730)	《天方性理》 Tianfang Xingli	This work discusses the Islamic theory of life and nature from a philosophical point of view. In Liu Zhi's words, it is "the book of reason" and "the book of understanding." The book is divided into two parts: "Beijing" and "Tuzhuan." Ten general plans are attached to this Sutra to illustrate its contents, which is like Zhou Dunyi's on his thoughts. Indeed, like other Islamic works in China, they all use Confucianism to expound the "Hui Confucianism" of Islamic doctrines.
	《天方典礼》 Tianfang Dianli	Consists of twenty volumes and twenty-eight chapters compiled by Liu Zhi concerning Arabic and Persian classics, as well as Chinese (especially Confucian) classics, and then elaborated in his style and

INTRODUCTION 13

		language. The work is a masterpiece of Islamic principles and Confucianism. This book, "although contained in the book of heaven, [is] not different from the Confucian code." Therefore, it has been listed in the catalog of *Siku Quanshu*.
	《天方至圣实录》 Tianfang zhi Shengshilu	The book consists of twenty volumes and nearly 300,000 words. It describes in detail the experiences and achievements of Muhammad's life. Volume 17 is a Ma Zhu work annotated by Liu Zhi. Liu Zhi said that book, together with "Xingli" and "Dianli," shows the whole world that it is the most important "Hankitabu."
	《真境昭微》(Zhenjing Zhaowei), 《五功释义》(Wugong Shiyi), 《真功发微》 (Zhengong Fawei），《天方礼经》(Tianfang Lijing), 《礼书五功义》(Lishu Wugongyi), 《天方字母解义》(Tianfang Zimu Jieyi), 《天方三字经注解》(Tianfang Sanzijing Zhujie), 《续天方三字经》(Xu Tianfang Sanzijing), 《天方三字幼义》(Tianfang Sanziyouyi), 《教典释难》(Jiaodian Shinan), 《五更月偈》(Wugengyue Jie), 《醒世归真》(Xingshi Guizhen), 《穆圣仪行录及遗嘱》(Mosheng Yixinglu ji YIshu)	
马德新 Ma Dexin (1794– 1874)	《四典要会》 Sidian Yaohui	This book has four volumes and about 50,000 words. The "four classics" refers to these four parts. Yaohui refers to "the key to entering the Tao." Like Wand Daiyu, Ma Zhu, and Liu Zhi, Ma Dexin dedicated his life to establishing the ideological system of "Hui Confucianism," of Islam in China.

	《大化总归》 Dahua Zonggui	This book about doctrinal theory was written by Ma Dexin and Ma Kaike, and is divided into two volumes. We should give full attention to the discussion in combination with the Confucian viewpoint. Ma Kaike spoke highly of the book and talked about its significance from the ideological standpoint of Hui and Confucianism.
	《宝命真经（古兰经）直解》(Baoming Zhenjing (QURAN) Zhijie),《回归要语》(Huigui Yaoyu),《天理命运说》(Tianli Mingyunshuo)《性命宗旨》(Xingming Zongyi)《天方信源蒙引歌》(Tianfang Xingyuan Mengyinge),《祝天大赞》(Zhu Tian Dazan) His works involve many fields such as epistemology, life science, dogmatism, pedagogy, linguistics, and history, which have greatly influenced modern Chinese Islam and theory.	
蓝煦 Lian Xu	《天方正学》 Tianfang Zhengxue	This book is a work of religious philosophy on doctrinal theory, consisting of seven volumes and more than 800,000 words. This book, together with those of Wang Daiyu, Ma Zhu, and Liu Zhi, "is the same in theory and explanation as the book of various foresight." Its purpose is to demonstrate that "Hui" and "Ru" can coexist in the world.

These works embody an ideological theoretical system. Logical thinking, theoretical discourse, and discussions of values all apply Confucianism to explain Islamic doctrine. In a history of more than 1,350 years, it can be said that the understanding and research of Islam by Chinese scholars, including Chinese Muslim scholars, includes multi-perspective and multi-dimensional research processes such as external description and internal interpretation, objective transcendence, and subjective intervention, which constitute the forerunners of modern research.

INTRODUCTION 15

In the 20th century, the revolution of 1911 overthrew the rule of the Qing Dynasty, transitioning China into a new historical period, that of the Republic of China. In a short period, great changes took place in China's social politics, economy, and culture: the overthrow of the autocratic monarchy, the abolition of the bureaucratic system, rituals, and the imperial examination system, and the gradual transition of China from a semi-feudal, semi-colonial society to a modern one. This period was not only one of internal and external trouble but also reflective of the rising revolutionary movement. Because Chinese Muslims were no longer under the high-pressure policy of the Qing Dynasty and were influenced by the revolutionary trend of thought, they gradually stepped out of being a closed state, and their national consciousness gradually increased. They began to advocate for equal political status, improvements of economic life, the development of culture and education, and the freedom of religious belief. During this period, some religious people spread the ideas and classics of the Wahhabi school, and founded the Ihwani school in Gansu, Qinghai, and Ningxia in the northwest, and later spread it to Henan, Shandong, Hebei, and Xinjiang. This was the second sectarian differentiation of Islam in China since the introduction of Sufism in the late Ming and early Qing dynasties. After these two divisions, the formation of the modern Chinese Islamic faction pattern was apparent.

By 1949, the sects of Islam in China were Gedi, Sufism menhuan (including Hufeiye, Jiadilinye, Zhehlinye, Kubulinye), Xidaotang, Ihwani, Selefiye, and Yichan. Most Chinese Muslims belong to the Suni Hanafi school; the basic beliefs and doctrines of different sects are the same, but some differences are present in the details of certain disciplines and rituals. Under the influence of the national bourgeoisie in modern China, a group of Muslim scholars advocated the reform of religious education, the implementation of "two links of scriptures," and the establishment of new schools. This promoted the transformation of Chinese Muslim Temple Scripture education to modern education.

When Islam was introduced into China, due to the different customs, social history, environment, and cultural backgrounds of various ethnic regions, two major systems of Islam and its culture were formed in relation to the dissemination, development, and evolution of Chinese ethnic groups (e.g., Hui) and Turkic ethnic groups (e.g., Uyghur). Today, as a foreign and national religion, Islam in China has become one of the five major religions in the country and has a certain historical and contemporary impact on the Chinese nation.

PART ONE.
PEOPLE, INSTITUTIONS, JOURNALS, AND ACADEMIC CONFERENCES

It appears that the history of academic research on Islam and Muslims in China has been relatively long. However, according to academic standards, the research on Islam and Muslims both domestically and internationally in China began only after the 1980s. Although there were some research achievements in the academic community before the 1980s, some of which had high academic and reference value, strictly speaking, a systematic disciplinary system had not been formed, and like other disciplines, it had experienced long-term pauses during the Cultural Revolution. In fact, academic research in its true sense began only after the reform, with only thirty years of research on academic history as the research object.

1 PEOPLE

The academic history of Islamic studies in China should start with the four major imams who made significant contributions to the study of Islam. These imams were proficient in Arabic and Persian Islamic scriptures, and some were both proficient in English and familiar with the laws and teachings of Islam as well. They had unique insights into the calendar, produced many Chinese Islamic translations, and are respected by Muslims in China, enjoying a high social status. Because most of the Muslim population in China did not know Arabic, they had great difficulties reciting scriptures and understanding the teachings, plus they had little knowledge of religious rituals. Therefore, these imams were needed to educate,

18 ISLAM IN CHINA AND THE ISLAMIC WORLD

explain, guide, and practice on their behalf. These imams also lead Muslims in religious activities. These four major Muslim scholars are:

Ha Decheng (1888–1943) was born in Nanzheng. He made a pilgrimage to Mecca and studied in Egypt. In 1924, he returned to China as imam of the mosque on Zhejiang Road in Shanghai and initiated the establishment of the "Chinese Muslim Society" with Ma Ganghou. At the same time, the journal *MONTHLY* was founded to expound Islamic doctrine. After twenty-eight years in Shanghai, he established the Islamic normal school and served as dean of educational affairs. He also organized Ma Jian and others to translate the Quran and other classical Islamic literature.

Wang Jingzhai (1879–1949) was born in Tianjin. In 1922, he went abroad to study at Al-Azhar University in Egypt, then studied in Turkey, India, and other places. After pilgrimage in 1923, he returned to China and founded China Arab University in Tianjin. In 1927, he hosted the *YIGUANG* monthly and later went to Beijing's Jiaozi Hutong Mosque as Imam. In 1937, he established the Chinese Hui Anti-Japanese Association in Henan Province. He translated many works, such as *The Interpretation of the Quran* and the *Arabic Chinese Dictionary*.

Da Pusheng (1874–1965) was born in Liuhe. In 1907, he and Wang Kuan founded the Muslim normal school in Beijing's Niujie Mosque, and he became the president of Shanghai's Islamic normal school in 1928. In 1952, he participated in the initiation of the Chinese Islamic Association and was elected as the deputy director. He was also Dean of the Islamic Scripture Academy.

Ma Songting (1895–1992), born in Beijing, was a student of Dapu. He once went to Mecca for pilgrimage and after returning to China, served as Imam of Xidan Mosque in Beijing. In 1925, he established Chengda normal school with Jinan and later founded *YUEHUA* magazine. He went to Egypt for further study. He served as Deputy Director of the China Association for Iraq

1. PEOPLE, INSTITUTIONS, JOURNALS, CONFERENCES   19

> and Vice President of Islamic Economic College. He is the author of *Islam and Life.*

In addition to these religious scholars, Muslim scholars also engage in Islam-related research in universities and research institutions:

> Jinjitang (1908–1978) was of Hui nationality and the Beijing Tongxian people, and a historian and educator of Islam in modern China. He had more than ten seminal articles on the historical problems of Chinese Islam, religious sects, the theory of Muslim nationality, and the history of Laici Mosque.

> Bai Shouyi (1909–2000), of Hui nationality, was a historian, educator, and social activist. His life's research was in the field of history, and he made outstanding achievements in the history of Islam and Hui nationality in China. He edited *The Outline of Chinese General History*, published in 1980.

> Ma Jian (1906–1978) was a professor in the Oriental Language and Literature Department of Peking University. His published works include *History of Arab Philosophy, Arabian Peninsula, General History of Arabia, Overview of Chinese Islam, Academic Movements of Muslim Sages, The Status of Arabic in International Politics, Sword of Muhammad, Brief Biography of the Holy Muhammad,* and the *Arabic Chinese Dictionary.* He also translated and published a Chinese version of the Quran.

At the beginning of the 20th century, most scholars studying Islam and Muslims in China were Chinese Muslim scholars, but there were also non-Muslim scholars such as Chen Tan[1] and Chen

---

[1] Chen Yuan, "A Brief History of Hui Hui's Entry into China," *initially published in the Monthly Journal of Chinese Studies at Peking University Research Institute*, Volume 25, No. 1, 1927, titled "The Origins and Flows of Hui Hui's Entry into China," later published in *the Eastern Journal*, Volume 25, No. 1928, changed to its current name. (陈垣，《回回教入中国史略》（初载《北京大学研究所国学门月刊》1927 年第 25 卷第 1 号，题为《回回教进中国的源流》，后刊于《东方杂志》1928 年第 25 卷第号，改为今名）

Hanzhang. [2] The work of these scholars has been widely recognized by the academic community. Their initial research focused on the history and classics of Islam in China, but later, under the influence of Western styles of learning, such as textual research historiography, Marxist historiography, and Western positivist historiography, they began to use new methods to study the history, doctrine, and law of Islam and Muslims abroad, as well as contemporary issues and many other fields. With their unremitting efforts, they established a solid theoretical and practical foundation for the establishment of various research institutions and the emergence of many outstanding scholars after the period of Chinese reform.

2 Institutions and Academic Journals

2.1 Institutions

In 1964, the Institute of World Religions of the Chinese Academy of Social Sciences was established as a state-level, specialized institution for religious academic research, with resources dedicated to Buddhism, Christianity, Islam, and Taoism, as well as religious research magazines and scientific research offices. Among them, the Islamic research office is the only academic research institution engaged in the study of Islam and its related topics, which can be regarded as the beginning of a new stage. However, many Chinese academic research institutions, including those supporting Islamic Studies, have suffered setbacks for more than ten years.

The departments set up by higher authorities and the funding sources of research institutions can be divided into the following categories:

Governmental agency	Department of Islam; Institute of World Religions; Chinese Academy of Social Sciences; Research on Islam – State Bureau of Religious Affairs

---

[2] Chen Hanzhang, 1926, "History of Chinese Islam," *Historiography and geoscience*, Vol.1, pp. 16–22.

1. PEOPLE, INSTITUTIONS, JOURNALS, CONFERENCES   21

Social science research institutions	Ningxia Institute of Social Sciences and Institute of Islamic States in the Middle East; Gansu Institute of Nationalities; Institute of Religion, Xinjiang Academy of Social Sciences
Scientific research institutions in colleges and universities	Department of Religious Studies, School of Philosophy and Religion, Central University for Nationalities, and related research departments in the School of Nationalities and Society; The related research departments of Northwest University for Nationalities; Southwest University for Nationalities; Central South University for Nationalities; Qinghai University for Nationalities; Department of Philosophy, Peking University; Shanghai Institute of Foreign Languages; Middle East Research Institute of Northwest University; Yunnan University; Xinjiang University; Xinjiang Normal University; other relevant research departments of colleges and universities.
Non-governmental	Xi'an Islamic Culture Research Association and other folk social and cultural research academic organizations

The Islam Research Office of the Chinese Academy of Social Sciences takes the leading position in the field of domestic Islamic research and has great influence in the world. Its research areas include Islamic history, Islamic Sharia, Sufism, Chinese Islam, Islam and international issues, ethnic issues, and so on. The Ningxia Institute of Social Sciences founded the quarterly *Journal of Hui Muslim Minority Studies* in 1991, which is still influential today. Another one of their many achievements is the establishment of the editorial department of *The Encyclopedia of Hui Nationality in China*.

In Gansu Province, there is the Provincial Institute for Nationalities. Established in 1959, the Institute is a scientific research institution specializing in ethnic and religious issues in Gansu and Northwest China. After the founding of the Institute for the Study of Nationalities, it organized a systematic survey of the ethnic minorities in Gansu Province, collected valuable first-hand information, and made a lot of progress in the area of ethnic studies. It has completed the "Five Series of Chinese Minority Issues,"[3] issued by the National Committee for Democracy and People's Livelihood, and successively compiled and published monographs and anthologies such as *Collection of Paintings in China's Ethnic Minority Areas*[4] and *Research on Muslim Social Problems in Northwest China.*[5]

In Xinjiang, there is mainly the Xinjiang Folk Culture Research Center of Xinjiang University and Xinjiang Islam Research Center of Xinjiang Normal University. The folk culture research center was established in 2007 based on the folklore teaching and research section of the College of Humanities. The center is known for its use of the latest foreign folklore theory, specializing in Turkic ethnic groups, Islam, and culture related research.

2.2 Academic Journals

Over the years, many Chinese research institutions and academic units in the field of Islamic Studies have sponsored their own journals to introduce the latest research results, academic trends, and relevant information. These academic journals can be divided

---

[3] "China's ethnic minorities," "A series of brief history of China's ethnic minorities," "A series of brief chronicles of China's ethnic minority languages," "A series of books on China's ethnic minority autonomous areas," "A series of social and historical investigation materials of China's ethnic minorities". China's State Commission for Ethnic Affairs began organizing editing in 1958 and in 1991. 400 copies of the original edition were published by more than 30 publishing houses across the country.

[4] Chief Editorial Committee of China ethnic minority area painting series, 1986, "Collection of paintings in ethnic minority areas of China," Ethnic Publishing House.

[5] Gao zhanfu, 1991, "Research on the social problems of Muslims in Northwest China," Ganzhen Nationality Press.

1. People, Institutions, Journals, Conferences   23

into the following categories according to the types of sponsoring departments:

Government office	The Institute of World Religions of the Chinese Academy of Social Sciences sponsored *Studies in World Religions* and *World Religious Cultures*; The State Administration of Religious Affairs sponsored *The Chinese Religion*
Social science research institutions	Ningxia Social Sciences publish *Ningxia Social Sciences* and *Journal of Hui Muslim Minority Studies*; Gansu Institute of Nationalities publish *Gansu Institute of Nationalities*; Xinjiang Social Sciences publish *Xinjiang Academy of Social Sciences*
University scientific research institutions	*The Arab World* published by Shanghai Institute of Foreign Languages; *Northwest Ethnic Studies* and *Chinese Hui Studies* by Northwest University for Nationalities; *Qinghai Ethnic Studies* by Qinghai Institute for Nationalities; *Middle East Studies* by the Institute of Middle East Studies at Northwestern University; *Journal of Central University for Nationalities*; *Journal of Northwest University for Nationalities*; *Journal of Northwest Second Institute for Nationalities*; *Journal of Yunnan University for Nationalities*; *Journal of Xinjiang University*
China Islamic Association	*Chinese Muslims* by the China Islamic Association; *Shanghai Muslims* by the Shanghai Islamic Association; *Shaanxi Muslims* by the Shaanxi Islamic Association; *Gansu Muslims* by Gansu Islamic Association; *Qinghai Muslims* by Qinghai Islamic Association; *Huiwei Muslims in Hunan Province* by Hunan Islamic Association; *Xinjiang*

	Muslims (Uyghur version, Kazak version) by Xinjiang Islamic Association, etc.
Non-governmental	*Research on Islamic Culture* sponsored by Xi'an Islamic Culture Research Association

These journals publish academic research on Islam and Muslims but there are also religious journals, university journals, and other periodicals that publish different types of Islam-related papers.

Studies in World Religions, founded in 1979, is the most authoritative academic journal in the field of religious studies in China. It is edited by Zhuo Xinping with assistant editor Huang Xianian and publishes important materials in religious studies at home and abroad. The representative Islamic academic journal is the *Journal of Hui Muslim Minority Studies*. The quarterly *Journal of Hui Studies* was approved by the State Press and Publication Administration in 1990 and officially established in 1991. It was originally sponsored by the Hui Islamic Institute, but the Ningxia Academy of Social Sciences took it over in 2001. These journals publish a large number of academic papers and related articles, and play an important role in promoting the development of domestic Islamic Studies.

3 ACADEMIC CONFERENCES

Before the period of Chinese reform and development, there were few academic conferences on Islam and Muslims in China. In February 1979, the World Religion Research Institute held a national conference on religious research planning in Kunming. This conference marks the beginning of Chinese academic conferences related to Islam. In the spirit of the conference, a symposium on Islamic Studies in the five northwest provinces was held in Urumqi in 1979. The Institute of World Religions agreed with the relevant institutions of the five northwest provinces to hold annual regular Islamic academic seminar.

1. People, Institutions, Journals, Conferences 25

The First Five Seminars on Islam in the Five Provinces and Regions in Northwest China						
Date & Place	Theme	Host	Participants	Papers	Published Proceedings	
November 10–20, 1980 / Yinchuan	Chinese Islam in Qing Dynasty	Ningxia Institute of Social Sciences	More than 80	47	"On Islam in China in the Qing Dynasty"	
October 10– 21, 1981 / Lanzhou	Spread and development of Islam in China and its historical role	Gansu Institute of Nationali ties	151	65	"Islam in China"	
August 18– 26, 1982 / Xining	Special characteristics of Islam in China; Evolution, differentiation, and social influence of Islamic sects and officials; Ethnic education in history; Islam and ethnic relations.	Religious Bureau of Qinghai Province	More than 120	More than 80	"Studies on Islam in China"	
November 22–26, 1983 / Xi'an	How Islam serves the construction of two civilizations	Shaanxi Academy of Social Sciences	88	102	"Collection of studies on Islam in China"	

August 22–27, 1986 / Urumqi	History of the spread and development of Islam in China		112	79	

The Seminar on Islam in the five provinces of northwest China was a national academic activity with far-reaching theoretical and practical significance that was directly related to Islam and Muslims in China and the world. However, the second round of Islamic academic seminars in the five northwest provinces has not been launched. Since 1983, the Symposium on Islamic Literature and History Along the Southeastern Coast has been held annually, and the National Symposium on the History of Hui Nationality has been held biannually.

To continue the momentum and promote the development of Islamic Studies, the World Institute of Islamic Studies held three national Islamic academic seminars in Beijing from 1987 to 1990.

Date	Theme	Participants
August 21–26, 1987	The disciplinary study of the history of Islam in China, sects of Islam in China, and the development of Islam after the Second World War	More than 60
September 12, 1990 (Under the name "Seminar on the History of Islam in China")	How Islam enriched and developed national culture after its entry into China and how to accept the influence of Chinese traditional culture	More than 40
October 19–21, 1990	Characteristics of Islam after WWII; The division of Islamic stages after the war; Issues related to the study of Islam in China	More than 80

1. PEOPLE, INSTITUTIONS, JOURNALS, CONFERENCES   27

Since 1998, with the development of Islamic academic research in depth and breadth, a series of significant seminars have been held.

Meeting name	Date/place	Theme	Host(s)
Academic Seminar "Islamic Revival Movement"	October 25–26, 1988 / Beijing	Rise of and reasons behind the Islamic revival movement, its current situation, characteristics, and influence	Institute of West Asia and Africa, Chinese Academy of Social Sciences, China Asian African Society, and China Middle East Society
International Seminar "Islam and Modernization in Northwest China"	October 8–11, 1991 / Xi'an	Islam, the foreign development of Northwest China, and the development of Muslim nationality; Islamic economic thought and modernization; Foreign Islamic Reform Movement and modernization	Northwestern University and Adenauer Foundation in Germany
Symposium "Islamic Culture and China"	October 14–17, 1991 / Jinan	The introduction, reasons for, and development of	Jinan Islamic Association; Department of Philosophy,

		Islam in China; problems in the dissemination and development of Islam in China	Shandong University; Shandong Oriental Philosophy Research Association
International Symposium "Maritime Silk Road and Islamic Culture"	February 21–26, 1994 / Quanzhou, Fujian	The spread and influence of Islamic culture in countries along the Silk Road; friendly relations between China and Muslim countries; Muslim contributions to navigation and trade	UNESCO Silk Road Project Organization, China Maritime Silk Road Research Center, and 8 other institutions jointly
Academic Seminar "Contemporary Islamic Revival Movement"	June 16–18, 1995 / Ma'anshan, Anhui	Development, nature, and impact of the Islamic revival movement after the Cold War	Middle East Research Center of Shanghai Institute of International Studies
Seminar "Islamic Arab Philosophy"	October 9, 1996 / Jinan	Ideological characteristics and historical influence of Islamic Arab philosophy	Department of Philosophy, Shandong University; Shandong Oriental Philosophy Research

1. PEOPLE, INSTITUTIONS, JOURNALS, CONFERENCES 29

			Association and Jinan Islamic Association

From 1996 to 1999, Xi'an Islamic Culture Research Association held three Islamic culture seminars in Xi'an:

Meeting name	Year	Theme	Papers and Published Proceedings
Islamic Culture and Real Life	1996	Contemporary Muslim national culture, education, science, and figures	30 papers submitted; *The Treatise on Islamic Culture* (published by Religious Culture)
Jing Tang Education	1997	Jing Tang education, Islamic education	71 papers submitted: *Research on Islamic Culture* (Ningxia People's Publishing House)
21st Century and Islamic Culture, Islamic Studies, and the Chinese Nation	1999	History, present situation, and future of Hui and Islamic culture	More than 60 papers submitted; edited as a collection on Islamic culture

The conference on Jing Tang education marked the first time this practical theme was discussed comprehensively and systematically, including the educational and related economic issues of concern to the Muslim public. Nearly 200 experts and scholars attended the Third Islamic Culture Seminar held in Xi'an, and 163 papers were received, promoting the study of Islam in China. The achievements of Islamic cultural research during this period are reflected in the topics and outcomes of the above-mentioned conferences. Since entering the 21st century, especially in the past few years, the number of conferences on Islamic research has decreased. Conferences with the theme of Islamic and Muslim studies include:

Meeting Name	Date / Place	Theme	Host(s)
Symposium on the History and Development of Islam in China	December, 2001 / Beijing	History, development, and future of Islam in China	Islamic Association of China
Seminar on the Current Research Status of Hui Studies and Islam	September 21, 2004 / Yinchuan	Trends and problems in Hui Studies and in the study of Hui Islam	Ningxia Academy of Social Sciences
Seminar on Chinese Scripture Jingtang Jiaoyu	January 21–22, 2007 / Lanzhou	Development, problems, countermeasures, and direction of Chinese Scripture Education	Sponsored by Lanzhou University's Institute of Islamic Culture
Symposium on Islam and Building a Harmonious Society	2006 年 10 月 October 2006	Muslims of all ethnic groups participate in building a harmonious society	Islamic Association of China
Symposium on the Worldview of Hui Confucianism and the Contemporary Value of	June 2011 / Beijing	The worldview of Hui Confucianism and Chinese Islam through four topics: literature and text, philosophy and theology, civilization and	Peking University

1. PEOPLE, INSTITUTIONS, JOURNALS, CONFERENCES   31

| Chinese Islamic Research | | culture, history and reality | |
| Symposium on Chinese Islam and Chinese Culture | December 2012 / Beijing | Islam and Chinese traditional culture through four topics: literature and text, philosophy and theology, civilization and culture, history and reality | Peking University |

Academic seminars with the word "Islam" in the title are rare. These conferences attract many scholars with interdisciplinary theory and interreligious vision that promote the development of Islamic research in China. A few interdisciplinary and interreligious conferences are listed below:

Meeting Name	Date / Place	Theme	Host(s)
International Symposium on Zheng He's Voyages to the West and Dialogue among Civilizations	June 30 to July 3, 2005 / Yinchuan	Zheng He made seven voyages to the west, visited more than 30 countries, and discussed issues such as establishing friendly relations with people of all countries and effectively promoting their economic development	Ningxia Academy of Social Sciences; Cultural Office of the Iranian Embassy in China
Nanjing University Harvard Yanjing Civilization	June 16–18, 2006 / Yunnan	Global significance of dialogue among civilizations; dialogue between Hui and Confucianism in China in the time of	Nanjing University, Harvard University, and

Dialogue Forum		globalization; east Asian knowledge in global development; global significance of indigenous knowledge in Chinese Muslim society; local knowledge and cultural innovation	Yunnan University
The Second International Symposium on Hui Studies	September 3–6, 2006 / Shahu, Ningxia	Hui studies in a global context; dialogue between civilizations and Hui Confucianism; discipline and methodology of Hui studies; history and reality of Hui nationality in Central Asia; history of communication between Chinese Muslims and Muslims in central Asia and west Asia	Chinese Hui society
Symposium on Religious Dialogue and Harmonious Society	June 5–6, 2007 / Lanzhou	Religious dialogue and harmonious society; history and present situation of Christianity in northwest China	Lanzhou University

PART TWO.
COLLATION AND PUBLICATION OF REFERENCE BOOKS AND HISTORICAL MATERIALS

1 REFERENCE BOOKS

The collation of reference books and historical materials has become an extremely important part of the discipline of Islamic Studies research over the past thirty years and has been highly regarded by various state and academic organizations. The proudest achievements in the research and publication of reference books are as follows:

Compiled by the Editorial Committee of *China Islamic Encyclopedia* Published by Sichuan Dictionary Publishing House		
The book is divided into three parts: frontier, example, and Islam		
	Entry classification directory	Islam, Islamic law, Islamic education, Islam, Tianfang religion, orthodox religion, Kaitian ancient religion, halal religion, Islam
	Teachings derived from the classics	The Quran, Haiting, Haitie, heting, fatiha, fadihai, ayeti qursi, the 18th section, the 18th surai, qurat, yinzil, zahur, the name of the Quran, gurani, Fogang, mshafu, juzwu, Hizbu, surai, sol, ayeti, ayat Quran chapter initials, muhakaem, mteshabih, menopause, nasih, mansuhh

Sunni Sutra	Summary of Quran interpretation, Tiberi Sutra annotation, Razi Quran annotation, the key to the mystery, Badawi Quran annotation, Ibn kesir Quran annotation, zhelalaini Quran annotation, concise Quran annotation, general theory of Quran studies
Shia scripture annotations	Aas Carey's notes, Jingyi Hui Jie, Sufi school notes, Quran note, the quintessence of the Quran, Ruha Bellani, Moore's Tai Chi Lai school notes, and Kashav's notes
Modern classics note	The Quran notes, the notes of the Quran, the Quran essence, Rhyme translation of the Quran, Tong's translation of the Quran;
Appendix	List of phonetic order of Chinese characters, Stroke index of the first character of the entry, Chronology of Islamic personnel, Genealogy of major Islamic dynasties, Genealogy of twelve imams of Shia, Profile of Chinese ethnic minorities who believe in Islam, Postscript

The *China Islamic Encyclopedia* is one of the key research projects of philosophy and social sciences during the national "Seventh Five-Year Plan" period (1986–90). This project has been planned, designed, organized, edited, and processed since 1987 and is the first large-scale specialized reference book to introduce comprehensive and systematic knowledge of Iran to China. The publication won the second National Book Award (1995) and the first National Dictionary Award (1995).[1]

The *Islamic Dictionary*, edited by Jin Yijiu, is a medium-sized research work that was difficult to compile. It includes 3,090 entries covering the history, theories, and current situation of Islam from eleven different aspects, and reflects the professional strength and quality of Islamic research in China. The dictionary

---

[1] Compiled by the Editorial Committee of China Islamic encyclopedia, 1994, "*China Islamic Encyclopedia*," Sichuan Dictionary Publishing House, p.773. (中国伊斯兰百科全书编辑委员会编写,《中国伊斯兰百科全书》, 四川辞书出版社出版, 1994 年)

2. COLLATION AND PUBLICATION OF BOOKS AND MATERIALS 35

is one of the most popular professional research tools in China because it has simple and concise explanations, accurate and fluent expression, vast content, and wide application.[2]

The Religious Dictionary (1998), under Editor in Chief Ren Jiyu, increased the number of entries to nearly 12,000 and the number of words by about 3.7 million. To live up to its name, the editorial board decided to change the project's title to the *Great Dictionary of Religion*. The book has 11,970 entries on topics related to religion, Buddhism, Christianity, Islam, Taoism, Confucianism, and many other traditions. For each religious system, it introduces its sectarian organization, historical figures, terminology, doctrines and theology, scriptures and works, major rituals, festivals, temples, sacred sites, and gods. The information is rich and the details appropriate. Islam has the most entries, and the citations of the Quran are based on Ma Jian's translation published by China Social Sciences Press.[3]

There is also *The Islamic Dictionary* (2001), which has 1,932 entries and is more convenient for professionals.[4]

Related to it, *The Religious Dictionary* was published in 1981, with a total of about 7,000 entries that cover topics in Buddhism, Christianity, Islam, Taoism, some ethnic minority religions in China, Chinese folk religions, and other religious traditions. This is the first book on religion published in New China. At the time, it met the needs of society and attracted the attention of academic and religious circles at home and abroad. There are two shortcomings to this dictionary: first, some of the resources used were slightly old and failed to reflect the religious situation of the time; second, the religious categories used in the book are not complete and need to be supplemented. Therefore, preparations

---

[2] Jin Yijiu (edited), 1997, "Islamic dictionary," Shanghai Dictionary Publishing House, p. 771. (金宜久, 《伊斯兰教辞典》, 上海辞书出版社, 1997 年)

[3] Ren Yuji (edited), 1998, "religious dictionary," Shanghai dictionary press. (任继愈(主编), 《宗教大辞典》, 上海辞书出版社, 1998 年)

[4] Jin Yijiu (edited), 2001, "little dictionary of Islam," Shanghai Dictionary Publishing House, p. 1 (directory). (金宜久, 《伊斯兰教小辞典》, 上海辞书出版社，2001 年)

36 ISLAM IN CHINA AND THE ISLAMIC WORLD

for revision had to be made soon after the publication of the dictionary.[5]

Indices of research data, theses, and ancient books include *Brief List of Chinese Islamic Thesis Data (1949–1980)*, *Important Materials Such as Bibliographic Indices of Ancient Islamic Books in Xinjiang*, and *Index of Hui Research Materials*.

2 COLLECTIONS OF HISTORICAL MATERIALS

An important focus in the study of Islam in China is the collection and sorting of historical data. This task falls into two categories: 1) to collect and arrange rare historical materials pertaining to Chinese Islam overall and 2) to compile localized Islamic history materials.

In 1994, Ma Baoguang edited *The Series of Chinese Hui Classics* that contains twenty-one kinds of Islamic Chinese texts, translated into both ancient and modern Chinese. It is divided into six volumes with about 3.5 million words. This is a large set of vernacular translations of ancient books and was a difficult project requiring a high level of skill on the part of the researchers.[6]

In 1998, the Office of the Planning Group for the Collation and Publication of Ancient Books of Ethnic Minorities in Ningxia photocopied and published the first volume of *The Compilation of Ancient Books of Hui and Chinese Islam*, which includes fifteen kinds of early Chinese Islamic documents divided into nine volumes and thread bound. This is a large collection of photocopies of ancient books.[7]

Another publication that deserves recognition is *Selected Reference Articles on the History of Islam in China (1911–1949)*

---

[5] Ren Yuji (edited), 1981, "The religious dictionary," Shanghai Dictionary Publishing House. (任继愈(主编),《宗教大辞典》,上海辞书出版社, 1981 年)

[6] Ma Baoguang (compiled), 1994, "Chinese Hui Classics Series," (internal data). (马宝光主编,《中国回族典籍丛书》,以内部资料出版, 1994 年)

[7] Ningxia minority ancient prose collation and publication plan, 1998, "The compilation of ancient books of Hui and Chinese Islam," Tianjin Ancient Books Publishing. (宁夏少数民族古籍整理出版规划小组办公,《回族和中国伊斯兰教古籍资料汇编》1998 年)

2. COLLATION AND PUBLICATION OF BOOKS AND MATERIALS 37

compiled by Li Xinghua and Ma Jinyuan (1985). The book contains 197 papers, investigations, essays, reports, and translations on the history and culture of Islam in China that were scattered throughout Chinese newspapers and series, totaling more than one million words. This volume enables previously scattered data to be collected and sorted in a systematic and comprehensive fashion, saves several historical documents, and provides rich reference materials for researchers.[8]

Yu Zhengui and Yang Huaizhong collected 580 ancient and modern documents and books, compiled them by classification, and wrote abstracts, thus making a systematic summary of Islamic literature before 1992 that is very useful.[9] In order to save and preserve the historical materials of the Hui nationality, they decided to systematically collect written and oral traditions in Chinese, Arabic, and Persian, and other texts related to the history of the Hui nationality throughout the country, including historical classics, biographies, genealogies, literary inscriptions, representative Islamic materials, menhuan sect materials, and modern Hui newspapers and periodicals. The materials collected date as early as the Tang and Song Dynasties and end with the founding of the people's Republic of China in 1949.[10] With the subsequent publication of *The Series of Chinese Hui Ancient Books*, more new materials and rare documents will be available to researchers.

The Collection of Chinese Religious Historical Documents is the first large-scale series of photocopies of ancient books in China that collects the historical documents of its major religions. The series has a total of 180 volumes, divided into five parts:

---

[8] Li Xinghua, Ma Jinyuan (edited), "Selected references to the history of Islam in China (1911–1949)," Ningxia people's publishing house, 2 books. (李兴华、马今源编，《中国伊斯兰教史参考文选编（1911-1949），1985 年)

[9] Yu Zhengui, Yang Yizhong, 1993, "Abstracts on the writing and translation of Chinese Islamic Literature," Ningxia people's publishing house, p.65. (余振贵、杨怀中，《中国伊斯兰文献著译提要》，1993 年)

[10] Ningxia minority ancient books sorting and publishing plan, 2000 "Chinese Hui ancient books series," p. 1 (Preface). (宁夏少数民族古籍整理出版规划小组，《中国回族古籍丛书》，2000 年)

"Buddhism Outside Tibet," "The Collection of Three Caves," "The Qingzhen Scripture," "The Eastern Gospel," and "The Folk Treasure Volume." It contains more than 1,100 types of religious classics, inscriptions, and documents from previous dynasties through the beginning of the 20th century. In this collection of Chinese religious historical documents, only the "Buddhism Outside Tibet" and "Three Caves Collection" volumes include Buddhist and Taoist documents from outside Tibet; the folk division contains literary scrolls; and the Qingzhen scripture and eastern gospel divisions are the first systematic and comprehensive compilation of historical documents of Chinese Islam and Christianity. All collections are drawn from domestic universities, public libraries, and museums, most of which are rare and isolated books on the verge of loss, or important documents and materials published for the first time.

This book is the first comprehensive and systematic collation of Chinese Islamic documents and classics, including nearly 200 kinds of important documents and about twenty-five million words published across twenty-five volumes. It not only includes the earliest engraved version of the Quran in Chinese history, the precious copy of the Quran from the Qing Dynasty, and the Hui astronomical calendar from the Ming Dynasty, it also publishes important folk copies that were often ignored in the past. It is an invaluable resource for the study of Islam in China, and its importance is self-evident in academic circles where it is highly valued. The documents compiled in this book cover a wide range of topics, from scripture translation to minor miscellaneous studies, from doctrinal interpretation to enlightenment reading, from astronomical calendar to medical drugs, from etiquette and law to Sufism, and from historical and geographical records to inscriptions and local chronicles. It significantly reflects the depth and breadth of the Islamic Chinese social culture, including the spread, development, and evolution of Islam in China, and demonstrates the relationship between religion and nationality, specifically the relationship between Islam and the various Chinese ethnic groups who adhere to Islam. It also enables researchers to explore the characteristics of Islamic culture, the integration of Islam with traditional Chinese society and

2. COLLATION AND PUBLICATION OF BOOKS AND MATERIALS 39

mainstream ideas, Muslim scholars' contributions to promoting religious teaching, the history of Chinese religion, the history of Chinese Islam, the history of Chinese ethnic relations, the history of Chinese Hui nationality, the history of Chinese thought and the history of cultural exchanges between China and foreign countries, all of which are essential in the academic study of Islam in China. [11]

Another achievement in this regard is *The Collection of Hui History* (1984), which contains sixty research papers from 1949 to 1979 with a comprehensive index of Hui history research papers from the same period.

Types of Publications	Names of Publications
Important local data sets	Xinjiang religious research materials; Abstract of historical materials of ethnic religion in Northwest China; Selected materials of Quanzhou Hui genealogy; Historical materials of Xidaotang; Historical materials of the Hui nationality in Sadian
Historical investigation reports	Tuomao people in Qinghai and their relationship with Islam; Investigation on the social history of Hui nationality in Yunnan; Investigation on Islam in Kashgar and Hotan areas of Xinjiang; Investigation on Yichan and Wahhab sects of Islam of Uyghur nationality in Xinjiang
Excavation and arrangement of ancient books	Biography of the Department of Confucian classics; Beijing Niu Jie Zhi Shu - Gang Zhi; Kremer's interpretation of enlightenment; Kublinye pedigree of Islam in China -- dawantau official; A brief history of Chinese Islam; A collection of the history of zehringer's orthodoxy; Taizi Gongbei Ma Ming and Qing Dynasties sages wear a brief; Halal

---

[11] Zhou xiefan, 2006, "preface to the halal ceremony," research on world religions, Vol.2, pp. 147–148. (周燮藩," 清真大典前言"《世界宗教研究，2006 年第 2 期)

	roots; Saidianchi genealogy; Ganjiaopu family tree in Nanhai; Selected genealogies of Hui nationality in Liaoning; Record of accumulated stones; Quanzhou Islamic religious stone carvings; Selected edition of Hebei halal steles, plaques and couplets

The collecting and sorting of precious documents has opened a new field for the study of Islam in China and enabled in-depth research. There are additional collections relating to more specific regions and topics, such as *Selected Papers on Quanzhou Islam* compiled by Quanzhou Overseas Transportation History Museum and Quanzhou History Research Association (Fujian People's Publishing House, 1983); *Quanzhou Islamic Stone Carvings* compiled by Quanzhou Overseas Transportation History Museum (jointly published by Ningxia People's Publishing House and Fujian People's Publishing House, 1984); *Research on Islamic Monuments in Guangzhou* compiled by Ma Jianchuang, et al. (Ningxia People's Publishing house, 1989); and *Selected Inscriptions of the Hui Nationality in Southern China* edited by Da Zhenyi and An Yonghan (Ningxia People's Publishing House, 1999) to give just a few examples.

Great progress has also been made in the comparison, collation, and publication of ancient Chinese books. These results show that there will be more and greater achievements in the collation and publication of ancient books in the coming years. Moreover, the digitization of books and materials is also being carried out. The database of the Institute of World Religions of the Chinese Academy of Social Sciences may be the fastest growing in terms of major of Islamic research. It promises to become an important tool for the study of Islam in China in the near future.

It should also be mentioned that *The Examination of Islamic Chinese Books*, translated by Yang Daye, has great reference value for the study and collation of Islamic Chinese classics. The original author, Leslie (Li Dunan), is an Australian Sinology expert specializing in Chinese Islamic classics from the late Ming and early Qing Dynasties. Because he mastered many languages and excelled at textual research, his analysis and conclusions are

2. COLLATION AND PUBLICATION OF BOOKS AND MATERIALS 41

credible. The first book of the series was published in 2001. Among its many contributions, the book compiles 440 valuable inscriptions with dates starting from the Yuan Dynasty. It also covers ten major areas of research: 1) Creation, 2) Rebuilding and repair of mosque inscriptions, 3) Doctrines and teachings, 4) History of religion, 5) Merit and virtue monuments, 6) Donation and student aid inscriptions, 7) Notice inscriptions of prohibition and negotiations, 8) Character inscriptions, 9) Religious dispute inscriptions of clan rules and religions, and 10) Muslim cemetery inscriptions.

This chapter summarized the academic achievements of scholars of Islam and Muslims in China from the perspective of academic history so as to establish a starting point for people trying to engage in Islamic research today. The second purpose is to provide later scholars with an understanding of the seminal resources available in Islamic Studies. Its more profound significance is to enable scholars to fully realize that combing and summarizing existing academic achievements is an indispensable part of the research process because it enhances awareness of both academic history and the norms of academic research.

This study is not limited to the religious aspects of Islam but includes research into its history, philosophy, politics, society, and culture, and analyzes the research trends in each period and each stage systematically. China's research on Islam and Muslims includes field reports, literature research, translation research, and folk research, to name just a few genres. I collect as many works and related materials as possible, classify and summarize them, read and understands them, then analyze and synthesize them. The outcome is a systematic, comprehensive, and in-depth description of the overall characteristics of China's research on Islam based on collection, collation, and analysis. It is to this description that I now turn.

PART THREE.
RESEARCH IN THE FIELD OF HISTORY

1 CENTERED AROUND THE STUDY OF ISLAMIC HISTORY IN CHINA

1.1 Before 1949

According to academic standards, there was no research in the field of Islamic history in China before the 20th century. At the beginning of the 20th century, scholarship in the history of Chinese Islam began to develop with some publications becoming foundational. Many of the works discussed below have been translated and cited by scholars in countries such as Japan and are seminal works in the study of Islam in China. Such examples of academic scholarship from the Republic of China period include:

Chen Hanzhang, "History of Chinese Islam," *History and Geoscience*, 1926, Issue 1, pp. 166–222（陈汉章，"中国回教史，"《史学与地学》，1926 年第 1 期，166-222 页）
Chen Yuan, "A Brief History of Hui Hui's Entry into China," initially published in the *Monthly Journal of Chinese Studies* at Peking University Research Institute, Volume 25, No. 1, 1927, titled "The Origins and Flows of Hui Hui's Entry into China," later published in *The Eastern Journal*, Volume 25, No. 1928, changed to its current name.（陈垣，"回回教入中国史略，"初载《北京大学研究所国学门月刊》1927 年第 25 卷第 1 号，题为"回回教进中国的源流"，后刊于《东方杂志》1928 年第 25 卷第号，改为今名）

Jin Jitang, *Research on the History of Chinese Islam*, published by Chengda Normal Publishing Department, 1935. (金吉堂, 《中国回教史研究》, 成达帅范出版部出版, 1935 年)

Chuan Tongxian, *History of Chinese Islam*, published by the Commercial Press, 1940. (傅统先, 《中国回教史》, 商务印书馆出版, 1940 年)

Ma Yiyu, *A History of Chinese Islam*, Changsha Commercial Press, first edition, 1941; Shanghai Commercial Press, revised edition, 1948. (马以愚, 《中国回教史鉴》, 长沙商务印书馆, 1941 年初版; 上海·商务印书馆, 1948 年修订本)

Bai Shouyi, *A Brief History of Islam in China*, published in Frontier Politics, 1943; published by the Commercial Press, revised in 1944; included in The History of Islam in China, published by Ningxia People's Publishing House, 1982. (白寿彝, 《中国回教小史》, 发表于《边政公论》杂志, 1943 年; 商务印书馆出版, 1944 年修订本; 收入《中国伊斯兰教史存稿》, 宁夏人民出版社出版, 1982 年)

Bai Shouyi, "Outline of Islamic History in China," Chongqing: Wentong Bookstore, first edition in August 1946; reprinted in March 1947. (白寿彝, 《中国伊斯兰史纲要》, 重庆文通书局, 1946 年 8 月初版; 1947 年 3 月再版)

Ma Liangjun, *Textual Research on the History of Islam*, Xinjiang Shiyin Publishing House, published in 1949; the full text of the fifth issue of *Xinjiang Religious Research Materials*, published by the Religious Research Institute of the Xinjiang Academy of Social Sciences, published in 1981; Xinjiang People's Publishing House, republished in 1994. (马良俊, 《考证回教历史》, 新疆石印出版社, 1949 年出版; 新疆社会科学院宗教研究所《新疆宗教研究资料》第 5 辑中全文刊印, 1981 年; 新疆人民出版社, 1994 年再出版)

Chen Yuan's article "A Brief History of Hui Hui's Entry into China" was based on a speech delivered by Chen Yuan in September 1927 at the Chinese Studies Department of Peking University Research Institute. In it, he specifically discusses the term "Islam," which is the religion of the entire Chinese Hui ethnic group, as well as the meaning of ethnic names. Although this article is not extensive, it marks the first time that Chinese

3. RESEARCH IN HISTORY

scholars used scientific methods to study the history of the Hui ethnic group and Islam. [1]

Jin Jitang's *Research on the History of Chinese Islam* is the manuscript of a lecture given at Chengda Normal School in Beiping. The book is divided into two volumes. The first volume is on Chinese Islamic history and discusses the differentiation between Hui and Huihe, as well as the introduction of Muslim ethnicity and Islam into China. It also describes the different titles of Islamic believers throughout history, the expressions of their translated names and meanings, and the differences between the Chinese and Islamic calendars. Based on his evaluation of published works on Islamic history, Jitang proposes the basic content, historical stages, organization, and methods of data collection used to discuss Chinese Islamic history. The second volume discusses issues like the period in which the Hui people lived abroad, the period of assimilation, and the period of being scattered throughout various regions of China. Jitang also investigates the origin of the term "hui hui" and the period when Islam was introduced into China. For example, distinguishing it from the Huihe people, it is believed that the Huihui people are neither descendants of the Huihe people nor the Han people. Instead, they come from different ethnic groups in Central and West Asia who share a belief in Islam, have resided in China for a long time, intermarry with each other, and reproduce to form the Hui people. [2] The book has clear viewpoints, rich historical materials, and detailed textual research. It is a highly academic monograph on the history of Islam in China.

---

[1] Chen Yuan, "A Brief History of Hui Hui's Entry into China," *initially published in the Monthly Journal of Chinese Studies at Peking University Research Institute*, Volume 25, No. 1, 1927, titled "The Origins and Flows of Hui Hui's Entry into China," later published in *the Eastern Journal*, Volume 25, No. 1928, changed to its current name. (陈垣, 《回回教入中国史略》（初载《北京大学研究所国学门月刊》1927 年第 25 卷第 1 号, 题为《回回教进中国的源流》, 后刊于《东方杂志》1928 年第 25 卷第号, 改为今名)

[2] Jin Jitang, "*Research on the History of Chinese Islam*," published by Chengda Normal Publishing Department, 1935. (金吉堂, 《中国回教史研究》, 成达师范出版部出版, 1935 年)

Tongxian's classic *History of Chinese Islam* is one of the large-scale volumes of the "Chinese Cultural History Series" organized by the Commercial Press. After its publication in 1940, the study of Chinese Hui and Islamic history officially entered the academic world of Chinese cultural research. This book was reprinted multiple times, becoming a reference work for scholars engaged in the study of Chinese Hui and Islamic history abroad.[3]

Ma Yiyu's *History of Chinese Islam* includes a biography of Muhammad and information on Islamic teachings, ritual and legal systems, the historical records of different dynasties, the origins of the Huihe people, the Huihui calendar, articles of merit, famous temples and ancient tombs, and so on. The book first provides a brief overview of the history of Islam, including the creation and transmission of Islam by Muhammad, the succession of the four great caliphs, the Eastern Great Edict, the Western Great Edict, and the Southern Great Edict. Second, it explains the teachings, laws, and religious systems of Islam. It also verifies the Chinese historical records on Islam, records the time and route of Islam's transmission to China, describes the ethnic groups that entered China, and discusses the important cultural contributions of Muslims throughout Chinese history. The book is accompanied by a chronology of Chinese dynasties, translations of important Islamic names and place names, as well as a comparison table in English and Chinese. At the end of the book, the appendix includes Ma Jiequan's essay "After the Examination of Islam" and the author's "Important Points of Islam." The book is a compilation of Chinese Islamic historical records like the *Compendium of Comprehensive Studies*. In addition to collecting relevant Chinese historical records and conducting on-site inspections of ancient tombs in various temples, the author selected 272 works for comparative research and wrote this book. It has a rigorous style with fluent and elegant writing.[4]

---

[3] Chuan Tongxian, "History of Chinese Islam," published by the Commercial Pres, 1940, p. 143 （傳统先，《中国回教史》，商务印书馆出版，1940 年，156 页）

[4] Ma Yiyu, "A History of Chinese Islam," Changsha Commercial Press, first edition, 1941; Shanghai Commercial Press, revised edition, 1948.

3. RESEARCH IN HISTORY

Bai Shouyi's *A Brief History of Chinese Islam* describes the sea and land transportation between China and Arab countries before the rise of Islam, the eastward arrival of large food merchants after the rise of Islam, and the economic and cultural exchanges between China and Arab countries. It also includes Chinese historical sources dating to the Tang and Song dynasties that pertain to Islam. The establishment of mosques and public cemeteries, the influx of many Hui people from the Yuan Dynasty to China, and the emergence of political, economic, and academic talents demonstrate the spread of Islam in China. Shouyi also discusses the discrimination and persecution of Muslims by the ruling classes of the Yuan, Ming, and Qing dynasties. He also describes the rise of mosque scripture education and the Chinese translation of Islamic scriptures during the Ming and Qing dynasties. The author believes that the history of Islam in China can be divided into two periods: the first period is the Tang, Song, and Yuan periods, with most of the Muslim population in China being foreigners. This is known as the transplant period in the history of Islam in China. The second period was the Ming and Qing dynasties when all ethnic groups of Muslims in China were part of the Chinese nation, with a significant increase in numbers compared to previous periods. However, they were discriminated against and persecuted by the feudal ruling class and literati, making it a difficult period in the history of Chinese Islam. Finally, the book describes the development of religious education and academic culture in the first half of the 20th century. The book is informative with clear viewpoints and provides a concise outline of Chinese Islamic history.[5]

In Bai Shouyi's second book, *Outline of Chinese Islamic History*, he discusses a wide variety of topics in the study of Islam

---

（马以愚，《中国回教史鉴》，长沙商务印书馆，1941 年初版；上海·商务印书馆，1948 年修订本）

[5] Bai Shouyi, *A Brief History of Islam in China*, published in Frontier Politics, 1943; published by the Commercial Press, revised in 1944; included in *The History of Islam in China*, published by Ningxia People's Publishing House, 1982, p. 141. （白寿彝，"中国回教小史"发表于《边政公论》杂志，1943 年；商务印书馆出版，1944 年修订本；收入《中国伊斯兰教史存稿》，宁夏人民出版社出版，1982 年, 141 页）

in China. These include, but are not limited to, the arrival of the Great Cannibal and his merchants in China during the Song Dynasty, the beginning of the migration of Islam into China, the political status of the Hui Hui in the Yuan and Ming dynasties, the contributions of the Hui in Chinese academia, the decline of Hui political status in the Ming and Qing dynasties, famous Hui scholars and officials during the Ming and Qing dynasties, Hui soldiers and villages in the Ming and Qing Dynasties, the promotion of temple education, religious academic movements, the tragedy of Hui in the Qing Dynasty, the cultural work of Hui in the late Qing Dynasty, and the growth of Islam despite adversity. The book is accompanied by a list of references at the end.

In November 1948, Wentong Book Company published a reference book for the book, *Reference Materials for the Outline of Chinese Islamic History*. This volume includes a total of 15 articles, including "Memories of Hui Scholars during the Ming and Qing Dynasties" and "Memories of Hui Generals during the Ming and Qing Dynasties," which are Bai Shouyi's essays. The last article is a compilation of historical materials, while the remaining articles are by the author himself and other famous scholars, including Chen Hanzhang's "History of Chinese Islam," Chen Yuan's "A Brief History of Hui Islam Entering China," Yang Zhijiu's "Origin and Evolution of the Word Hui Hui," Pang Shiqian's "Evolution and Textbook of Chinese Muslim Temple Education," Zhao Zhenwu's "Overview of Chinese Muslim Culture in the Past 30 Years," as well as the author's "Battle of Talos and Its Influence," "Activities of the Great Food Merchants in China during the Song Dynasty," "Hui People and Islam in the Yuan Dynasty," "Record of Qingjing Temple in the Wei Wu Jian," "Record of Rebuilding Huaisheng Temple," "Liuzhou Islam and Ma Xiong," etc. Each chapter includes images of select artifacts, such as the epitaph of Mahachi in Kunyang, Yunnan and the earliest Chinese edition of the Quran. *The Compendium* and *Materials* complement one another and systematically outline the development of Islam in

3. RESEARCH IN HISTORY

China, making it a representative work for studying the history of Islam in China.[6]

Textual Research on the History of Islam is an academic work on Islamic and Hui history written by the late Ma Liangjun, a renowned religious figure, former head of Islam in Xinjiang, and member of the Standing Committee of the China Islamic Association. This book was originally written in classical Chinese and contains many scriptural languages. It was translated it into vernacular Chinese in the 36th year of the Republic of China.[7]

In addition to these representative achievements, the *Yu Gong* periodical edited by Gu Jiegang in the 1930s was an academic publication on historical geography, border history, and ethnic studies. It was founded in March 1934 and ceased publication in July 1937 with a total of seven volumes and eighty-two issues published. Two of the most notable are the "Islamic and Hui Special Account" (Volume 5, Issue 11, 1936) and the "Islamic Special Account" (Volume 7, Issue 4, 1937), which published over 40 papers and dozens of communications related to Hui Islam by scholars such as Chen Yuan and Bai Shouyi, as well as distribution advertisements and catalogs in Hui newspapers such as *Yuehua* and *Chenxi*, expanding the influence of Hui Islamic research. The articles on the history of Islam in China include:

> Gu Jiegang, "Hui Han Issue and Current Work," Volume 7, Issue 4. (顾颉刚，" 回汉问题和目前应有的工作，" 第七卷第四)

---

[6] Bai Shouyi, "Outline of Islamic History in China" ,Chongqing: Wentong Bookstore, first edition in August 1946; reprinted in March 1947, p. 37 (白寿彝，《中国伊斯兰史纲要》，重庆文通书局，1946 年 8 月初版；1947 年 3 月再版, 73 页，)

[7] Ma Liangjun, *Textual Research on the History of Islam*, Xinjiang Shiyin Publishing House, published in 1949; the full text of the fifth issue of *Xinjiang Religious Research Materials*, published by the Religious Research Institute of the Xinjiang Academy of Social Sciences, published in 1981; Xinjiang People's Publishing House, republished in 1994, p. 244 (马良俊，《考证回教历史》，新疆石印出版社，1949 年出版；新疆社会科学院宗教研究所《新疆宗教研究资料》第 5 辑中全文刊印，1981 年；新疆人民出版社，1994 年再出版, 244 页）

Nazhong, "Preface to Islam and Arab Civilization," Volume 7, Issue 10. (纳忠，"回教与阿拉伯文明序目，"第七卷第十期）

Jin Jitang, "On the Muslim Ethnic Group," Volume 5, Issue 11. (金吉堂，"回教民族说，"第五卷第十一期）

Bai Shouyi, "From the Battle of Talas to the earliest Chinese records of Islam," Volume 5, Issue 11. (白寿彝，"从怛逻斯战役说到伊斯兰教之最早的华文记录，"第五卷第十一期）

Wang Riwei, "Examination of Islam Entering Xinjiang," Volume 4, Issue 2. (王日蔚，"伊斯兰教入新疆考，"第四卷第二期）

Chen Yuanan, "Examination of the Western Huihu in Congling," Volume 4, Issue 5. (陈援庵，"葱岭西回鹘考"，第四卷第五期）

Wang Riwei, "Discussing the Names of Huihe, Huihui, and Other Names with Mr. Chen Yuan'an," Volume 4, Issue 10. (王日蔚，"与陈援庵先生论回纥回回等名称，"第四卷第十期）

Feng Chengjun, "Preface to Zheng He's Expedition to the West," Volume 2, Issue 1. (冯承钧，"伯希和撰郑和下西洋考序，"第二卷第一期.）

Feng Chengjun, "Annotations on Yingya Shenglan," Volume 2, Issue 6. (冯承钧，〈瀛涯胜览校注〉序，"第二卷第六期）

Xia Bi, "The Years and Years of Zheng He's Seven Ambassadors Traveling to the Western Regions and the Countries They Passed Through," Volume 2, Issue 8. (夏璧，"郑和七使西洋往返年月及其所经诸国，"第二卷卷第八期）

Dan Huapu, "On the Geographical Relations at the Beginning of the 'Hui Rebellion' in Shaanxi and Gansu," Volume 5, Issue 11. (单化普，"说陕甘'回乱'初起时之地理关系，"第五卷第十一）

Zhao Zhenwu, "Overview of Chinese Islamic Culture in the Past 30 Years," Volume 5, Issue 11. (赵振武，"三十年来之中国回教文化概况，"第五卷第十一期）

Ma Songting, "Chinese Islam and Chengda Normal School," Volume 5, Issue 11. (马松亭，"中国回教与成达师范学校，"第五卷第十一期）

Pang Shiqian, "History and Textbook of Chinese Islamic Monastery Education," Volume 5, Issue 11. (庞士谦，"中国回教寺院教育之沿革及课本，"第五卷第十一期）

3. Research in History

Yi Jun, "A Muslim Academic Group," Volume 6, Issue 2. （易君，"一个回教学术团体，"第六卷第二期）

Hu Shiwen, "Current Situation of the Hui People in Chengdu," Volume 7, Issue 4. （虎世文，"成都回民现状，"第七卷第四期）

Lu Zhenming, "Kaifeng Muslim Tan," Volume 7, Issue 4. （卢振明，"开封回教谭"（第七卷第四期）

Wang Shaomin, "Overview of the Hui People in Baotou, Suiyuan," Volume 7, Issue 4. （王绍民，"绥远包头的回民概况，"第七卷第四期）

Dai Pengliang, "The Situation of Hui People in Botou Town, Jiaohe, Hebei," Volume 7, Issue 4. （戴鹏亮，"河北交河泊头镇回民状况，"第七卷第四期）

Yiguang, "Overview of Hui People in Cangxian County, Hebei Province," Volume 7, Issue 4. （益光"河北沧县回民概况，"第七卷第四期）

Tai'an Muslim Association, "Shandong Tai'an Mosque Survey Form," Volume 7, Issue 4. （泰安回教公会，"山东泰安清真寺调查表，"第七卷第四期）

Zheng Daoming, "Overview of the Hui People in Zheng County, Henan Province," Volume 7, Issue 4. （郑道明，"河南郑县回民概况，"第七卷第四期）

Ma Quanren, "The Status of Islam in Shayan Town, Xinye, Henan," Volume 7, Issue 4. （马全仁，"河南新野沙堰镇回教状况，"第七卷第四期）

Ma Youyao, "Mingde Middle School in Kunming, Yunnan," Volume 7, Issue 4. （马有曜，"云南昆明的明德中学，"第七卷第四期）

Ma Xuchu, "Overview of the Hui People in Yuxi, Yunnan," Volume 7, Issue 4. （马旭初，"云南玉溪的回民概况，"第七卷第四期）

Wang Mengyang, "Overview of the Hui People in Beiping City," Volume 7, Issue 4. （王梦扬，"北平市回民概况，"第七卷第四期）

Wang Riwei, "Research on the Changes of Uyghur (Entangled) Ethnic Names," Volume 7, Issue 4. （王日蔚，"维吾尔（缠回）民族名称变迁考，"第七卷第四期）

> Yuan Fuli, "Kazakh Ethnic Group in Xinjiang," Volume 7, Issues 1-3. (袁复礼，"新疆之哈萨克民族，"第七卷第一、二、三合期)
>
> Deng Wang Wei, "Catalogue of Papers on Chinese Islam in Muslem World (1-2)," Volume 7, Issue 4. (登王伟，"Muslem World 中关于中国回教之论文目录(1-2)，"第七卷第四期)
>
> Bai Shouyi, "On the Creation of Mosque Steles," Volume 7, Issue 4. (白寿彝，"关于创建清真寺碑"，第七卷第四期)
>
> Wang Jingzhai, "Fifty Years of Self Study," Volume 7, Issue 4. (王静斋，"五十年求学自述"（第七卷第四期)
>
> (Japan) Sanghara Zhizang, "Creating a Mosque Stele" (Translated by Mou Runsun), Volume 5, Issue 11. ((日本)桑原骘藏，"创建清真寺碑"（牟润孙译）第五卷第十一期)
>
> (Japan) Sanghara Zhizang, "Food Taboos for Muslims in Chinese Books" (translated by An Mutao), Volume 5, Issue 11. ((日本)桑原骘藏，"中国书中回教徒之食物禁忌"（安慕陶译），第五卷第十一期)
>
> Schader et al., "The Activities of Arab Merchants on the Chinese Sea Before the 13th Century" (translated by An Wenzhuo), Volume 5, Issue 11. ((德国)夏德等之，"十三世纪前中国海上阿拉伯商人之活动"（安文倬译），第五卷第十一期)
>
> (Germany) Xia De et al., "A Textual Study of Zhao Rushi's Great Edict in the Chronicles of Various Kingdoms" (translated by Mou Yuan), Volume 7, Issue 4. ((德国)夏德等之，"赵汝适大食诸国志考证"（牟沅译），第七卷第四期)
>
> (Russian) Gaudefroy Demorabynes, "Research on Islam among Westerners in the Last Fifty Years" (translated by Han Rulin), Volume 7, Issue 4. ((俄国)Gaudefroy-Demorabynes 著，"近五十年西人之回教研究"（韩儒林译），第七卷第四期)
>
> (Russia) E. Bretgchueider, "Records of Islam in Middle Ages Chinese Books" (translated by Bai Shouyi) (ibid.), Volume 7, Issue 4. (俄国)E•Bretgchueider 著，"中世纪中国书中的回教记录"（白寿彝译）（同上），第七卷第四期)等。

These published papers can be divided into subfields such as comprehensive research, early Islamic studies of the Hui ethnic group, historical figures and events, Hui culture and education, and a brief introduction to Islam among the Hui ethnic groups in

3. RESEARCH IN HISTORY

various regions. *Yu Gong* also places great emphasis on the collection and translation of research materials on Hui Islam. For example, in the eleventh issue of the fifth volume of the periodical, there were eight pictures of Chengda Normal School and rubbings of the tombstones of the sages of Niujie Mosque in Beiping, the tombstones of the Islamic sages unearthed in Hangzhou, the tombstones of the founding mosques, and the stone inscriptions of Huang Tingjian in Taiyuan Mosque.[8]

Research papers on Islam published in various publications during the Republic of China period include:

> Liu Fengwu, "Introduction of Islam to China," "Relationship between Muslims and Chinese History," "Contribution of Muslims to Chinese Medicine," etc. (刘风五的"回教传入中国时期"、"回教徒与中国历代的关系"、"回教徒对于中国医药的贡献"等)
>
> Xue Wenbo "Relationship between the Ming Dynasty and the Hui People" (薛文波的"明代与回民之关系")
>
> Yang Zhijiu "The Origin and Evolution of the Word 'Hui Hui'" (杨志玖的"'回回'一词的起源和演变")
>
> Li Yan "Relationship between Islam and Chinese Li Arithmetic" (李俨的"伊斯兰教与中国李算之关系")
>
> Liu Mingshu "Hui Hui and Yuan Dynasty Opera" (刘铭恕的"回回与元代之戏曲")
>
> Wang Jingzhai "Review of Chinese Islamic Canon Education" and other papers. (王静斋的"中国回教经堂教育的检讨"等论文)

The above are just a few examples of papers published during the Republic of China period. Some study the historical context of Islam's introduction to China from different perspectives and methods, some investigate and study Islam and Muslims in China from a sociological perspective, and some introduce research from foreign countries such as Japan. Taken together, they reflect the trends in Islamic academic research during the Republic of

---

[8] *"Yu Gong"* Two of them are the "Islamic and Hui Special Account" (Volume 5, Issue 11, 1936) and the "Islamic Special Account" (Volume 7, Issue 4, 1937), which published over 40 papers.

China period and impacted the theoretical and practical aspects of Islamic research in later decades.

1.2 After the Establishment of the People's Republic of China

After the establishment of the People's Republic of China, research in this field encountered various setbacks during the period of the Cultural Revolution (1966–1976). Until the reform and opening, research on Islam and Muslims in China continued to expand and the results were published, forming new trends in studying Islam and Muslims. The research on the history of Islam in China is introduced in the following interrelated fields.

1.2.1

First, the main research achievements in the field of history include:

Feng Jinyuan, *Islam in China*, Ningxia People's Publishing House, 1991. (冯今源, 《中国的伊斯兰教》, 宁夏人民出版, 1991 年)
Qin Huibin, *Islam in China*, Commercial Press, 1997. (秦惠, 《中国的伊斯兰教》, 商务印书馆, 1997 年)
Li Xinghua, Qin Huibin, Feng Jinyuan, and Sha Qiuzhen, *The History of Islam in China*, Chinese Academy of Social Sciences Press, 1998. (李兴华、秦慧彬、冯今源、沙秋真合著《中国伊斯兰教史》, 中国社会科学院出版社, 1998 年)
Qin Huibin, *Islamic Annals*, People's Publishing House, 1998. (秦惠彬, 《伊斯兰教志》, 上海人民出版社, 1998 年)
Mi Shoujiang, *A Brief History of Islam in China*, Religious Culture Press, 2000 edition. (米寿江, 《中国伊斯兰教简史》, 宗教文化出版社, 2000 年)
Sha Qiuzhen, *Islam in China*, Chinese Publishing House, 2002. (沙秋真, 《伊斯兰教在中国》, 华文出版社, 2002 年)
Yang Guiping and Ma Xiaoying, *Islam Changming*, Religious Culture Press, 2007. (杨桂萍、马晓英合著, 《清真长明》, 宗教文化出版社, 2007 年)

3. Research in History

Feng Jinyuan's *Islam in China* begins with an introduction to the topic, including various views on the timeline of when Islam entered China, then dedicates the following chapters to mosques in China, the different Islamic sects in China, the culture of Chinese Muslims, and the Jingtang education of Chinese Islam. The author considers Islam a foreign religion that is deeply rooted in the land of China, making China's Islamic culture an important part of Chinese national culture. Only by studying its distinct Chinese style and characteristics can we truly understand China's Islam and the importance of various Muslim ethnic groups in the history of China and thus contribute to the unity of the Chinese nation.[9]

Qin Huibin's *Islam in China* begins with an overview of the history of Chinese Islam from the Tang through Qing dynasties and includes chapters on Chinese Islamic doctrine, the main scriptures, rituals, systems, and customs of Islam, outstanding contributions in the sciences and technology, and special topics related to the ethnic groups in China that ascribe to Islam.[10]

Mi Shoujiang's *A Brief History of Islam in China* focuses on the rise and development of Islam with commentary on major historical events. It includes analyses of the rise and development of Islam, the peaceful preaching of the Tang and Song Silk Road, the large dispersion and small concentration of Muslims in the Yuan and early Ming dynasties, and the nationalization of Islam in China, plus five chapters on the development of Islam in contemporary China. In addition to religious content, the book also provides an overview of the politics, economy, military affairs, culture, art, and customs across West Asia, North Africa, East Africa, Southwest Europe, Central Asia, and South Asia over the past 1,400 years, providing a systematic and concise

---

[9] Feng Jinyuan, "Islam in China," Ningxia People's Publishing House, July 1991. (冯今源, 《中国的伊斯兰教》, 宁夏人民出版社, 1991 年 7 月)
[10] Qin Huibin, "Islam in China," Commercial Press, 1997. (秦惠彬, 《中国的伊斯兰教》, 商务印书馆, 1997 年, 1 页（目录）)

introduction to the Islamic dynasties established in various periods and regions.[11]

The book *Islam Changming*, co-authored by Yang Guiping and Ma Xiaoying, covers many important topics. It starts with an overview of the rise and development of Islam in general and Islam in China in particular before moving onto issues such as Islam and Chinese ethnic minorities, Chinese Islamic sects, culture and education, philosophy and ethical thought, literature and architectural art, and the beliefs and customs of Chinese Muslims, including religious life, marriage and funeral customs, initiation names, and initiation ceremonies. This book systematically explores the history, denominations, cultures, religious beliefs, and customs of the ten Chinese ethnic minorities deeply influenced by Islam, and examines China's Islam from the perspective of the relationship between ethnicity and religion, looking at the relationships between minority ethnic groups in which the majority of members ascribe to Islam. The book also discusses the philosophy and ethical ideas of Chinese Islam, as well as the impact of Islam on Chinese Muslims.[12]

Of the above listed monographs, the most important for the academic study of Islam in China is *The History of Islam in China*, co-authored by Li Xinghua, Qin Huibin, Feng Jinyuan, and Sha Qiuzhen. In addition to these books, many articles have been published on the study of the dynastic history of Islam in China, such as:

Qin Huibin, "The Development of Islam during the Five Dynasties Period," *World Religious Studies*, 1989, Issue 1. (秦惠彬，"伊斯兰教在五代时期的发展，"《世界宗教研究》，1989 年第 1 期)
Qiu Shusen, "The Spread of Islam in Beijing and Northwest China during the Yuan Dynasty," *Hui Studies*, 2001, Issue 1. (

---

[11] Mi Shoujiang, "A Brief History of Islam in China," Religious Culture Press, 2000. (米寿江，《中国伊斯兰教简史》，宗教文化出版社，2000 年、1 页（目录））

[12] Yang Guiping and Ma Xiaoying (co-authored), "Islam Changming," Religious Culture Press, 2007. (杨桂萍、马晓英合著，《清真长明》，宗教文化出版社，2007 年、1 页（目录））

邱树森: "元代伊斯兰教在中国北京和西北的传播"（《回族研究》，2001 年第 1 期）
Liu Chengyou, "Islam of the Yuan Dynasty with Elevated Status and Clear Attachment to Confucianism," *Journal of Hubei University for Nationalities*, Issue 1, 2002. （刘成有, "地位上升而又明确附儒的元代伊斯兰教," 《湖北民族学院学报》，2002 年第 1 期）
Ge Zhi, "Islam and Muslims in Ming Dynasty Society," *World Religious Studies*, Issue 1, 2002. （葛状, "明代社会中的伊斯兰教和穆斯林" 《世界宗教研究》，2002 年第 1 期）
Chen Guoguang, "Islam among the Uyghurs in the Qing Dynasty," *Xinjiang Social Sciences*, 2002, Issue 2-3. （陈国光, "清代维吾尔族中的伊斯兰教,"《新疆社会科学》，2002 年第 2-3 期）
Zhou Yaoming, "On the Spread of Islam in the Helong Region during the Song Dynasty," *Gansu Ethnic Studies*, 2004, Issue 4. （周耀明: "试论宋代伊斯兰教在河陇地区的传播"（《甘肃民族研究》，2004 年第 4 期）

The article "The Development of Islam during the Five Dynasties Period" argues that during the Five Dynasties period, the pattern of dissemination of Islam in China shifted from the west to the south. Islam is strongly influenced by traditional Chinese culture in the southeast, while in the west this influence is relatively mild. In the article, Qin Huibin proposes that there is a "belief ladder," that is, the veracity of Chinese Muslim belief shows a gradual decline from west to east.[13]

1.2.2

Ma Tong and Yu Zhengui have achieved the most outstanding results in specialized historical research.

Ma Tong, *A Brief History of Chinese Islamic Sects and the Menhuan System*, Ningxia People's Publishing House, 1983. （马通, 《中国伊斯兰教派与门宦制度史略》，宁夏人民出版社，1983 年）

---

[13] Qin Huibin, "The Development of Islam during the Five Dynasties Period," World Religious Studies, 1989, Issue 1. （秦惠彬, "伊斯兰教在五代时期的发展," 《世界宗教研究》，1989 年第 1 期）

> Yu Zhengui, *Chinese Political Power and Islam in Past Dynasties*, Ningxia People's Publishing House, 1996. （余振贵，《中国历代政权与伊斯兰教》，宁夏人民出版社，1996 年）

Ma Tong's book *A Brief History of Chinese Islamic Sects and the Menhuan System* is divided into two parts: the first part provides an overview of the history of Islam, while the second part comprehensively records the various systems and major historical events of the three major Islamic sects and the four major Sufi schools and their clans. Research for the book involved firsthand investigation into oral accounts, family histories, local chronicles of sects, and the officials in charge of those sects. The appendix also preserves historical records and the overview and lineage of Islamic sects and eunuchs in China. The author explores the close relationship between Islam and certain ethnic minorities in China, as well as the widespread influence of its sects. Overall, it provides a detailed introduction to the development of Islam in China and its sectarian system.[14]

Yu Zhengui's *Chinese Political Power and Islam in Past Dynasties* is divided into four sections: the Islamic policy of promoting overseas trade during the Tang Dynasty and the emergence of regional Islamic attacks in the northwest (mid-7th to mid-12th century), Islamic policy established on the basis of ethnic integration during the Yuan and Ming dynasties and the birth of Muslim ethnic groups (mid-12th to mid-17th century), Islamic policies of the Qing Dynasty that influenced the great cause of China's reunification and the stability of western ethnic regions (mid-17th century to 1911), and the policies of various groups towards Islam during the Republic of China period (1911–1949), each of which are further divided into four parts. This book, which covers Islam in China in chronological order from the Tang Dynasty to the pre-founding period, elaborates on the relationship between Islam and politics in various historical periods, especially the close relationship between Islam and social stability in the northwest region since the late Ming and early

---

[14] Ma Tong, *A Brief History of Chinese Islamic Sects and Menhuan System*, Ningxia People's Publishing House, 1983. （马通，《中国伊斯兰教派与门宦制度史略》，宁夏人民出版社，1983 年，目录（391 页））

3. RESEARCH IN HISTORY

Qing dynasties. From the perspective of the overall development of Chinese history, this book constitutes a comprehensive and systematic study of the policies of previous regimes regarding Islam. Based on historical facts, the author supports some traditional views but also explores issues rarely discussed by his predecessors, such as the Islamic policies during the Republic of China period.[15]

1.2.3

Islam in China is divided into Hui and other ethnic groups that have the Chinese language family as their main source of Islamic tradition, and Uyghur and other ethnic groups that have the Turkic language family as their main source. Most of these groups are located in the mainland and Xinjiang regions. From a historical perspective, there are significant differences between these two regions when it comes to the introduction of Islam into China. After the reform and development, the compilation of historical materials on Islamic history in various regions prompted an important step in the field. Research papers, survey reports, and other projects continued, and have been published one after another. For example:

Quanzhou Museum of Overseas Transportation History and Quanzhou History Research Association, eds., *Selected Essays on Islamic Studies in Quanzhou*, People's Publishing House, 1983. (泉州海外交通通史博物馆和泉州历史研究会合, 《泉州伊斯兰教研究论文选》, 福建人民出版社, 1983 年.)
Gansu Institute of Ethnic Studies, ed., *Research on Islam in Northwest China,* Gansu Ethnic Publishing House, 1985. (甘肃民族研究所编《西北伊斯兰教研究》, 甘肃民族出版社, 1985 年)
Liu Zhengyan and Wei Liangtao, *A Study of the Western Regions and the Zhuo Family*, China Social Sciences Press, 1998. (刘正演和魏良弢合著, 《西域和卓家族研究》, 中国社会科学出版社, 1998 年)

---

[15] Yu Zhengui, Chinese Political Power and Islam in Past Dynasties, Ningxia People's Publishing House, 1996. (余振贵, 《中国历代政权与伊斯兰教》, 宁夏人民出版社, 1996 年, 目录 (480 页))

Li Jinxin, *A Brief History of the Islamic Khanate in Xinjiang*, Religious Culture Press, 1999. (李进新,《新疆伊斯兰汗朝史略,宗教文化出版社,1999 年》)
Wu Yiye, ed., *Historical Manuscripts of the Hui and Islam in Nanjing*, Islamic Association of Nanjing, 1999. (伍贻业主编,《南京回族、伊斯兰教史稿》,南京市伊斯兰教协会,1999 年.)
Bai Xianjing, ed., *Selected Materials of Historical Figures of the Hui Ethnic Group in Southern China*, Guangxi Ethnic Publishing House, 2000. (白先经等 主编,《中国南方回族历史人物资料选编》,广西民族出版社,2000 年.)
Chen Huisheng, ed., *History of Islam in Xinjiang China*, People's Publishing House, Xinjiang, 2000. (陈慧生主编,《中国新疆地区伊斯兰教史》,新疆人民出版社,2000 年.)

Chen Huisheng's edited volume, *History of Islam in Xinjiang China*, is a significant achievement in the study of regional Islamic history. The editor in chief is a scholar at the Institute of Religion, Xinjiang Academy of Social Sciences. After 1979, he organized personnel to translate and organize many materials, conducted multiple on-site interviews, and published many high-level papers, making special contributions to the study of Islam in China.[16] The volume edited by Wu Yiye, *Historical Manuscripts of the Hui and Islam in Nanjing*, highlights the history and culture of the southern Hui ethnic group in Nanjing and has high reference value. It also demonstrates that Chinese scholars pay attention to the study of Islam in the south.[17]

There are also specialized studies in the history of Islam in China. One example is Shuijingjun's *The History of Chinese Muslim Women's Temples* (2002), a specialized history related to the

---

[16] Chen Huisheng (Chief Editor), *History of Islam in Xinjiang, China*, People's Publishing House, Xinjiang, 2000. (陈慧生主编,《中国新疆地区伊斯兰教史》,新疆人民出版社,2000 年)

[17] Wu Yiye (Edited), *Historical Manuscripts of the Hui and Islam in Nanjing*, Islamic Association of Nanjing, 1999. (伍贻业主编,《南京回族、伊斯兰教史稿》,南京市伊斯兰教协会,1999 年)

3. RESEARCH IN HISTORY

history of Chinese Muslim women.[18] In recent years, Li Xinghua has published a series of articles on "Islamic Studies in Famous Cities and Towns in China" in publications such as *Hui Studies*. This research focuses on the centers of Muslim settlement in China, such as Linxia, Zhuxian Town, Datong, Nanjing, Xi'an, Kafeng, and Lanzhou. The author dedicates an article to each center, detailing the history, significance, and current situation of Islam in that place, and situates it within the history and reality of Islam in China.[19]

The advancement of the historical study of the Hui ethnic group is also evident through the long-term research of Bai Shouyi. In addition to his books *Records of Hui Figures* (four volumes)[20] and *History of Chinese Hui Ethnic Groups* (2003),[21] he has also published important collections through the People's Publishing House of Ningxia.

Compiled by the Institute of Ethnic Studies of the Chinese Academy of Social Sciences and the Institute of Ethnic Studies of the Central University for Nationalities, *Collected Works on the History of the Hui Ethnic Group*, 1984. (中国社会科学学院民族研究所和中央民族大学民族所合编的,《回族史论集》, 1984 年)

Yang Huaizhong, *Commentary on the History of the Hui Ethnic Group*, 1991. (杨怀中,《回族史论稿》, 1991 年)

Li Songmao, *Research on Hui Islam*, 1993. (李松茂,《回族伊斯兰教研究》, 1993 年)

---

[18] Shui Jingjun: "History of Chinese Muslim Women's Temples", Shuijing Jun, Sanlina Bookstore, 2002 pp. 398. (水镜君：『中国清真女寺史』三聯書店、2002 年、398 页)

[19] Li Xinghua, "Research on Islam in Famous Cities and Towns in China," Research on Hui Ethnic Groups, 2009, Vol 4, pp. 24–36. (李兴华,《中国名城名镇伊斯兰教研究》《回族研究》)

[20] Bai Shouyi, Records of Hui Ethnic Figures, Ningxia People's Publishing House, 2000, pp. 1978. (白寿彝,《回族人物志》（上下本），宁夏人民出版社、2000 年、1978 页)

[21] Bai Shouyi, "History of Chinese Hui Ethnic Groups," Zhonghua Book Company, 2003, p. 766. (白寿彝,《中国回回民族史》, 中華書局、2003 年、766 页)

> Yang Huaizhong and Yu Zhengui, eds., *Islam and Chinese Culture*, 1995. （杨怀中　余振贵　主编，《伊斯兰与中国文化，1995 年》
>
> Yu Zhengui, *Chinese Political Power and Islam*, 1996. （余振贵，《中国历代政权与伊斯兰教》，1996 年）
>
> Mian Weilin, *Introduction to the Islamic Religious System of the Hui Ethnic Group in China*, 1997. （勉维霖，《中国回族伊斯兰宗教制度概论》，1997 年）
>
> Ding Hong, *A Hundred Years of Chinese Muslims*, 1996. （丁宏，《百年中国穆斯林》，1996 年）

Since China's reform and development, there have been about a thousand articles and papers published on Islam in the field of Hui Studies. One of the most hotly debated issues is the relationship between the introduction and development of Islam in China and the formation of the Hui ethnic group. Representative contributions to this issue include:

> Lin Song, "On the decisive role of Islam in the formation of the Hui ethnic group in China," *Social Science Front*, 1983, Issue 3. （林松，"试论伊斯兰教对形成中国回族所起的决定性作用"，《社会科学战线》，1983 年第 3 期）
>
> Ma Ruling, "Further Discussion on the Relationship between Islam and the Formation of the Hui Ethnic Group," *Journal of Ningxia University*, 1984, Issue 3. （马汝领，"再论伊斯兰教与回回民族形成的关系，"《宁夏大学学报》，1984 年第 3 期）
>
> Nan Wenyuan, "On the Leading Role of Islamic Culture in the Formation of the Hui Nationality," *Hui Studies*, 1991, Issue 3. （南文渊，"论伊斯兰文化在回族形成中的主导作用，"《回族研究，1991 年地 3 期》

Lin Song's paper states that, "whatever one's perspective, no characteristic of the Hui ethnic group can exist completely without the influence of Islam,"[22] arguing that Islam plays a

---

[22] Lin Song, "On the decisive role of Islam in the formation of the Hui ethnic group in China," *Social Science Front*, 1983, Issue 3. （林松，"试论伊斯兰教对形成中国回族所起的决定性作用"，《社会科学战线》，1983 年第 3 期, 200－210 页）

3. RESEARCH IN HISTORY

decisive role in the formation of the Hui ethnic group. Ma Ruling takes this further and insists that Islam plays a leading role in the formation of Hui ethnic consciousness. [23] Nan Wenyuan demonstrates that the prosperity and development of Islam in China at the end of the Yuan Dynasty and the beginning of the Ming Dynasty encouraged Islamic culture to play a leading role in the formation of Hui nationality. Some scholars hold that without the spread of Islam in China, the Hui ethnic group would not have formed and that the history of the Hui ethnic group is equivalent to the history of Islam. [24] Others hold that the role of Islam is secondary while national consciousness is primary. The consensus is that the formation and development of the Hui ethnic group cannot do without Islam. Based on this understanding, Islam has become an extremely important component of Hui Studies.

The following table focuses on works that discuss the impact of Islam on the Hui people. The main papers include:

Ding Mingjun, "A Brief Discussion on the Influence of Islam on Hui Art," *Hui Studies*, 1992, Issue 2. (丁明俊，"略论伊斯兰教对回族艺术的影响，《回族研究》，1992 年第 2 期）
Nan Wenyuan, "The Impact of Islam on Hui Education," *Qinghai Ethnic Studies*, 1992, Issue 3. (南文渊，"伊斯兰教对回族教育的影响，"《青海民族研究》，1992 年第 3 期)
Liang Xiangming, "A Brief Discussion on Islamic Morality and Its Role in the Formation of Hui Traditional Morality," *Ningxia Social Sciences*, 1998, Issue 1. (梁向明，"略论伊斯兰教道德及其在回族传统道德形成中的作用"，《宁夏社会科学》，1998 年第 1 期）
Xiao Mang: "The Impact of Islamic culture on Hui Business Activities," *Journal of Southwest University for Nationalities*,

---

[23] Ma Ruling, "Further Discussion on the Relationship between Islam and the Formation of the Hui Ethnic Group," *Journal of Ningxia University*, 1984, Issue 3. (马汝领，"再论伊斯兰教与回回民族形成的关系"《宁夏大学学报，1984 年第 3 期. 32—37 页）

[24] Nan Wenyuan, On the Leading Role of Islamic culture in the Formation of the Hui Nationality, Hui Studies, 1991, Issue 3. (南文渊，"论伊斯兰文化在回族形成中的主导作用"《回族研究》，1991 年地 3 期, 31—38 页.)

2000, Issue 12.（肖芒，　"伊斯兰文化对回族商业活动的影响"，《西南民族大学学报》，2000 年第 12 期.）
Ding Hong, "On the Significance of Strengthening the Study of Islamic culture from the Perspective of Hui Han Ethnic Relations," *Journal of Northern University for Nationalities*, 2002, Issue 1.（丁宏，　"从回汉民族关系角度谈加强伊斯兰文化研究的重要意义"，《北方民族大学学报》，2002 年第 1 期）
Tao Hong and Bai Jie, "Hui Clothing Culture and Islam," *Hui Studies*, Issue 3, 2000.（陶红和白洁，　"回族服饰文化与伊斯兰教"，《回族研究》，2000 年第 3 期）
Li Lin, "A Brief Account of Islam's Activities in the Tang Dynasty," *Hui Studies*, Issue 4, 2001.（李林，　"伊斯兰教在唐代活动述略——"，《回族研究》，2001 第 4 期.）
Chen Guoguang, "Islam among the Uyghurs in the Qing Dynasty, *Xinjiang Social Sciences*, Issue 1, 2002.（陈国光，　"清代维吾尔族中的伊斯兰教"，《新疆社会科学》，2002 年第 1 期）
Zhou Yaoming, "On the Spread of Islam in the Helong Region during the Song Dynasty," *Gansu Ethnic Studies*, Issue 4, 2004.（周耀明，　"试论宋代伊斯兰教在河陇地区的传播"，《甘肃民族研究》，2004 年第 4 期.）

Publications from the perspective of ethnic history also occupy important positions.

2 CENTERED AROUND THE STUDY OF WORLD ISLAMIC HISTORY

Compared to the amount of research on the history of Islam and Muslims in China, Chinese research on the history of world Islam is lacking. Before the 20th century, there was no research to speak of. In the first half of the century, only the following two books were published:

Shuizi Li, *A Brief History of World Islam*, Beiping Niujie Halal Book Newspaper, 1923; Reprinted in 1930.（水子立，《世界回教史略》，北平牛街清真书报社，1923 年，1930 年再版）
Yuan Dongyan, *A Brief History of the Development of Islam*, 1946.（袁东演，《回教发展史略》，1946.）

3. Research in History

Shuizi Li's *A Brief History of World Islam* is in classical Chinese, divided into two volumes. The first volume covers the creation of Islam and the rise and fall of the Arab Empire, the rise of the Ottoman Empire, a brief biography of Muhammad, and the histories of the Arab Empire, Wenmian government, the East and West Arab Empire, the Crusades, and Turkey. The second volume provides a brief account of modern Arab history and the development of Islam in other regions, such as China, India, the Southern Islands, and Africa, including the relationship between Islam and various religions. It concludes with a discussion of the future of Islam in the world. The book starts with the year of Muhammad's passing and describes historical events marked by the number of years since.[25] This book is a groundbreaking work on the systematic study of world Islamic history, with rich content and abundant information. It had a widespread influence among Muslim youth in the 1920s and 30s and became a must read.

As in any academic field, the translation and quotation of foreign Islamic and Muslim research is an important part of academic history. The study of world Islam over the past 20 years can be said to have started with the translation and introduction of foreign works into Chinese, including those listed here:

A Brief History of Islam by Henri Massé, translated by Wang Huaide and Zhou Zhenxiang, Commercial Press, 1978. （《伊斯兰教简史》, （法国）昂里·马塞 著，王怀德和周祯祥 译，商务印书馆，1978 年. ）
General History of Arabia by Philip Khuri Hitti, translated by Ma Jian, Commercial Press, 1979. （《阿拉伯通史》（美国）菲利普·胡里·希提 著，马坚 译，商务印书馆，1979 年. ）
A Brief History of Islam by Said Fiaz Mahood, translated by Wu Yungui, China Social Sciences Press, 1981. （《伊斯兰教简史》, （巴基斯坦）赛义德·菲亚兹·马茂德著，吴云贵等译，中国社会科学出版社，1981 年. ）

---

[25] Shuizi Li, "A Brief History of World Islam," Beiping Niujie Halal Book Newspaper, 1923; Reprinted in 1930. （水子立, 《世界回教史略》, 北平牛街清真书报社，1923 年, 1930 年再版）

The Arabs in History by Bernard Lewis, translated by Ma Zhaochun and Ma Xian, Chinese Publishing House, 1981. (《历史上的阿拉伯人》（（美国）伯纳德·刘易斯 著，马肇椿、马贤 译，华文出版社，1981 年。）
History of Arab Islamic Culture by Ahmed Amin, translated by Nazhong, et al., Commercial Press, 2007. (《阿拉伯——伊斯兰文化史》（（埃及）穆罕默德·艾敏 著，纳忠等 译，商务印书馆，2007 年。）
The History of Islamic Nations and States by Carl Brockelmann, published by the Commercial Press, 1980. (《伊斯兰教各民族与国家史》（（德国）卡尔·布罗克尔曼著，商务印书馆出版，1980 年。）

Henri Massé, author of *A Brief History of Islam* (1930), was a professor at the University of Paris. He once served as President of the Paris Modern Oriental School and is one of the famous French Orientalists of his time. The Chinese translation, published by Commercial Press in 1978, is based on the Russian translation of the sixth edition of the French. The book is divided into 16 chapters, each with a subheading style that provides a summary of the content, and includes maps related to different periods. The text is followed by a personal name index, a list of places in Russian, and a glossary of commonly used Islamic terms. The book introduces pre-Islamic Arabia, summarizes the emergence and spread of Islam throughout the world, and elaborates on the development of Islamic doctrine, teachings, sects, culture, and religious philosophy. The book also includes information on politics, economy, military affairs, culture, art, and folk customs, reflecting the spread and development of Islam in West Asia, North Africa, East Africa, Southwest Europe, Central Asia, the South Asian subcontinent, and Southeast Asia over the past 1,400 years. It gives a systematic and concise introduction to the Islamic dynasties established in various periods and regions, including their origins. There are many comments on the history of East-West relations, especially in the modern history section.[26]

---

[26] *A Brief History of Islam*, written by Henri Masse of France, translated by Wang Huaide and Zhou Zhenxiang, Commercial Press, 1978. (《伊斯

3. RESEARCH IN HISTORY

67

The 10th edition of *The General History of Arabia* (2 vols.) is one of Hiti's most important works. It was published in 1937 and subsequently revised or reprinted. By 1970, it had reached its tenth edition. The first volume includes the first thirty-three chapters, starting from the early Arabs, describing the rise of Islam, the birth of Arab countries, the rise and fall of the Arab Empire, and the achievements of Arabs in cultural and scientific fields. The second volume includes the last nineteen chapters, which mainly discuss the Arab countries established in Europe, other Muslim countries, the Ottoman Empire, and the new trends in the development of Arab countries up to the twentieth century. At the same time, it also introduced the achievements of Arabs in cultural and scientific fields, as well as their influence on the West.[27] It is an indispensable reference book for understanding the development of the Arab world.

The Arabs of History by British American scholar Bernard Lewis is divided into 10 chapters: Pre–Islamic Arabia, Muhammad and the Origins of Islam, Conquest Periods, Arab Kingdoms, Islamic Empire, Islamic Uprising, Arab Culture in Europe, Islamic Culture, Arab Decline, Western Influence, and Chronology of Events.[28]

History of Arab Islamic Culture by Ahmed Amin, an Arab scholar in Egypt, is an eight-volume series with one volume dedicated to each of the following eight periods: the Dawn Period, Near Noon Periods I-III, and Noon Periods I-IV. The book covers a wide range of topics, including politics, economy, society, culture, academic activities, and sectarian development in Arab Islamic countries, and is an important resource for studying Islamic history and culture. The author objectively narrates from

---

兰教简史》, （法国）昂里·马塞 著，王怀德和周祯祥 译，商务印书馆，1978 年, 249 页）

[27] *General History of Arabia*, written by Philip Khuri Hitti, translated by Ma Jian, Commercial Press, 1979. （《阿拉伯通史》（美国）菲利普·胡里·希提 著，马坚 译，商务印书馆，1979 年， 649 页）

[28] *The Arabs in History*, written by Bernard Lewis, translated by Ma Zhaochun and Ma Xian, Chinese Publishing House, 1981. （《历史上的阿拉伯人》（（美国）伯纳德·刘易斯 著，马肇椿、马贤 译，华文出版社，1981 年，目录（211 页））

a neutral perspective, selecting major historical moments to showcase the macro context of Islam's development, and narrates the development of the Arabs in history, as well as their status, characteristics, and achievements in different historical periods. The series showcases the long history of Arabs and their contributions to human civilization during Islam's development, and objectively evaluates the ideas of Arab culture and Islamic philosophy in various periods with a rigorous attitude. It is the most authoritative Arab history of half a century.[29]

Carl Brockelmann, author of *History of Islamic Nations and States*, was professor of Semitic language at universities such as Konisburg, Halle, and Berlin in Germany, and an Islamic philologist and historian. The book covers the origins of various Islamic countries and their connections. For example, that the kings of Iraq and Jordan were brothers of the Hashemite family – historically enemies of the ruling family of Saudi Arabia. It systematically discusses the issues faced by Arabs and the Arab Empire, the Islamic Empire including its collapse, Ottoman Turks as the leading force of Islam, Islam in the 19th century, and Islamic countries after the First World War.[30]

These translated works are rich in information and detailed in content. Some reflect the views of Muslim scholars, while others reflect the views of the wider international academic community. Many others have not yet been fully translated by later generations.

In the 1980s, Jin Yijiu published two important introductory books on Islam:

> Jin Yijiu, *Introduction to Islam*, Qinghai People's Publishing House, 1987. (《伊斯兰教概论》, 青海人民出版社, 1987 年.)

---

[29] Ahmed Amin, translated by Nazhong, *History of Arab Islamic Culture*, Commercial Press, 2007. (《阿拉伯——伊斯兰文化史》（（埃及）穆罕默德・艾敏 著, 纳忠等 译, 商务印书馆, 2007 年, 共 8 册本、目录）

[30] *The History of Islamic Nations and States*, (Germany) Carl Brockelmann, published by the Commercial Press, 1980. (《伊斯兰教各民族与国家史》,（德国）卡尔・布罗克尔曼著, 商务印书馆出版, 1980 年, 目录（650 页））

3. RESEARCH IN HISTORY

> Jin Yijiu, *History of Islam*, Chinese Academy of Social Sciences Press, **1989.** (《伊斯兰教史》, 中国社会科学院出版社, 1989 年.)

Introduction to Islam covers the rise and spread of Islam, its basic scriptures and belief system, Shariah, sects, schools, dogmatics, Sufi mysticism, social life (i.e., politics, economy, ethics, culture), modern and contemporary Islamic social thought and movements, Islam in China, etc. At the end of the book, there are seven appendices and indexes, which are highly useful. The book is objectively and fairly written with detailed historical materials and is characterized by its readability. It is systematic in its introduction, which enhances its value for understanding and studying Islam.[31]

Jin Yijiu's *History of Islam* is divided into four parts and fourteen chapters. The first part, the rise of Islam, consists of two chapters describing the history from the early stages of Islam to the period of the four major caliphs. The second part, the comprehensive development of Islam, consists of five chapters that deal with the general situation of early Islam, the formation of the Islamic system, the emergence and development of various branches of Islam, the rise of sects, schools, Sufi mysticism, and their mutual disputes and interactions, and the formation and disintegration of the Khalifa system. The third part discusses the dissemination, development, and characteristics of Islam in North Africa and Spain, Central Asia, South Asia, Southeast Asia, East Africa, West Africa, and China, with a total of five chapters. The fourth part on modern Islam consists of two chapters, outlining the social movements, political and religious relations, and development trends since the 18th century. This book provides a comprehensive and systematic introduction to the historical emergence, development, and dissemination of Islam. In terms of time periods covered, the book starts with pre-Islamic Arabia and ends with the current situation of Islam in various countries. The content is divided into sects and covers basic topics in Islamic religious practice and culture. The book also provides a profound analysis of Islam's relationship with politics, society, economy,

---

[31] Jin Yijiu, *Introduction to Islam*, Qinghai People's Publishing House, 1987. (《伊斯兰教概论》, 青海人民出版社, 1987 年 1 页 · 目录 (454 页)).

70   ISLAM IN CHINA AND THE ISLAMIC WORLD

and culture, and offers many new insights into important historical events and academic issues.[32]

The general history of Islam is foundational to the study of Islam in China and directly related to the construction of the academic discipline. In order to improve academic research of Islam in China, we not only need to continue to translate and introduce relevant works from foreign academic circles, we also need to continuously accumulate information, organize resources, conduct research on core topics, and compile Islamic history monographs that reflect the views and achievements of Chinese scholars. After more than ten years of unremitting efforts, China has made significant progress in the study of world Islam. Nowadays, we have several academic works on Islamic studies and established connections within the international academic community, laying a solid foundation for in-depth research in various fields of world Islam.

Jin Yijiu's *History of Islam* is a product of this background. Yu Zhengui and Yang Jinzhong state, "this book is rich in content, reliable in argumentation, concise in description, and has absorbed the latest research achievements of Islamic scholars from both domestic and foreign countries in the past 10 years. Its role far exceeds the scope of textbooks, and it is a good teaching book for contemporary Chinese scholars to understand Islamic history."[33] Three years later, another volume of the same name was published:

Wang Huaide and Guo Baohua, *History of Islam*, Ningxia People's Publishing House, 1992. (王怀德、郭宝华合著，《伊斯兰教史》，宁夏人民出版社，1992 年.）

Wang Huaide and Guo Baohua's *History of Islam* presents Islam as one of the world's major religions, with a history spanning 1400 years. *History of Islam* provides a detailed account of the

---

[32] Jin Yijiu, *History of Islam*, Chinese Academy of Social Sciences Press, 1998. (《伊斯兰教史》，中国社会科学院出版社，1998 年，目录（619 页））
[33] Yu Zhengui, Yang Jinzhong: " Summary of translation Chinese Islamic Literature," Ningxia People's Publishing House, 1993 edition, page 398. (余振贵、杨怀中，《中国伊斯兰教文献译著大要》，宁夏人民出版社，1993 年版，第 398 页。.）

3. RESEARCH IN HISTORY

71

development of Islam, giving readers a comprehensive understanding of its international, national, and mass characteristics. Given the vast populations affected by Islam, its existence and development have inevitably had a huge impact on the world. We should fully understand the long-term and complexity, strengthen our research on it, and focus on explaining its origin and development based on the historical conditions under which it emerged and gained dominance. Over the past 1400 years, many Muslim scholars have written books and expounded on Islam from various aspects based on their own beliefs, and the book introduces these aspects. Simply put, this is an introductory work based on history, which may be more suitable as a textbook.[34]

Research on historical topics has also been carried out, and a number of quality academic works have emerged:

Ma Mingliang, *A Brief History of Islam*, Economic Daily Press, 2001. (马明良,《简明伊斯兰教史》,经济日报出版社,2001 年.)
Wang Yujie, *Islamic History of Iran*, Ningxia People's Publishing House, 2006. (王宇洁,《伊朗伊斯兰教史》,宁夏人民出版社,2006 年)
Wu Yungui and Zhou Xiefan, *Islamic Thought and Movement in Modern Times*, Social Science Literature Press, 2001. (吴云贵,周燮藩合著,《近现代伊斯兰教思潮与运动》,社会科学文献出版社,2001 年)

Ma Mingliang's *A Brief History of Islam* is divided into two parts, "The Rise and Spread of Islam" and "Islam in China." The first part is divided into the Muhammad era (610–632 AD) and the rise of Islam, The Four Orthodox Caliphate eras (632–661), the consolidation of Islam (i.e., Abu Bakr era [632–634], Omar era [634–644], Uthman era [644–656], and Ali era [656–661]), The Umayyad era (661–750), the Abbasid era (750–1258), the early period of the Ottoman Turkey era (14th century to modern times), the spread of Islam in the Indian subcontinent and Southeast Asia,

---

[34] Wang Huaide and Guo Baohua (co-authored), *History of Islam*, Ningxia People's Publishing House, 1992. (王怀德、郭宝华合著,《伊斯兰教史》,宁夏人民出版社,1992 年, 482 页.)

East Africa, and West Africa, and Modern Islam and the challenge of the West. The second part, "Islam in China," is divided into the Tang and Song Dynasties, the Mongol Yuan period, the Ming and Qing dynasties, Islam amidst setbacks, the development of Islam in the Xinjiang region, the contributions of ancient Chinese Muslims in technology and culture (e.g., astronomy, calendar, medicine, architectural engineering, literature), and the Republic of China period. *A Brief History of Islam* systematically elaborates on the development of Islam from its birth to the modern Islamic revival movement, nearly 1,400 years from 610 AD to the 1990s. It has comprehensive discussions of major political events, important historical figures, Islamic culture, and sectarian origins, and an in-depth analysis of the rise and fall of the Islamic world.[35] This book also has many insights into the formation and development of Chinese ethnic minorities such as Hui, Salar, Uyghur, Dongxiang, and Baoan, and provides a new summary of the development of Islam in China against the backdrop of the general history of Islam.

Wang Yujie's *Islamic History of Iran* provides an overview of Shia Islam and elaborates on the history of Shia before they relied on Iran as a country to develop and strengthen. It includes an overview of Shi'ism, the establishment and development of Shia Islam in Iran from the 18th to the early 20th century, the Shia Islam of the Pahlavi dynasty, the Islamic Revolution, and the Practice of the Islamic Republic. Temporally, the book starts with Ali, the first imam in the Shia lineage. The main approach is to narrate Shia history in chronological order from the Safavid, Kaga, and Pahlavi dynasties to the Islamic Republic of Iran. From the establishment of Shia as the state religion in Iran to the later 20th century when it was once again established as the state religion, the relationship between religion and Iran's political destiny was determined.[36]

---

[35] Ma Mingliang, "A Brief History of Islam," Economic Daily Press, 2001. (马明良, 《简明伊斯兰教史》, 经济日报出版社, 2001 年, 1 页·目录 (647 页))

[36] Wang Yujie, "*Islamic History of Iran,*" Ningxia People's Publishing House, 2006. (王宇洁, 《伊朗伊斯兰教史》, 宁夏人民出版社, 2006 年, 1 页·目录 (192 页))

3. Research in History

73

The book *Islamic Thought and Movement in Modern Times*, co-authored by Wu Yungui and Zhou Xiefan, is dedicated to the study of Islamic reform and revival, Islamic modernism, and the Revival Movement, covering various social trends and movements in the modern Islamic world, such as pan-Islamism, Islamic modernism, nationalism, socialism, and Islamic fundamentalism. As such, it is a history of modern Islam. The authors not only use history to shed light on current realities, they also clarify the historical background of various ideological trends and movements that emerged during the colonial and post-colonial periods, thus creating a summary of previous research.[37]

In terms of the study of Islamic history in various regions of the world, African Islamic studies have always been ignored by the Chinese academic community, and there are no domestic scholars currently specializing in African Islamic studies. At present, research on Islam in Africa is limited to African history, culture, and politics, and is a by-product of research on Africa in general. No Chinese scholar has yet conducted thematic research on Islam in Africa, especially in Sub-Saharan Africa. As for the study of the Islamic movement in West Sudan, current domestic academic works fall under the study of the history of Africa in general, usually as a single chapter on the theme of social revolution, not religion, and tend to focus on content rather than analysis.

The National Social Science Foundation Youth Project "Research on the Islamic Movement in West Sudan," led by Li Weijian, has partially filled this gap. This project takes the Islamic movement in West Africa in the 19th century as the theme, adopts a writing method that combines history and theory, narrates the history of the Islamic movement, and conducts an analysis of it. The content is organized along three themes: the causes and background of the Islamic Movement in West Africa in the 19th century, the nine large-scale Islamic Jihad movements that occurred in West Africa in the 19th century, and the results and

---

[37] Wu Yungui and Zhou Xiefan (Co-authored), "*Islamic Thought and Movement in Modern Times*," Social Science Literature Press, 2001. (吴云贵，周燮藩合著，《近现代伊斯兰教思潮与运动》，社会科学文献出版社，2001 年, 1 页·目录（493 页））

nature of the Islamic movement in the 19th century. The authors of the study point out that the Islamic movement in West Africa greatly improved the living situation and state of Islam in the region. These researchers put forward their own views on the basis of current and preceding research, and supported the idea that religion was the most fundamental attribute of the 19th century West African Islamic movement. This movement was essentially an Islamic revival movement with the New Sufi Mission as the carrier. The Islamic Ummah class seized power through this movement, hoping to make sharia the basic social system and legal norm of West African society, and Islam still plays an important role in the political, economic, and cultural aspects of West Sudan. This research project provides a necessary model for Chinese researchers to understand the process of globalization and increasing political, economic, and cultural exchanges with African countries. Islam maintains strong momentum in Africa, forming a distinctive Islamic culture. Africa holds a very important position in China's foreign exchanges and faces increasing competition from other countries. Cultural understanding is the foundation of political and economic exchange and can promote such exchange. Therefore, the study of African Islam not only deepens China's understanding of African history and culture, but also contributes to China's exchanges with Africa. [38]

---

[38] The National Social Science Foundation Youth Project "Research on the Islamic Movement in West Sudan" led by Li Weijian. (李维健主持的国家社科基金青年项目《西苏丹伊斯兰运动研究》)

PART FOUR.
RESEARCH IN THE FIELD OF RELIGION—CENTERED ON CHINESE ISLAMIC STUDIES

Islamic teaching can be defined as the academic attribute of religious study related to Islam and can include studies in a variety of areas, such as tafsir, hadith, fiqh, dogmatics, and sectarian movements. Wu Yungui states in his monograph *Islamic Doctrine* that Islamic doctrine is an advanced course in the discipline of Islamic religion, and students generally begin to learn it after understanding the basics of sutra, hadith, and shariah. Islamic theology is an internal discipline of Islamic faith, and the prerequisite for learning it is to be convinced of the correctness and universality of Islamic belief.[1]

Doctrine is a traditional Islamic discipline of interpreting faith through rational thinking. Islamic doctrine has always been valued by Chinese Muslims and has been the main content of scripture education and Chinese translations since the Ming and Qing dynasties. Li Lin analyzes the history of academic research in this area: "Contemporary Chinese scholars' research on Islamic righteousness did not gradually recover until the 1980s, and their research methods were limited to the framework of philosophical research. Since China entered the development transformation period in 2000, there have been changes in the academic study of

---

[1] Wu Yungui, *Islamic Doctrine*, China Social Sciences Press, 1995, 138 pages. (吳雲貴，《伊斯兰教义学》，中国社会科学出版社、1995.)

Islamic doctrine. Not only have new publications emerged, but the religious characteristics of Islamic doctrine have gradually been recognized and are no longer limited to the scope of philosophical research. Some of these studies reflect the unique purpose and care of research in religious doctrine. Other traditional aspects of Islam, as well as modern humanities and social sciences, have posed major challenges to contemporary Islamic dogmatism and its research, but these challenges contain opportunities for self-transcendence and self-transformation."[2]

Islamic law is also an important component of Islamic teaching. As Li Lin has demonstrated, the study of Islamic law in contemporary China has gone through three periods of creation, reconstruction, and development since 1949, forming a disciplinary system with a focus on Chinese characteristics and practical dimensions. Currently, it is facing a methodological transformation regarding how to make research into Islamic law a modern academic discipline. Influenced by traditional Islamic law scholars and modern Western Islamic law scholars, this field has formed two major academic traditions, namely the "Traditional School" and the "Academic School." In the future, research on Islamic law in China should transcend the differences between these two schools, integrate the strengths of both, and form a contemporary Chinese Islamic law research system with its own style.[3]

---

[2] Li Lin, "Issues and Reflections on Contemporary Islamic Studies in China," *Chinese Muslims*, Issue 3, 2011, pp. 18–21. (李林，"当代中国伊斯兰教义学研究的问题和反思"《中国穆斯林》, 2011 年第 3 期，18–21 页）

[3] Li Lin, "Issues and Reflections on Contemporary Islamic Studies in China," *Chinese Muslims*, Issue 3, 2011, pp. 18–21. (李林，"当代中国伊斯兰教义学研究的问题和反思"《中国穆斯林》, 2011 年第 3 期，18–21 页）

4. RESEARCH IN RELIGION—CHINESE ISLAMIC STUDIES   77

1 CENTERED AROUND RESEARCH ON ISLAMIC TEACHING IN CHINA

1.1 Menhuan and Sects

In China, the study of sects and menhuan in Islamic teaching occupies an extremely important position. After the introduction of Islam to China, China's Islam gradually evolved into its own unique sectarian system known as the "Three Major Sects" and "Four Great Menhuan." The so-called "Three Major Sects" include Gettymus, Ihwani, and Siddhartha. The "Four Great Menhuan" or "Four Great Sufi Schools" include Hufuye, Gadlinye, Zheheye, and Kubuye. Research in the field of sects and menhuan did not progress until after China's reform and opening, and its research methods and other aspects were not fully developed. Since the beginning of the 21st century, there have been numerous developments in this field of research; not only has there been an increase in publications, but a relatively systematic disciplinary system has also been formed. The most representative publications of the pre-21st century period are the following two books by Ma Tong:

Ma Tong, *A Brief History of Chinese Islamic Sect Menhuan System*, Ningxia People's Publishing House, 1983. (马通, 《中国伊斯兰教派门宦制度史略》, 宁夏人民出版社, 1983 年)
Ma Tong, *Tracing the Origin of Chinese Islamic Sect Menhuan*, Ningxia People's Publishing House, 1986. (马通, 《中国伊斯兰教派门宦溯源》, 宁夏人民出版社, 1986 年)

The first part of *A Brief History of Chinese Islamic Sect Menhuan System* provides an overview of the history of Islam, while the second part comprehensively records the various systems and major historical events of the three major Islamic sects and the four major menhuan. The contents of the book are derived from a variety of sources, including oral traditions and interviews, family histories, and local chronicles of some sect and gate menhuan leaders. The appendix of this book includes an overview table of sects and menhuan, and the lineage of Islamic sects and eunuchs in China. The author explores the close relationship between Islam and certain minority ethnic groups in China, discusses the development and influence of the various forms of Islam in China, and provides a detailed introduction to the development of Islam in China and its eunuch system.[4]

In *Tracing the Origin of Chinese Islamic Sect Menhuan*, the content is divided into: Su Fei, Yi Chan, and Menhuan; Heda Yetong Rashi and Ma Shouzhen; Huazhe Abudu Dong Laxi and Qi, Ma, and Xian Sanmen; Ma Mingxin and Abdul Al Harig Azezi Al Misjieji; Ma Lingming and the Babu faction; Xidaotang and Baidaotang; Wahhabiya and Ihwani. There are also chapters on Islamic historical sites along the southeast coast and Gongbei in the northwest region. This book explores the historical origins of the Islamic denominations in China, specifically of the Sufis, Hedaye Tongrashi, and Huazhe Abdul Dongrashi factions, and their relationship with the menhuan.[5]

These two books are comprehensive, systematic, and scientific in their knowledge and exploration, and provide readers with a robust understanding of the emergence, development, and social role of Chinese Islamic sects and menhuan. Together they have laid a solid foundation for the study of Chinese Islamic sects and received high praise from Ma Tong's academic peers. For historical reasons, there are almost no records of this aspect of Chinese Islamic history, and there were no monographs introducing the Islamic sects and menhuan in China until Ma Tong's volumes. Their publication was undoubtedly a breakthrough in the study of Islam in China. Famous historian Bai Shouyi commented that Ma Tong's books, "after years of hard work and collection of relevant rich materials, has opened up a new field in the history of Islam and the Hui ethnic group in

---

[4] Ma Tong, *A Brief History of Chinese Islamic Sect Menhuan System,* Ningxia People's Publishing House, 1983. （马通，《中国伊斯兰教派门宦制度史略》，宁夏人民出版社，1983 年，391 页）

[5] Ma Tong, Tracing the Origin of Chinese Islamic Sect Menhuan, Ningxia People's Publishing House, 1986. （马通，《中国伊斯兰教派门宦溯源》，宁夏人民出版社，1986 年，166 页）

4. RESEARCH IN RELIGION—CHINESE ISLAMIC STUDIES 79

China." [6] Ma Tong's work is the most academically valuable masterpiece in China's thirty years of reform and opening.

Another scholar with outstanding research in sectarian studies is Mian Weilin.

Mian Weilin, *Summary of Ningxia Islamic Sects*, Ningxia People's Publishing House, 1981. (勉维霖，《宁夏伊斯兰教派概要》，宁夏人民出版社，1981 年)
Mian Weilin, *Introduction to the Islamic Religious System of the Hui People in China*, Ningxia People's Publishing House, 1997. (勉维霖，《中国回族伊斯兰宗教制度概论》，宁夏人民出版社，1997)

Summary of Ningxia Islamic Sects is an introduction to the five sects and menhuan of Islam in Ningxia based on the author's investigation in the late 1950s. Due to its brevity and limited circulation, it has not received much attention. The content of this book was later incorporated into the edited volume *Introduction to the Islamic Religious System of the Chinese Hui Ethnic Group*, edited by Mian Weilin. The book covers topics as varied as the Five Merits of Destiny, festival celebrations, family and life etiquette, marriage system, funeral system, dietary system, the organizational structure of mosques, religious leadership system, temple system, Jingtang Jiaoyu, the introduction of Sufism, Sufi doctrine, and Sufi ritual. There are chapters on the inheritance of Sufi religious positions and traditions, Sufi clerical power and economic structure, the Ihwani Reformation Movement, the Ihwani Reformation Proposition, Selefiya, the Western Daoist Muslim Family, the Hui Islamic Cultural Movement, and the development and characteristics of contemporary Hui Islam. The author comprehensively discusses the historical evolution of the Islamic religious system of the Hui ethnic group, including faith and merit, social and family life, organization and education, Sufism, the Hui Islamic Reformation Movement, and contemporary Hui Islam, all of which are involved in scientific

---

[6] Ma Tong, *A Brief History of Chinese Islamic Sect Menhuan System,* Ningxia People's Publishing House, 1983. (马通，《中国伊斯兰教派门宦制度史略》，宁夏人民出版社，1983 年，「白寿彝氏序文」)

analysis and research.[7] From this book, one can see that trends in Hui Islam shift in different eras as it strives to adapt to the social environment.

After Mian Weilin's publications, a batch of papers and monographs appeared in which significant progress was made in the collection and organization of literature. The research field continued to expand and attracted the attention of the international academic community. Important papers on individual eunuchs and historical events include:

> Yang Huaizhong, "On the Uprising of Zheheye Muslims in the 18th Century" (杨怀中, 《论十八世纪哲赫耶穆斯林的起义》)
>
> Chen Huisheng, "On the Struggle and Influence between the Baishan School and the Heishan School in the Qing Dynasty" (陈慧生, 《试论清代白山派和黑山派之间的斗争及其影响》)
>
> Ma Chen, "Ma Yuanzhang and the Revival Activities of the Zhehelinye Sect" (马辰, 《马元章与哲赫林耶教派的复兴活动》)
>
> Ma Fuhai, "The Beginning and End of Lin Yemen's Official Yang Men in Ga" (马福海, 《嘎的林耶门宦杨门始末》)
>
> Feng Jinyuan, "On the Issues of the Menhuan Sect" (冯今源, 《 关于门宦教派问题的》)

The above batch of papers are all published in *Collected Papers of the Islamic Academic Conference of the Five Northwest Provinces* previously discussed. Among the officials of various sects, there has been a fruitful collection of materials and research on Xidaotang. Xidaotang is one of the three major sects of Islam in China and is known as the Han School in academia due to its emphasis on the localization of Islamic transmission methods. The following papers were the first to introduce this field:

> Guan Lianji, "Overview of the History of Xidaotang," *World Religious Studies*, Issue 3, 1982. (关连吉, " 西道堂历史概述, " 《世界宗教研究》, 1982 年第 3 期)

---

[7] Mian Weilin, *Introduction to the Islamic Religious System of the Hui People in China*, Ningxia People's Publishing House, 1997. (勉维霖, 《中国回族伊斯兰宗教制度概论》, 宁夏人民出版社, 1997, 1 页 · 目录 (460 页))

> Zhu Gang, "A Review of the Belief in Chines Islamic Xidaotang," *Journal of Qinghai University for Nationalities*, Issue 4, 1982. （朱刚，"中国伊斯兰教西道堂信仰述评，"《青海民族学院学报》，1982 年第 4 期）

In this regard, there are also some thesis studies, such as Li Kuan's "Other's Vision and Self Elaboration – A History of Islamic Research on Xidaotang." In this paper, the research group was divided into two categories: Xidaotang people and non-Xidaotang people. The subjects jointly wrote the history of Xidaotang, and this study compares their research. Their perspectives on the Xidaotang people complement each other; while there are similarities and inconsistencies, overall, their works are positive affirmations and elaborations of Xidaotang and its spirit. It is this exchange and interaction between the "self" and the "other" that promotes the development of Xidaotang and enriches its research history.[8]

In 1987, *Historical Materials Collection of Xidaotang* was jointly edited by the Institute of Ethnic Studies of Qinghai University for Nationalities and the Institute of Northwest Ethnic Studies of Northwest University for Nationalities. To this day, it is the only book that discusses Xidaotang specifically. It is a compilation of sixteen materials and articles related to the study of Xidaotang from the Ming Dynasty to the 1980s, making it a mandatory and valuable reference book for studying Xidaotang. More recently, a book titled *Appreciation of Ma Qixi's Poetry Union* by Zhonghua Publishing House reflects new viewpoints in the academic community.[9]

In May 1994 and July 1995, two groups of scholars were invited to conduct academic research at Xidaotang for nearly half a month each. This was unparalleled in the history of Islamic

---

[8] Li Kuan's "Other's Vision and Self elaboration – A History of Islamic Research on Xidaotang" (2012 Master's Thesis from Central University for Nationalities). （李寛，《他者眼光与自我阐述—伊斯兰教西道堂研究史》2012 年中央民族大学修士学位論文）

[9] Min Shengguang, *Appreciation of Ma Qinxi's Poetry Union*, Zhonghua Book Company Publishing House, 2004, pp. 299. （敏生光，《马启西诗联赏识》，中华书局，2004 年，299 页。）

research in China, and the success of the investigation has been well published and influential to this day. Related papers include:

Zhang Shihai, "The History and Current Situation of the Hui Ethnic Group in Lintan," *Gansu Ethnic Studies*, Issue 3, 1993. (张世海，"临潭回族的历史与现状，"《甘肃民族研究》，1993 年第 3 期)

Lu Jinxian and Lu Juxian, "Chinese Islamic Xidaotang," *Arab World*, Issue 2, 1994. (陆进贤、陆聚贤，"中国伊斯兰教西道堂，"《阿拉伯世界》，1994 年第 2 期)

Gan Minyan, "Investigation of the History and Current Situation of the Islamic Xidaotang in Gansu Province – Focusing on How Islam Adapts to Social Development," *Northwest Ethnic Studies*, Issue 21, 1994. (甘敏岩，"甘肃伊斯兰教西道堂历史与现状调查——以伊斯兰教如何与社会发展相适应为主，"《西北民族研究》，1994 年 2 期)

Ma Deliang and Yu Qian, "Analysis of the Influence of Liu Zhi's Thought on Xidaotang," *World Religious Studies*, Issue 1, 1995. (马德良、于谦，"刘智思想对西道堂影响浅析，"《世界宗教研究》，1995 年第 1 期)

Jin Yijiu, "The Influence of Liu Zhi's Thought on Chinese Muslims," *Gansu Ethnic Studies*, Issue 3–4, 1996. (金宜久，"刘智思想在中国穆斯林中的影响，"《甘肃民族研究》，1996 年第 3-4 期)

Ding Hong, "Xidaotang Model - Social Practice of a Religious Faction and Reflections on It," *Journal of Central University for Nationalities*, Issue 5, 1996. (丁宏，"西道堂模式——一个宗教派别的社会实践及带给我们的思考，"《中央民族大学学报》，1996 年第 5 期)

Ma Ping, "The 'Pueblo' of the Hui People in China—A Study of the Xidaotang Nailaitidafangzi, Lintan, Gannan," *Hui Studies*, Issue 2, 1997. (马平，"中国回族的"普埃布洛"—甘南临潭西道堂尕路提大房子研究，"《回族研究》，1997 年第 2 期)

Ma Ping, "The Group Study of the 'Qiusouma' of the Hui People in Larenguan, Gannan Tibetan Area," *Collection of Islamic Culture*, China Social Sciences Press, 2001. (马平，"甘南藏区拉仁关回族"求索玛"的群体研究，"《伊斯兰文化论集》，中国社会科学出版社，2001 年)

4. RESEARCH IN RELIGION—CHINESE ISLAMIC STUDIES   83

The authors of "Chinese Islamic Xidaotang" (Lu Jinxian and Lu Junxian) were national religious workers who worked in the Gannan ethnic area for more than twenty years and wrote this paper based on surveys, interviews, and data collection. They argue that Xidaotang has unique insights and measures in various aspects such as Chinese socialist culture, education, and economic construction. This research is worthy of attention by philosophers, religious experts, and sociologists alike.[10]

The article "Investigation of the History and Current Situation of the Islamic Xidaotang in Gansu Province – Focusing on How Islam Adapts to Social Development" by Gan Minyan focuses on the objective laws of religious development in history and the continuous changes in religion in relation to social change.[11]

Ma Deliang's and Yu Qian's "Analysis of the Influence of Liu Zhi's Thought on Xidaotang" demonstrates how Islam has spread, rooted, blossomed, and borne fruit in the land of China, going through a long historical process and a difficult path of development, and finally integrating with traditional Chinese culture. Islamic educators in the Ming and Qing dynasties interpreted classic Islamic works in Chinese and expounded the basic spirit of Islam. The study also discusses issues that have had an impact on fields such as the study of Xidaotang.[12]

In "Xidaotang Model – Social Practice of a Religious Faction and Reflections on It," Ding Hong presents Xidaotang as a Chinese Islamic sect that emerged in Lintan, Gansu, during the Guangxu period of the Qing Dynasty. Its members are mainly Hui, including Salar, Dongxiang, and some Han and Tibetan who have

---

[10] Lu Jinxian and Lu Juxian, "Chinese Islamic Xidaotang," *Arab World*, Issue 2, 1994. （陆进贤、陆聚贤， "中国伊斯兰教西道堂" 《阿拉伯世界》，1994 年第 2 期，48－50 页）

[11] Gan Minyan, "Investigation of the History and Current Situation of the Islamic Xidaotang in Gansu Province - Focusing on How Islam Adapts to Social Development," *Northwest Ethnic Studies*, 1994, Issue 21. （甘敏岩，"甘肃伊斯兰教西道堂历史与现状调查—以伊斯兰教如何与社会发展相适应为主" 《西北民族研究》，1994 年 2 期，42－47 页）

[12] Ma Deliang and Yu Qian, "Analysis of the Influence of Liu Zhi's Thought on Xidaotang," *World Religious Studies*, 1995, Issue 1. （马德良、于谦， "刘智思想对西道堂影响浅析" 《世界宗教研究》，1995 年第 1 期）

converted to Islam. There are tens of thousands of followers throughout provinces such as Gansu, Qinghai, Ningxia, and Xinjiang. As a religious sect, Xidaotang formed a unique pattern during its establishment and development, and is the only Islamic sect in China that has not been directly influenced by a foreign Islamic school of thought. The founder of Xidaotang, Ma Qixi, firmly believed in Islam and was also a scholar.[13]

In "The 'Pueblo' of the Hui People in China—A Study of the Xidaotang Nailaitidafangzi, Lintan, Gannan," Ma Ping argues that there were large houses used for collective life in Xidaotang's history. Through this folk heritage, we can see the unique cultural charm and influence of Xidaotang as an Islamic community in maintaining group interests in specific organizational forms under specific historical conditions.[14]

The above papers have analyzed and studied the early history of Xidaotang, whether it was a sect or menhuan. When it comes to Xidaotang, Gao Zhanfu's achievements are relatively concentrated:

> Gao Zhanfu, "The Influence of Liu Zhi's Religious Thoughts on the Xidaotang Sect," *Ningxia Social Sciences*, 1990, Issue 2. (高占福，"刘智宗教思想对西道堂教派的影响，"《宁夏社会科学》，1990年第2期)
>
> Gao Zhanfu, "The Religious Thought of Liu Zhi and Its Impact on the Economic Development of Xidaotang," *Northwest Ethnic Studies*, 1993, Issue 1. (高占福，"刘智的宗教思想对西道堂经济的发展，"《西北民族研究》，1993年第1期。)
>
> Gao Zhanfu, "Investigation and Research on the 'Big Family Organization' of Xidaotang," *Gansu Ethnic Studies*, 1999, Issue

---

[13] Ding Hong, "Xidaotang Model - Social Practice of a Religious Faction and Reflections on It," Journal of Central University for Nationalities, 1996, Issue 5. (丁宏，"西道堂模式—1个宗教派别的社会实践及带给我们的思考"《中央民族大学学报》，1996年第5期，49—53页)

[14] Ma Ping, "The 'Pueblo' of the Hui People in China – A Study of the Xidaotang nailaitidafangzi, Lintan, Gannan, *Hui Studies*, 1997, Issue 2. and (马平，"中国回族的普埃布洛"—甘南临潭西道堂尕路提大房子研究"《回族研究》，1997年第2期，1—19页)

> **2.** (高占福，"关于西道堂 '大家庭组织' 的调查与研究》，" 《甘肃民族研究》，1999 年第 2 期)

At the end of the Qing Dynasty and the beginning of the Republic of China, the Chinese Islamic sect Xidaotang appeared at the foot of Xifeng Mountain in the old city of Lintan, Gansu. It has received great attention from various sectors of society since its formation, which is not uncommon in the history of Chinese Islam. Xidaotang has attracted widespread attention among the numerous sects of Islam in China for two main reasons: first, its main religious ideas come from the teachings of Liu Zhi, a scholar native to Nanjing, and did not develop under foreign influence like other sects. Commenting on the relationship between Liu Zhizong's religious ideology and the origin of Xidaotang, Ma Mingren's economic activities in revitalizing Xidaotang, and the history and current situation of Xidaotang, Gao Zhanfu's research also involves sociology.

Ma Fuchun, the eldest son of Ma Mingren, the third bishop of Xidaotang, and the current bishop of Xidaotang, Min Shengguang, have also written:

> Ma Fuchun, "The Impact of Mr. Liu Jielian's Religious Translation on the Future Islamic Sects," Arab World, 1983, Issue 1. (马富春，"刘介廉先生的宗教译著对以后伊斯兰教派的影响，" 《阿拉伯世界》，1983 年第 1 期)
>
> Min Shengguang, "Liu Zhi's Thought and Xidaotang," Hui Studies, 1991, Issue 4. (敏生光，"刘智思想与西道堂，" 《回族研究》，1991 年第 4 期)
>
> Min Shengguang, "The Impact of the Uma System in Islam on the Xidaotang," World Religious Studies, 1995, Issue 1. (敏生光，"伊斯兰教 '乌玛' 制度对西道堂的影响，" 《世界宗教研究》，1995 年第 1 期)

In the late Ming and early Qing dynasties, Chinese Islamic educators such as Wang Daiyu, Ma Zhu, and Ma Dexin devoted their lives to the translation of Islamic teachings. With their proficiency in multiple languages, including Chinese, Arabic, and Persian, and their tireless research and verification, they wrote books such as *Zhengjiao Zhenquan, Qingzhen Daxue, Qingzhen*

Zhinan, and *Dahua Zonggui*. Ma Qixi, Ma Mingren, Min Zhidao, and others were influenced by scholars such as Liu Zhi to establish or inherit the Xidaotang. These papers examine the historical activities of Xidaotang from an academic perspective. [15] Ma Fuchun's paper provides comments on the religious translations of senior scholars such as Liu Jielian, while Min Shengguang's article explores the relationship between Islamic ideology and the development of Xidaotang.

Papers that trace the origin of Xiben menhuan to the Yichan sect in Xinjiang and reveal the orthodox origins of the Asufi sect include:

Wang Shouli, "Research on Xinjiang Yichan School," *Research on Xinjiang Social Sciences*, 1983, Issue 3. (王守礼，"新疆依禅派研究,"《新疆社会科学研究》，1983 年 3 期)

Chen Guoguang, "A Study of the 25th Hui Dynasty to the Central Plains: On the Dissemination of Xinjiang Islamic Mysticism in the Mainland," *World Religion Research*, 1985, Issue 1. (陈国光，"回回 25 世到中原考—关于新疆伊斯兰神秘主义在内地传布问题,"《世界宗教研究》，1985 年第 1 期)

Chen Guoguang, "Ishakye in the History of Islam in Xinjiang – Also on the Source of the Chinese Philosopher Ninye Menhuan," *World Religious Studies*, 1987, Issue 1. (陈国光，"新疆伊斯兰教史上的伊斯哈克耶—兼论中国哲赫忍耶门宦的来源,"《世界宗教研究》，1987 年第 1 期)

Chen Guoguang, "The Central Asian Nahe Xi Ban Di Order and the Northwest Gate Officials in Xinjiang, China," *World Religious Studies*, 1988, Issue 1. (陈国光，"中亚纳合西班底教团与中国新疆和卓、西北门宦,"《世界宗教研究》，1988 年第 1 期)

Zhou Xiefan, "The Sufi Order of Islam and the Chinese Imperial Household," *World Religious Studies*, 1991, Issue 4. (周燮藩，"伊斯兰教苏菲教团与中国门宦,"《世界宗教研究》，1991 年第 4 期)

---

[15] Ma Fuchun, "The Impact of Mr. Liu Jielian's Religious Translation on the Future Islamic Sects," Arab World, 1983, Issue 1. (马富春，"刘介廉先生的宗教译著对以后伊斯兰教派的影响"《阿拉伯世界》，1983 年第 1 期, 93－98 页)

4. RESEARCH IN RELIGION—CHINESE ISLAMIC STUDIES 87

> Wang Huaide, "The Evolution of the Sufi School and the Characteristics of the Formation of the Menhuan System," in *Collection of Materials from the Islamic Academic Seminar (Xi'an Conference) in the Five Northwest Provinces (Regions)*, ed. Historical Literature Department of Gansu Provincial Library, 1983. (王怀德，"苏菲派的演变与门宦制度形成的特点"，载《西北五省（区）伊斯兰教 学术讨论会（西安会议）资料汇集》，甘肃省图书馆历史 文献部辑订，1983 年)
>
> Wang Huaide, "A Brief Discussion on the Formation and Characteristics of the Yichan School," in Jin Yijiu, *Selected Books on Contemporary Chinese Religious Studies: Islamic Volume*, Ethnic Publishing House, January 2008. (王怀德，"略论依禅派的形成及其特点，" 载金宜久 编《当代中国宗教研究精选丛书：伊斯兰教卷》，民族出版社，2008 年 1 月出版)
>
> Pan Zhiping, *Rise and Fall of Central Asia and Xinjiang Hezhou*, China Social Sciences Press, June 1991. (潘志平，《中亚和新疆和卓的盛衰》，中国社会科学出版社，1991 年 6 月)
>
> Liu Zhengyin, "The Activities and Political Background of Islamic Sects in the Western Regions before the Rise of the Hezuo Family," World Religious Studies, 1991, Issue 4. (刘正，"和卓家族兴起前伊斯兰教派在西域的活动及其政治背景，"《世界宗教研究》1991 年第 4 期)

There are also papers that combine the study of the Sufi order with the study of Sufism, thus merging with the study of world Islam. Due to the recognition that the menhuan was a branch of the Sufi order in the northwest of China, the difference between the menhuan and the sect is unclear. Gedimu, also known as "Lao Jiao" or "Zun Gu Pai" in China, refers to the Chinese Muslim community that maintains the tradition formed after the entry of Islam into China and is different from the menhuan and sects that emerged after the late Ming and early Qing dynasties.

> Feng Zenglie, "Eight Discussions on the 'Ge Di Mu'," *Journal of Northwest University for Nationalities*, 1984, Issue 1. (冯增烈，"'格底目' 八议，"《西北民族学院学报》，1984 年第 1 期)
>
> Feng Jinyuan, "Preliminary Exploration of the Islamic Jiaofang System in China," *World Religious Studies*, 1984, Issue 1. (冯今

> 源，"中国伊斯兰教教坊制度初探，"《世界宗教研究》，1984 年第 1 期）
>
> Li Xinghua, "Preliminary Exploration of the History of Gedimu," *Gansu Ethnic Studies*, 1985, Issue 1 and 2. （李兴华，"格底木史初探，"《甘肃民族研究》，1985 年第 1、2 期）

In "Preliminary Exploration of the Islamic Jiaofang System in China," Feng Jinyuan begins with the fact that Islam has been in China for over a thousand years since the early Tang Dynasty. The religious organizational systems introduced over the centuries not only have the characteristics of Islam, but preserve the beliefs, systems, and traditional customs of Islam. They also have many Chinese characteristics and played an important role in the formation and development of the Chinese Hui ethnic group. Studying these systems is one of the more important aspects of studying Islam in China.[16]

Ihwani, also known as the "Xinxing Sect" or "Zun Jing Sect" in China, refers to a new denomination that emerged in the late 19th century, with the call of "teaching based on scriptures" and "respecting scriptures to reform customs." Related papers include:

> Ma Kexun, "Ma Wanfu, an Advocate of the Islamic Ihwani Faction in China"（马克勋， "中国伊斯兰教依赫瓦尼派的倡导者——马万福"）
>
> Ma Zhanbiao, "On Ma Wanfu and His Yihuani Sect"（马占彪，"试论马万福及其依赫瓦尼教派"）
>
> Liu Dewen, "The Relationship between Islam in China and the Wahhabism"（刘德文，"中国伊斯兰教依赫瓦尼与瓦哈比派的关系"）

In "Ma Wanfu, an Advocate of the Islamic Ihwani Faction in China," Ma Kexum shares that Ma Wanfu was named Nuhai (1853–1934). Ma Wanfu may be regarded as a famous scholar and activist of Islam in modern China who played an important role in advocating for the Ihwani faction and the "Reformation"

---

[16] Feng Jinyuan, "Preliminary Exploration of the Islamic Jiaofang System in China," *World Religious Studies*, 1984, Issue 1. （冯今源，"中国伊斯兰教教坊制度初探"《世界宗教研究》，1984 年第 1 期）

4. RESEARCH IN RELIGION—CHINESE ISLAMIC STUDIES   89

of Islam, and had a significant influence among Muslims both domestically and internationally. However, there is no systematic written record of his life and deeds. In the paper, Ma Kexun organizes and records what can be known about Ma Wanfu (Orchard) through surveys and interviews with his relatives and Ihwani insiders.[17]

2 JINGTANG JIAOYU (MOSQUE EDUCATION)

Hu Dengzhou, a Shaanxi scholar in the Ming Dynasty, founded the Chinese Muslim religious education system. At first, he taught out of his home and advocated for studying the classics. Beginning with his second disciple, he moved from a private home to the mosque and recruited more disciples to learn scriptures. The purpose was to cultivate monks and imams for mosques in various regions and to impart religious knowledge to Muslims. This education has a history of over 400 years and continues to this day. Over the centuries, scriptural education constantly improved and adapted to the times; however, few updates have been made since the 20th century, especially in the northwest region, which retains the status of the Middle Ages. Thus, scripture education has difficulty finding acceptance compared to the mainstream education system.

In academic research, scholars who do and do not identify as Muslim study the issue of Muslim religious education to varying degrees, but there are few publications on scripture education. The most representative work comes from Ma Jian:

> (Syria) K. A. Totah, *History of Muslim Education*, trans. Ma Jian, Commercial Press, 1946. （（叙利亚）托太哈,《回教教育史》, 马坚译, 伊斯兰文化学会编辑, 商务印书馆, 1946 年版, 一五六頁）

This book is divided into chapters that discuss the development of Islamic education, including schools, teachers, students, curriculum, teaching methods and school etiquette, Arabic

---

[17] Ma Kexun, "Ma Wanfu, an Advocate of the Islamic Ihwani Faction in China" (马克勋, "中国伊斯兰教依赫瓦尼派的倡导者—马万福")

educational masterpieces, Arab women and education, Arab educational philosophy, and Arab contributions to education.[18]

There are also several articles regarding Islamic education in China, such as Wang Jingzhai's "Review of Chinese Islamic Jingtangjiaoyu," Long Shiqian's "The Evolution and Topics of Chinese Islamic Monastery Education," and Hilarentin's papers such as "A Study of Jingtng Language." Like research in other fields, there were no significant research achievements during the Cultural Revolution, and it was not until the 1980s that papers were published:

> Feng Zenglie, "Islamic Jingtang Education in Shaanxi During the Ming and Qing Dynasties," *Journal of Ningxia University*, 1981, Issue 1–2. (冯增烈，"明清时期陕西伊斯兰教的经堂教育，"《宁夏大学学报》，1981 年第 1-2 期）

In Feng Zenglie's paper, the origin and rise of Jingtang jiaoyu are elucidated, and the relationship between the organization of mosques and the structure of Jingtang jiaoyu is discussed. It also provides a clear introduction to the courses taught in Jingtang jiaoyu education, Jingtangyu language, and the Jingtang script "Xiaoer Jing," plus the historical context of important figures such as Hu Dengzhou and his disciples. The article comprehensively explores the Islamic education system in China.

One of the greatest research achievements of the 1980s was the publication of the Confucian genealogy covering the Kangxi period of the Qing Dynasty compiled by Hui Muslim scholar Zhao Can:

> (Qing Dynasty) Zhao Can, *Genealogy of Classics Department*, People's Publishing House, Qinghai, July 1989. (（清）赵灿《经学系传谱》，青海人民出版社，1989 年 7 月）

The aim of Zhao Can's work is to provide a record of the famous Islamic scripture masters of the Hui and Salar ethnic groups in China during the Ming and early Qing dynasties, as well as their

---

[18] (Syria) K. A. Totah, *History of Muslim Education*, translated by Ma Jian, editor of Islamic culture Society, Commercial Press, 1946. (（叙利亚）托太哈，《回教教育史》，马坚译，伊斯兰文化学会编辑，商务印书馆，1946 年版, 156 页）

4. RESEARCH IN RELIGION—CHINESE ISLAMIC STUDIES 91

academic relationships and social activities. The manuscript was completed during the Kangxi period of the Qing Dynasty (1662 to 1722), and only four manuscripts were circulated. In 1987, Yang Yongchang and Ma Jizu jointly completed the sorting, annotation, and punctuation of the manuscript. The main text records the genealogy of twenty-seven famous scripture masters, including Mr. Hu Lao, Mr. Feng Haier, Hai Wenxuan, She Yunshan, Huangfu Jing, and others. The preface encourages the study of Islamic teachings and precepts, and there are two chapters devoted to She Yunshan's methods of gathering disciples and teaching scriptures. All the teachers listed in the volume were religious scholars who were considered by the public as excellent in both character and learning.[19] This volume is an important work that studies the development of scripture education, as well as the thoughts of scripture teachers and scholars.

The sixth National Hui History Seminar held in Jinan in 1990 focused on the history of Hui education, and the conference papers were edited and published under the name of the Shandong Provincial People's Committee:

> *Collected Works on the History of Chinese Hui Education,* Shandong University Press, 1991. (《中国回族教育史论集》，山东大学出版社，1991 年)

Many of these articles involve scripture education. In addition, periodicals such as *Chinese Muslims* have published introductions and research articles on Jingtang jiaoyu and famous scripture teachers.

> Wang Yongliang, "The Emergence and Early Forms of Hui Scriptural Education," *Chinese Muslims*, 1993. (王永亮，"回族经堂教育的产生和早期形态，"《中国穆斯林》，1993)

There have also been relevant publications in the 21st century, such as:

---

[19] (Qing Dynasty) Zhao Can, *Genealogy of Classics Department,* People's Publishing House, Qinghai, July 1989. ((清) 赵灿《经学系传谱》，青海人民出版社，1989 年 7 月，目录)

Zhang Xueqiang, *History of Northwest Hui Education*, Gansu Education Press, 2002. （张学强，《西北回族教育史》，甘肃教育出版社，2002 年）
Yang Wenjiong, "Women's Education: The Expansion of Jingtangjiaoyu and the Shift of the Center of Gravity in Cultural Communication," *Hui Studies*, Issue 1, 2002. （杨文炯，"女学：经堂教育的拓展与文化传播承角色的重心位移，"《回族研究》，2002 年第一期）
Wang Fuping, "Hai Sifu's Contribution to Chinese Jingtangjiaoyu," *Hui Studies*, Issue 4, 2007. （王伏平，"海思福对中国经堂教育的贡献"《回族研究》，2007 年第四期）

Zhang Xueqiang's book *History of Northwest Hui Education* promotes the development of ethnic education and Hui ethnic studies, but more importantly, supports Hui ethnic education in the Northwest region through historical research.[20] The content is divided into chapters and sections covering: Northwest Hui and Northwest Hui Education; The education of the ancestors of the Northwest Hui ethnic group during the Tang, Song, and Yuan dynasties; Menhuan education of the Northwest Hui ethnic group during the Ming and Qing dynasties; The teachings and rituals of Islamic Sufi menhuan in Ganning and Qinghai during the Qing Dynasty; The development of education for the Northwest Hui ethnic group during the Republic of China period (1912–1949); Hui education in the Shaanxi Gansu Ningxia Border Region; and factors that affect the historical development of education for the Hui ethnic group in northwest China. It also includes chapters on developing education for the Hui ethnic group in the northwest and suggestions for future study.

In Yang Wenjiong's paper, "Women's Education: The Expansion of Jingtang jiaoyu and the Shift of the Center of Gravity in Cultural Communication," documents the rise and development of women's schools as an extension of traditional canon education in urban Muslim communities in the northwest

---

[20] Zhang Xueqiang, "History of Northwest Hui Education," Gansu Education Press, 2002. （张学强，《西北回族教育史》，甘肃教育出版社，2002 年，303 页）

4. RESEARCH IN RELIGION—CHINESE ISLAMIC STUDIES 93

region, which became a remarkable cultural phenomenon. Yang Wenjiong traces the history of female mosque students, analyzing their context in urban areas of northwest China.[21]

In Wang Fuping's 2007 paper, "Hai Sifu's Contribution to Chinese Jingtangjiaoyu," he examines the life of Hai Sifu (1832–1920), a famous Hui Muslim scripture writer and translator of the late Qing and early Republic of China periods who transcribed, annotated, and translated many Islamic scriptures throughout his life and devoted himself to the cause of Islamic education in China. The year 2007 marked the 88th anniversary of Hai Sifu's death, and this article commemorates his life by providing an overview of Mr. Hai Sifu's contributions to Islamic scripture education in China.[22]

Also in 2007, the Seminar on Chinese Jingtang Jiaoyu was held in Lanzhou. Attendees gave papers and speeches focused on the development, problems, solutions, and future directions of Chinese Jingtang jiaoyu, featuring titles (by unidentified authors) such as:

"Creation and Cultural Revitalization: Historical Enlightenment from the Local Growth of Islam in China"（"创制与文化振兴—伊斯兰教中国本土生长的历史启示"）
"Centennial Development of Jingtangjiaoyu"（"经堂教育的百年发展"）
"Current Situation and Reflection on Jingtangjiaoyu"（"经堂教育的现状与思考"）
"Future Development Direction of Jingtangjiaoyu"（"经堂教育未来发展的方向"）

---

[21] Yang Wenjiong, "Women's Education: The Expansion of Jingtangjiaoyu and the Shift of the Center of Gravity in Cultural Communication," *Hui Studies*, Issue 1, 2002. (杨文炯，"女学：经堂教育的拓展与文化传播承角色的重心位移"《回族研究》，2002 年第 1 期，25—33 页)

[22] Wang Fuping, "Hai Sifu's Contribution to Chinese Jingtangjiaoyu," *Hui Studies*, Issue 4, 2007. (王伏平，"海思福对中国经堂教育的贡献"《回族研究》，2007 年第 4 期，101—103 页)

> "New Theory, New Perspective, and New Realm of Jingtangjiaoyu Development" ("经堂教育发展的新理论、新视角、新境界")[23]

also,

> Ding Shiren, *Chinese Islamic Jingtangjiaoyu (Mosque Education)*, Gansu People's Publishing House, 2013. (丁士仁,《中国伊斯兰经堂教育》, 甘肃人民出版社, 2013 年)

Ding Shiren's *Chinese Islamic Jingtangjiaoyu (Mosque Education)* is divided into three volumes. The first volume is a theoretical volume with more than thirty scholarly articles discussing Jingtang jiaoyu. The second volume is dedicated to context and sorts out the historical trajectory, academic schools, regions, and major events of in the development of Jingtang jiaoyu. The final volume is a biographical volume that features the life stories of renowned Islamic masters who have devoted themselves to the education of Jingtang in various mosques over the centuries, cultivating people, morality, and heart, preaching, imparting knowledge, and enlightening wisdom, all without seeking fame or fortune. They gained knowledge and benefit from teaching and were well known among the people. This work enables to reader to cherish the memory of our predecessors, see examples for future generations, achieve sustainable performance, and inherit Jingtang jiaoyu.[24]

In recent years, Xiaojing (i.e., Xiaoerjing)—the practice of writing Chinese in Arabic script—has gradually attracted scholars' attention. Chinese Muslims refer to Arabic and Persian as "Xiaohua Jingdian" and widely adopt both languages in Islamic Jingtang jiaoyu in China. Since around 2000, Liu Yingsheng from Nanjing University has organized a research group on the topic of Xiaojing that has gone to the northwest multiple times to collect

---

[23] All papers included in the *Symposium on Chinese Canon Education* (not officially published, internal materials) (均载入《中国经堂教育问题研讨会》论文集(没有正式出版, 内部资料))

[24] Ding Shiren, Chinese Islamic Jingtangjiaoyu (mosque education), Gansu People's Publishing House, 2013. (丁士仁,《中国伊斯兰经堂教育》, 甘肃人民出版社, 2013 年, 目录(336 页))

4. RESEARCH IN RELIGION—CHINESE ISLAMIC STUDIES 95

relevant literature. The following publications are representative of their work:

Liu Yingsheng, "Several Issues on the 'Xiaojing' script commonly used among some Muslim ethnic groups in China," *Hui Studies*, Issue 4, 2001. (刘迎胜, "关于中国部分穆斯林民族中通行的 '小经' 文字的几个问题," 《回族研究》, 2001 年第 4)

Han Zhongyi, "Research on the Relationship between Xiaojing Scriptures and Islamic Issues," *World Religious Studies*, Issue 3, 2005. (韩中义, "小经文献与伊斯兰教相关问题研究," 《世界宗教研究》, 2005 年第 3 期)

Han Zhongyi, "A Preliminary Study on the Related Issues of Xiaojing Literature and Linguistics," *Northwest Ethnic Studies*, Issue 1, 2007. (韩中义, "小经文献与语言学相关问题初探," 《西北民族研究》, 2007 年第 1 期)

Han Zhongyi and Zhu Liang, "Investigation on the Printing and Publication of Chinese Muslim Classics Literature - Taking the Xiaojing 'Kaidani' as an Example," *Journal of Northern University for Nationalities* (Philosophy and Social Sciences Edition), Issue 4, 2012. (韩中义、朱亮, "关于中国穆斯林经学文献印行的考察—以小经《开达尼》为例," 《北方民族大学学报（哲学社会科学版）》, 2012 年第 4 期, 118-125 页)

Hu Long, "'Xiaojing' 《Zhengda Guangming》 and Pu'er Ma Imam," *Hui Studies*, Issue 3, 2006. (虎隆, "'小经'《正大光明》与普洱马阿訇," 《回族研究》, 2006 年第 3 期).

Hu Long, "Also Talking about 'Xiaojing' and Opening the Yidane," *Hui Studies*, Issue 1, 2007. (虎隆, "也谈 '小经'开以达尼," 《回族研究》, 2007 年第 1 期)

In Liu Yingsheng's, "Several Issues on the 'Xiaojing' script commonly used among some Muslim ethnic groups in China," he discusses the name, meaning, and usage of Xiaojing characters, and the academic significance of collecting Xiaojing reading materials and carrying out Xiaojing research in Hui and Islamic studies. As part of his research, the author collected Xiaojing

96 ISLAM IN CHINA AND THE ISLAMIC WORLD

reading materials in Gansu, Xiaojing works recorded in literature, and various glossaries and reference works.[25]

In "Research on the Relationship between Xiaojing Scriptures and Islamic Issues," Han Zhongyi gives the Xiaojing, which are Arabic alphabetic characters used by Hui and other nationalities. The documents written with the Xiaojing have rich contents that are important to the study of Islam in China, as explained in this article.[26]

In the discussion "A Preliminary Study on the Related Issues of Xiaojing Literature and Linguistics," Han Zhongyi proposes that studying the issues related to Xiaojing literature and linguistics can provide meaningful insight into the many difficulties encountered in previous studies on "Jingtang vocabulary" (i.e., small scripture vocabulary) and its grammar, syntax, and so on, which provided a lot of reference tools for further research. The article builds on previous research in an attempt to gain more insight.[27]

In the article "Investigation on the Printing and Publication of Chinese Muslim Classics Literature – Taking the Xiaojing 'Kaidani' as an Example," Han Zhongyi and Zhu Liang make the case that there are certain channels for Chinese Muslims to inherit basic Islamic knowledge, but scholars have not paid enough attention to this issue in their research. The authors illustrate the methods of folk knowledge dissemination in China by taking a version of the Chinese Islamic scripture (Kaidani) as an example

---

[25] Liu Yingsheng, "Several Issues on the 'Xiaojing' script commonly used among some Muslim ethnic groups in China," Hui Studies, Issue 4, 2001. (刘迎胜，"关于中国部分穆斯林民族中通行的'小经'文字的几个问题"《回族研究》，2001 年第 4 期, 20－26 页)

[26] Han Zhongyi, "Research on the Relationship between Xiaojing Scriptures and Islamic Issues," World Religious Studies, Issue 3, 2005. (韩中义，"小经文献与伊斯兰教相关问题研究"《世界宗教研究》，2005 年第 3 期, 35－40 页)

[27] Han Zhongyi, "A Preliminary Study on the Related Issues of Xiaojing Literature and Linguistics," Northwest Ethnic Studies, Issue 1, 2007. (韩中义，"小经文献与语言学相关问题初探"《西北民族研究》，2007 年第 1 期, 164－175 页)

and explores the publication, translation, version changes, and proofreading of folk print texts in Confucian literature. [28]

In the article "Also Talking about 'Xiaojing' and Opening the Yidane," Hu Long focuses on issues that have arisen in recent years among scholars studying Islam and the Xiaojing and Kaidani, which have been widely circulated in the Muslim community in northwest China. Based on the principles of seeking truth from facts, evidence-based statements, and reason in historical research, this article clarifies some of the issues involved in the original Tashkent version of "Elimination of the Sutra" by investigating its author, writing time, printing location, content, translation, and version, as well as its relationship with the Xiaojing—the Pinyin script created by Hui Muslims. [29]

---

[28] Han Zhongyi and Zhu Liang, "Investigation on the Printing and Publication of Chinese Muslim Classics Literature - Taking the Xiaojing 'Kaidani' as an Example," Journal of Northern University for Nationalities (Philosophy and Social Sciences Edition), Issue 4, 2012, pp. 118–125. (韩中义、朱亮，"关于中国穆斯林经学文献印行的考察—以小经《开达尼》为例"《北方民族大学学报（哲学社会科学版）》, 2012 年第 4 期，118-125 页)

[29] Hu Long, "Also Talking about 'Xiaojing' and Opening the Yidane", Hui Studies, Issue 1, 2007. (虎隆，"也谈 '小经' 开以达尼"《回族研究》, 2007 年第 1 期，119−123 页)

PART FIVE.
RESEARCH IN THE FIELD OF RELIGION—CENTERED ON WORLD ISLAMIC STUDIES

1 RESEARCH ON THE QURAN

The academic history of Islamic teaching abroad should start with an analysis of foreign achievements. There is no doubt that translation and annotation work on the Quran is the most important area of Islamic Studies as the Quran is a fundamental classic of Islam. Chinese translations are certainly helpful for research. Since the 1920s, new translations have been continuously available, and to this day, there are still new translations near publication.

Ji Juomi's classical Chinese translation of the Quran (a line bound stone engraved version) was completed in 1920. The first edition was printed and distributed by Shanghai Ailiyuan Guangcang Academy in 1931. （姬觉弥总其事的文言体《汉译古兰经》（系线装石刻本）在 1920 年完成。1931 年的初版由上海爱丽园广仓学馆印刷并发行）
The translation of the Quran by Wang Jingzhai (1979–1945) is an important work after 20 years of study. （王静斋（1979-1945）的译本《古兰经译解》是历经 20 年潜心钻研重要著作之一）
The Quran translated by Ma Jian (1906–1978) was published in China in 1981. The translation is faithful to the original classic and has become the most influential Chinese translation of the Quran in the world. （马坚（1906-1978）的《古兰经》于

1981 年在中国出版发行，译文忠实经典原著，成为世界最有影响力的汉译《古兰经》）.
Shi Zizhou (1978–1969), after retirement, translated the Quran from the English version and wrote notes. （时子周（1978-1969），退休后自英文版翻译《古兰经》，撰写注释）
Tong Daozhang (1918–1982) translated and annotated the Quran from the English version in his later years. His translation of the Quran into Chinese has a certain influence on overseas Chinese Muslims. （仝道章（1918-1982），晚年自英文版译注《古兰经》，其《古兰经中阿文对照详注译本》在海外华文穆斯林中有一定影响）
Li Jingyuan (1914–1983), who translated and introduced the Quran from the English version in his later years, died before the book was completed. His son, Zhang Chengqian, continued his legacy and spent 20 years proofreading and translating the manuscript. In 2001, he completed the notes to the Quran and officially published it in 2004 (World Chinese Publishing House). （李静远（1914-1983），晚年自英文版译介《古兰经》，书未成逝世。其子张承迁继其遗志，用 20 年时间校译书稿，于 2001 年完成《古兰经注释》，正式出版于 2004 年（世界华人出版社））.
Ma Zhonggang, finalized in 2005, is a Chinese translation of the Quran annotated with the hadith. （马仲刚，2005 年定稿于《古兰经简注》是一部以《圣训》注释《古兰经》的中文译本）.
Ma Jinpeng (1913–2001) spent nearly ten years of his later translating and annotating the Quran. （马金鹏（1913-2001）晚年致力于《古兰经》的研究和译注，用近十年时间完成《古兰经译注》一书）.
Kong Dejun (1972–) translated notes to the Quran and notes to Ibn Kaiser's Quran （孔德军（1972-）其译著《古兰经注》和《伊本·凯西尔《古兰经》注》）
Sub Ji and Wang's Chinese version. To facilitate the understanding of Chinese readers, the Chinese translation of the Quran often includes a large number of notes in or after the text. （分姬和王的古代汉语版和其余的现代汉语版本。为方便中国读者理解，汉译《古兰经》在译介经典原文的同时，常在文中或文后附有大量中文注释。）

5. RESEARCH IN RELIGION—WORLD ISLAMIC STUDIES   101

Chinese Translation of the Quran was written by General Ji Juemini, drafted by Imam Li Yuchen, and mutually referenced and modified by Chinese scholar Fan Kangfu and Arab writer Imam Xue Ziming. It was completed in 1920, then printed and distributed by Shanghai Ailiyuan Guangcang School in 1931. The book is a thread bound print version with 114 chapters, and the volume number, chapter name, and translation and proofreading unit name are marked at the opening. The book states that, in all cases, the translation is based on the original Arabic text, with Muhammad Ali's English translation and Sakamoto Kenichi's Japanese translation as references, so as to make it concise and accurate without losing its truth. This one of the earliest Chinese translations of the Quran.[1]

Wang Jingzhai (1879–1945) devoted his entire life to Islamic academic research and the translation of Islamic scriptures. *The Interpretation of the Quran* is one of Wang Jingzhai's most important works and the culmination of twenty years of dedicated research. He translated and published the Quran in three different versions: Classical Chinese, Jingtang language, and vernacular Chinese. The vernacular translation is accompanied by explanations and 1,943 annotations, and is considered one of the most practical Chinese translations of the Quran.[2]

Ma Jian (1906–1978) is a modern Muslim scholar and translator in China whose most important and influential work is his modern Chinese version of the Quran. Ma Jian's translation of the Quran is faithful to the classic original work with concise and fluent writing and a simple, fresh style that is highly praised by academic and Muslim readers alike. Mr. Ma Jian's modern Chinese version of the Quran was published and distributed in

---

[1] *Chinese translation of the Quran* (a line bound stone engraved version), Ji juomi was completed in 1920. The first edition in 1931 was printed and distributed by Shanghai ailiyuan guangcang Academy. (《汉译古兰经》（系线装石刻本）姬觉弥在 1920 年完成。1931 年的初版由上海爱丽园广仓学馆印刷并发行)

[2] *The translation of the Quran*, translated by Wang Jingzhi, Shanghai Shuixiang Printing Library, 1946. reprinted by Dongfang Publishing House, 2005, 872 pages. (『古兰经译解』, 王静斋　訳本、上海水祥印书馆、1946 年（再版東方出版社、2005 年、872 页。）

China in 1981 with over 100,000 copies printed. In 1987, on the recommendation of the Hajj Ministry of the Kingdom of Saudi Arabia, Ma Jian's translation of the Quran was promoted worldwide as an excellent Chinese translation, making it the most influential Chinese translation of the Quran in the world to date.[3]

Shi Zizhou (1879–1969), the translator of the English version of the Quran, is a modern Chinese Muslim scholar. After retirement, he translated the English version of the Quran, wrote annotations, and completed the book *Interpretation of the Quran in Mandarin*, which is approximately 700,000 words. It has had a widespread influence among Muslim believers in Hong Kong and Taiwan.[4]

Tong Daozhang (1918–1982), another translator of the English version of the Quran, is a modern Chinese Muslim scholar, translator, and journalist. In his early years, he studied abroad and lived in the United States beginning in the 1950s. He served as the editor in chief of the Southeast Asian magazine *Islamic Light*. In his later years, he translated and annotated the English version of the Quran, and his detailed annotated version of the Quran in Arabic had a certain influence among overseas Chinese Muslims.[5]

Jing Yuan (1914–1983) was a modern Muslim scholar and translator in China. In his later years, he translated and introduced the English version of the Quran but passed away before completing the book. His son, Zhang Chengqian, continued his legacy by finishing his father's project, spending twenty years translating manuscripts, proofreading, and writing annotations. In 2001, he completed *Translation and Annotation of the Quran*,

---

[3] Quran, translated by Ma Jiang, China Social Science Publishing,1998, pp.493. (『古兰经』馬堅　訳本、中国社会科学出版社、1981年、493 页)

[4] Interpretation of the Quran in Mandarin, published by the Council of the Institute of Islamic Studies of the Chinese Academy of Sciences, Shi Zizhou (translated and annotated from the English version), pp. 1958, 908. (《古兰经国语译解》，時子周（自英文版译注）中华学术院回教研究所理事会出版，1958，908 页)

[5] *Detailed Annotated Translation of Arabic in the Quran*, translated by Shan Mu Shi, Tong Daozhang (translated from the English version), published by Yilin Publishing House in 1989 (『古兰经中阿文对照详注译本』（美）闪目氏・全道章（自英文版译注）译林出版社、1989 年)

5. RESEARCH IN RELIGION—WORLD ISLAMIC STUDIES   103

which is 1.6 million words. After its 2004 publication by World Chinese Publishing House, it sparked strong reactions among the public and academia.[6]

Ma Zhonggang, a contemporary Muslim scholar in China, is the translator of *Annotations to the Quran*. In his early years, he studied British and American literature. In 1982, he enrolled in the China Islamic Scripture Academy and, after graduation, taught at the Kunming Islamic Scripture Academy where he taught the Quran and the Hadith while translating and writing *Annotations*. Finalized in 2004, *Annotations* is a Chinese translation of the Quran annotated with the Hadith. Its defining features are that each page of scripture has annotations to the Holy Sermon at the end, the explanatory text is concise and easy to understand, easily confused personal pronouns are annotated in detail, and square brackets indicate difficult to understand scriptures so as to differentiate between the scripture and annotations. These features distinguish it from previous translations.[7]

Ma Jinpeng (1913–2001) is a modern Chinese Islamic scholar, translator, and associate professor at Peking University. In his early years, he studied at Beijing Chengda Normal School and Aizihar University in Egypt. After returning to China, he specialized in Islamic academic research, translation, and Arabic teaching. Ma Jinpeng devoted his entire life to academic pursuits, writing extensively in fields such as language, religion, history, and culture. In his later years, he spent nearly a decade completing his translation of the Quran, which was influential in the academic community.

Kong Dejun (1972–), a young Islamic scholar and translator in contemporary China serving as an imam, translated *Annotations*

---

[6] The Quran (Annotations to the Quran), translated and introduced by Li Jingyuan, published by World Chinese Publishing House in 2004. (《古兰经注释》, 李静远（自英文版译介，其子张承迁继其遗志），世界华人出版社，2004 年出版)

[7] Brief Annotations of the Quran, by Ma Zhonggang (Chinese translation of the Quran annotated with the Holy Sermon), Religious and Cultural Publishing House, 2005. (『古兰经简注』馬仲剛（以《圣训》注释《古兰经》的中文译本），宗教文化出版社、2005 年.）

to the Quran. He has also authored works such as *A Comparative Study of Islamic Human Rights and Western Human Rights, A Brief History of Islamic Revival,* and *The Faith of Muslims.* His translated works, *Annotations to the Quran* and *Annotations to the Quran by Ibn Kecil* have had a wide influence in the academic community.[8]

2 RESEARCH ON SHARIA AND DOCTRINES

To study the translation and annotation of the Quran, it is necessary to study Islamic law. Sharia, which is Arabic for "the path," is based on the Quran and hadith, and makes legal provisions for life and behavior. It is described by Muslims as "the entire commandment of Allah for human life." In a certain sense, without understanding Islamic law, one cannot understand Islam.

Research on Islamic law in the Chinese academic community started relatively late and has a relatively weak foundation. In the early stages of research, only a few publications emerged. For example:

> "Wei Ga Ye," Translated by Wang Jingzhai, published by Tianjin Yiguangyue Newspaper in 1931 and 1935 respectively. (《伟嘎业》，王静斋翻译，天津伊光月报社，1931 年、1935 年分别印行了上、下集)
>
> *Selected and Explained Wei Ga Ye,* Translated by Wang Jingzhai and compiled by Ma Saibei, published by Tianjin Ancient Books Publishing House in 1986. (王静斋 编译 马塞北 整理《选择详解伟嘎业》，天津古籍出版社，1986 年改作出版)
>
> *Chinese Translation of Ereshad*, Translated by Ding Yun, published in 1934 by the Mosque of Beiping. (丁蕴译，《汉译伊雷沙德》北平清真南寺，1934 年印行)
>
> *Comparison between Islamic Inheritance Law and Other Inheritance Laws* by Abdul Mutyadi, translated by Lin Xingzhi, Commercial Press, November 1946. (阿卜杜勒·穆泰阿迪 著、林兴智翻译《回教继承法与其他继承法之比较》，商务印书馆，1946 年 11 月)

---

[8] "Notes to the Quran," "Notes to the Quran" by Ibn Kesir ," written by Kong Dejun, China Social Sciences Press, 2005. (『古兰经注』『伊本·凯西尔《古兰经》注』孔德军訳着、中国社会科学出版社、2005 年)

5. RESEARCH IN RELIGION—WORLD ISLAMIC STUDIES 105

> *History of Islamic Law*, by Hu Zuli, translated by Pang Shiqian, published by Yuehua Cultural Service in 1950. （（埃及） 胡祖利著、庞士谦译《回教法学史》，月华文化服务社，1950 年）

Comparison between Islamic Inheritance Law and Other Inheritance Laws is a seminal work on Islamic law by author Abdul Mutyadi and was originally written in Arabic. It was first translated by Xiong Zhenzong in 1942 and serialized in *Islamic Culture* (vol.1, issues 2-4), a quarterly magazine published in Chongqing, but it was not initially published as a book. A different translation by Lin Xingzhi was released by Commercial Press in November 1946. The content of this book is divided into the basic content and theory of Islamic inheritance law, the inheritance laws of a variety of other cultures, and comparisons of Islamic inheritance laws with various ancient and modern inheritance laws. The author's primary argument is that faith cannot be the reason for the excellence of a certain law; it must have a theoretical basis. The author's basic viewpoint is that Islamic inheritance law is superior to other inheritance laws, and he goes to great lengths in support of his viewpoint. This book is one of the few works on Islamic law translated into Chinese and is important for studying Islamic legal thought.[9]

History of Islamic Law discusses the development of Islamic shariah from the time of Muhammad to the present.[10] It covers topics such as the teachings of the Mu Sheng era, the Quran, basic teachings in the Quran, political background, the Quran and the Sermon, key legislative points for this week, features of this week, the host of the teaching method, the establishment of legal schools, hypothetical issues, this week's jurist, a Hanafi jurist, the current status of dissection this week, and simplifying deviations in work.

---

[9] Abdul Mutyadi, "Comparison between Islamic Inheritance Law and Other Inheritance Laws," translated by Lin Xingzhi, Commercial Press, November 1946). （阿卜杜勒·穆泰阿迪 著、林兴智翻译《回教继承法与其他继承法之比较》，商务印书馆，1946 年 11 月，目录）

[10] (Egypt) Hu Zuli, translated by Pang Shiqian, "History of Islamic Law," published by Yuehua Cultural Service in 1950. （（埃及） 胡祖利著、庞士谦译《回教法学史》，月华文化服务社，1950 年、目录）.

> Jin Yijiu (editor), *An Introduction to Islam*, People's Publishing House, 1987. (金宜久主编,《伊斯兰教概论》, 青海人民出版社, 1987 年)

An Introduction to Islam was compiled by four scholars from the Islamic Research Office of the Institute of World Religions at the Chinese Academy of Social Sciences and edited by Jin Yijiu. Although the book is not a monograph on law, it provides a systematic introduction to various aspects of teaching law and is a good starting point for understanding and studying Islamic law in general.

Later, Wu Yungui was recognized as a scholar in the field of teaching methodology and has successively published translation and research works in China Social Sciences Press, such as:

> Noel J. Coulson, *A History of Islamic Law*, translated by Wu Yungui, China Social Sciences Press, 1986. (库尔森 著 吴云贵 译,《伊斯兰教法律史》(该书原本初版于 1964 年、1971 年重印, 1978 年出版通俗本), 中国社会科学出版社, 1986 年翻译版出版)

> Wu Yungui, *Outline of Islamic Shariah Law*, China Social Sciences Press, 1993. (吴云贵,《伊斯兰教法概略》, 中国社会科学出版社, 1993 年)

> Wu Yungui, *Dharma of Allah - Islamic Shariah*, China Social Sciences Press, 1993. (吴云贵,《真主的法度——伊斯兰教法》, 中国社会科学出版社, 1993 年)

> Wu Yungui, *Contemporary Islamic Law*, China Social Sciences Press, 2003. (吴云贵,《当代伊斯兰教法》, 中国社会科学出版社, 2003 年)

Originally composed in English by British scholar Noel J. Coulson, *A History of Islamic Law* is one of the more famous works in the modern West on the history of the Islamic legal system. It covers the origins of Islamic law, the doctrine and practice of teaching during the Middle Ages, and three articles on modern Islamic law. The first article starts with an analysis of the legislation of the Quran, then outlines the progression of Islamic law from the ancient Arab tribal customs through the four dynasties of the Caliphate, the Umayyad period, and the first half of the Abbasid period, to the formation of the four major Sunni schools of law,

5. RESEARCH IN RELIGION—WORLD ISLAMIC STUDIES   107

and the theoretical system of "classical" law. The second article reviews the theory and judicial practice of medieval Islamic sharia starting in the 10th century, introduces the legal theories of various sects, and analyzes the interrelationships between state power, Islamic society, and sacred law. Taking the invasion of Islamic countries by European colonizers in the 19th century as the upper limit, the final article reviews modern Islamic law, including the impact of foreign laws on Islamic law, and the inheritance and reform of Islamic tradition. Overall, this book is a fundamental reference work on the history of the Islamic legal system.[11] It is particularly popular in English speaking Western countries and an important reference.

Dharma of Allah – Islamic Shariah discusses the origin of Islamic law, the content of legal provisions, the legal theoretical viewpoints of different sects and schools, and the trends of modern legal reform. It covers the emergence and development of Islamic shariah and the judicial system of medieval Islamic law with chapters on the modern reform of Islamic law, including the historical background of the reform, commercial law, criminal law, civil law, marriage and family law, inheritance law, reform of the judicial system, revision of the theoretical system of Islamic law, and fundamentalist views on Islamic law.[12]

Contemporary Islamic Law presents the argument that a religion's form and function are deeply constrained and influenced by the social environment in which it operates. The development and evolution of religion itself, in turn, has positive and negative effects on social processes. Religions create indispensable conditions for their survival and development in this two-way interaction with human society. Wu Yungui

---

[11] Coulson, *The History of Islamic Law*, translated by Wu Yungui (originally reprinted in 1964 and 1971, and published as a popular version in 1978), and, China Social Sciences Press, published as a translation in 1986. (库尔森 著 吴云贵 译, 《伊斯兰教法律史》（该书原本初版于 1964 年、1971 年重印，1978 年出版通俗本），中国社会科学出版社，1986 年翻译版出版, 目录)

[12] Wu Yungui, Dharma of Allah - Islamic Shariah, China Social Sciences Press, 1993. (吴云贵,《真主的法度—伊斯兰教法》, 中国社会科学出版社，1993 年, 目录）

accomplishes this by presenting studies of local Islamic law issues.[13] The book begins with an overview of traditional Islamic law, then covers topics such as traditional Islamic political theory, the reform trend of Islamic law, modern Islamic political ideology, fundamentalism and Islamic law, the Iranian Revolution and Islamic law, state power and official Islamization, interpretation of mufti, fatwa, Islamic shariah, and Islamic law in a multicultural society, with chapters on religious extremism and its relation to Islamic law.

During this period, other scholars' translations and research results were subsequently published.

Interpretation of Weigaye's Shariah – Introduction to Islamic Shariah, Sai Shengfa translated, Ningxia People's Publishing House, 1993. （赛生发　译《伟嘎业教法经解—伊斯兰教法概论》，宁夏人民出版社，1993 年）
Weigaye Dharma Sutra, Ma Zhengping Translated, Religious Culture Press, 1999. （马正平　翻译《伟嘎耶教法经》，宗教文化出版社，1999 年）
Gao Hongjun, "Islamic Law: Tradition and Modernization," Social Science Literature Publishing, October 1996; Tsinghua University Press, revised version in September 2004. （高鸿钧：《伊斯兰教法：传统与现代化》（社会科学文献出版，1996 年 10 月出版；清华大学出版社，2004 年 9 月修订本）
Islamic Philosophy of Law, edited by Zhang Bingmin, Ningxia People's Publishing House, 2002. （张秉民　主编《伊斯兰教法哲学》，宁夏人民出版社，2002 年）
Islamic Law, translated by the Youth Translation Group, 1998, published internally. （青年翻译组翻译的《伊斯兰教法》，上、中、下，1998 年，内部出版发行）

Oubaidu La's *Weigaye Dharma Sutra* is an academic masterpiece in Islamic law and one of the commonly used teaching materials for Sunni Muslims. This book is an annotated version of the *Al*

---

[13] Wu Yungui, Contemporary Islamic Law, China Social Sciences Press, 2003. （吴云贵，《当代伊斯兰教法》，中国社会科学出版社，2003 年、目录）

5. RESEARCH IN RELIGION—WORLD ISLAMIC STUDIES   109

Wiqayah of his grandfather, Burkhan Shariat Mahmud, that consists of four volumes: the clean book, the marriage law book, the trade book, and the signed slave book. The simplified version of *Weigaye Dharma*, also known as *Mukhtser Weigaye*, is one of the commonly used teachings of Sunni Muslims. There is also a translated version of Wang Jingzhai's Chinese anthology titled *Weijiaye* that was published in Tianjin in 1931 and a new version compiled by Marseille North, titled *Selected Translation and Detailed Explanation of Weijiaye*, published by Tianjin Ancient Books Publishing House in 1986. Ma Zhengping's translation of *Weigaye Dharma Sutra* is the most complete translation so far and is valued within the academy for sorting out ancient books of Islamic culture in a way that facilitates its study.[14]

Islamic Philosophy of Law, edited by Zhang Bingmin, covers the Arab world before the emergence of Islamic philosophy, the emergence of the Quran, the formation and development of Islamic philosophy, and its current state. It provides a clear overview of Islamic philosophy from the perspective of historical evolution and a description of its basic laws and characteristics with special emphasis on its historical, social, and political aspects. It also explores the background of the emergence of Islamic philosophy from different perspectives and examines the philosophical ideas of different schools and representative figures.[15]

Entering the 21st century, the performance of Islamic law in China continues to deepen, and there have been some papers with the theoretical depth characteristic of the times. Representative works include:

Ma Zongzheng, "Theological Rule of Law Concept in Religious Law Culture – And the Influence of the Localization of Islamic Law in China on the Construction of Rule of Law Concept,"

---

[14] *Interpretation of Weigaye's Shariah - Introduction to Islamic Shariah*, Sai Shengfa translated, Ningxia People's Publishing House, 1993. （赛生发 译《伟嘎业教法经解—伊斯兰教法概论》, 宁夏人民出版社，1993 年）

[15] *Islamic Philosophy of Law*, edited by Zhang Bingmin, Ningxia People's Publishing House, 2002. （张秉民 主编《伊斯兰教法哲学》, 宁夏人民出版社，2002 年, 目录（389 页））

Northwest Ethnic Studies, 2006, Issue 1.（马宗正，"宗教法文化中的神学法治理念—兼及伊斯兰教法中国本土化对法治理念建构之影响，"《西北民族研究》，2006 年第 1 期）
Lv Yaojun, "The formation, development, and strictness of Islamic law in the context of 'Izhitihad'," *Journal of Northwest Second Ethnic University*, Issue 3, 2005.（吕耀军，"'伊智提哈德'与伊斯兰教法的形成、发展及严格，"《西北第二民族学院学报》，2005 年第 3 期）
Ma Jinhu, "The Ideological Origins of the Difficulties in Creating Islamic Law," *Journal of Chang'an University*, Issue 2, 2005.（马进虎，"伊斯兰法创制困难的思想渊源，"《长安大学学报》，2005 年第 2 期）
Ma Mingxian, "The Revival and Reform of Contemporary Islamic Law," *West Asia and Africa*, Issue 1, 2005.（马明贤，"当代伊斯兰法的复兴与改革，"《西亚非洲》，2005 年第 1 期）
Min Jing, "A Brief Introduction to Islamic Law and Its Practical Significance", *World Religious Culture*, Issue 2, 2005.（敏敬，"伊斯兰法浅识及其现实意义"，《世界宗教文化》，2005 年第 2 期）
Yang Jingde, "Analysis of the Relationship between Islamic Law and Islamic Shariah," *Journal of Yunnan University for Nationalities*, 2003, Issue 3).（杨经德，"伊斯兰法与伊斯兰教法关系辨析"，《云南民族大学学报》，2003 年第 3 期）
Zhu Hong, "Islamic Law in the Face of Legal Globalization", *Human Rights*, Issue 4, 2003.（朱虹，"面对法律全球化的伊斯兰法形态"，《人权》，2003 年第 4 期）

Taken together, the above publications demonstrate that research on Islamic law in China has matured into a specialized field of considerable scale with a focus on its characteristics and practical dimensions in China.

Another important area of research is Islamic doctrine, which is based on classical evidence and aims to deny opposing views and clarify difficult issues in a way that confirms the basic tenets of doctrine. Doctrine is a traditional Islamic discipline formed by Muslims in the process of interpreting faith through rational thinking. Islamic doctrine has always been valued by Chinese Muslims and has been the main content of scripture

5. Research in Religion—World Islamic Studies   111

education and Chinese translation since the Ming and Qing dynasties. Li Lin analyzes the history of academic research in this area as follows: "Contemporary Chinese scholars' research on Islamic doctrine did not gradually recover until the 1980s, and their research methods were limited to the framework of 'philosophical research.' Since entering the 'development transformation' period in 2000, there have been new changes in the study of Islamic doctrine. Not only have a number of new achievements emerged, but the religious characteristics of Islamic doctrine have gradually been recognized and are no longer limited to the scope of philosophical research. Some of these studies reflect the unique purpose and care of religious doctrine research. Other traditional [forms of] Islam, as well as modern humanities and social sciences, have posed major challenges to contemporary Islamic dogmatism and its research, but these challenges contain opportunities for self-transcendence and self-transformation of the two."[16] In the general study of Islam as a religion, dogmatism or theology is indispensable.

Chinese research on Islamic doctrine is based on the translation and annotation of foreign publications. For example:

Omar Neseif's Commentary on Selden Din Tafetasani, "*Interpretation of the Neseif Canon*" (Sharh al Aqa id al Nasafiyyah) （欧麦尔·奈赛斐 著 赛尔顿丁·太费塔萨尼 注释：《奈赛斐教典诠释》）
Translated by Yang Zhongming, "*Annotations on the Teaching Heart Sutra*" , published by Xiuzhen Jingshe in Beiping, 1924. （杨仲明 译，《教心经注》，北平秀真精舍出版，1924 年）
Translated by Ma Jian, "*The Great Righteousness of Doctrine*" (translated and published in Kunming (vernacular Chinese translation), 1945). （马坚译，《教义学大刚》，昆明翻译出版（白话文汉译本），1945 年）

---

[16] Li Lin, "Issues and Reflections on Contemporary Islamic Studies in China," *Chinese Muslims*, Issue 3, 2011, pp. 18–21 （李林「当代中国伊斯兰教义学研究的问题与反思」『中国穆斯林』，2011 年第 3 期，18-21 页）

> Translated by Ma Jian, *"Interpretation of the Scripture,"* reprinted by Shanghai Wentong Book Company in 1951. （马坚译，《教典诠释》，上海文通书局，1951 年再版）

Ma Jian's translation of *Interpretation of the Scripture* is an interpretation of *Sharh al-'Aqa'id al-Nasafiyya*, written by Seldundin Teftassani (1312–1389), and is respected as a classic by Chinese Muslims. It is an authoritative resource for understanding ideas of Islamic righteousness, philosophy, ethics, Arab literature, and rhetoric. This book uses logical reasoning to demonstrate the existence, uniqueness, and origin of Allah, Islamic cosmology and epistemology, and Sunni ideas on issues such as Allah and the world, faith and rebellion, predestination and freedom, and human abilities and behavior. It also discusses the significance of sending prophets and surrendering to the Quran, the succession of the four great caliphs, and the election of imams, as well as issues related to the doctrine and system of Islam. This book was introduced to China at the end of the 16th century and is widely used as a textbook for Jingtang jiaoyu. Liu Zhi once included this book in his reference list of *Tianfang Dianli* and titled it *Explanation of Difficulties in Scripture*. In 1870, Ma De published this book and called it *Interpretation of Difficult Scriptures in the Scripture*. In 1893, Ma Lianyuan published an abridged version of this book called *Tianfangshinanyaoyan*. In 1924, Xiuzhen Jingshe in Beiping published an ancient Chinese translation by Yang Zhongming known as *Jiaoxinjingzhu*. In 1945, Ma Jian translated and published a vernacular Chinese translation in Kunming, dividing the translation into eighteen chapters and seventy-nine sections, known as the "Outline of Doctrine." In 1951, when Shanghai Wentong Book Company reprinted it, Ma Jian renamed it *Interpretation of the Scripture*.

After the 1980s, scholar Wu Yungui made outstanding achievements in the area of religious thought. He has successively published papers and research works in publications such as:

> "Basic Signs of the Formation of Sunni Religious Thought," *World Religious Studies*, 1984, Issue 3. （"逊尼派宗教思想形成的基本标志，"《世界宗教研究》，1984 年第 3 期）

5. RESEARCH IN RELIGION—WORLD ISLAMIC STUDIES 113

> "Three Early Documents of Islamic Doctrine," *Hui Studies*, No. 4, 1993)（"伊斯兰教义学的三部早期文献" 《回族研究》，1993 年第 4 期）

> Wu Yungui, *Islamic Doctrine* , China Social Sciences Press, 1995.（吴云贵，《伊斯兰教教义学》，中国社会科学出版社，1995 年）

Islamic Doctrine is a Chinese paraphrase of the Arabic language *Kaila*. Its meaning refers to the use of human rational thinking and intuition based on natural philosophy to demonstrate the connotation and extension of Islamic beliefs, enabling Muslims to better understand the Quran, believe in Allah, and fulfill their mission of governance. Doctrine did not arise during the prophet Muhammad's era but during the post-disciple era. During the Abbasid period, a group of scholars who studied various Greek and religious philosophies under the premise of adhering to Islamic belief emerged among Muslims and gradually began to form doctrine. Islamic didactics is an advanced area in Islamic religious discipline, and students generally begin to learn it after the basics of Islamic law, hadith, and sutra annotation. Islamic theology is an internal discipline of Islamic faith, and the prerequisite for learning it is to be convinced of the correctness and universality of Islamic beliefs.[17] Wu Yungui's *Islamic Doctrine* is the first monograph by a Chinese scholar on the study of doctrine, briefly introducing representative schools of thought and their belief systems in various periods in Arab Islamic countries. The writing is simple and clear, which is important in the study of dogmatism.

The academic study of Islamic doctrine is growing steadily in China, with an increasing number of articles and monographs in publication. Additionally, books on philosophy generally include chapters on doctrine.

3 RESEARCH ON SECTS AND DOCTRINES

If we say that Shia is undoubtedly a sect, then it is the second largest sect in Islam with about 10% of Muslims worldwide

---

[17] Wu Yungui, *Islamic Doctrine* , China Social Sciences Press, 1995. （吴云贵，《伊斯兰教教义学》，中国社会科学出版社，1995 年，目录（138 页））

114   ISLAM IN CHINA AND THE ISLAMIC WORLD

ascribing to it, with the majority of Shia Muslims living in neighboring countries such as Iran, Iraq, Lebanon, India, and Pakistan. Its contrast with Sunni gives Islam a diverse appearance.

For a long time, research on the Shia faction did not receive sufficient attention from the Chinese academic community, but after the Islamic Revolution in Iran, scholars began to publish translations, works, and papers related to Shia Islam. Since the 1990s, a considerable number of works have appeared in this field, and in 2003, Shia became a momentary hot topic. Currently, a fair amount of historical research into Shia factions, doctrines, laws, and religious systems has been published from a political perspective, but overall, Shia research in China is still lagging.[18]

At present, there are few publications on Shia in China. One representative project is *Religion and the State: A Study of Contemporary Islamic Shia* by Wang Yujie.

> Wang Yujie, *Religion and the State: A Study of Contemporary Islamic Shia*, Social Science Literature Press, 2006. (王宇洁，《宗教与国家：当代伊斯兰教什叶派研究》，社会科学文献出版社，2006年)

This book studies Shia and Shi'ite history in the Middle Eastern countries where it is prevalent, with attention to the various movements and revolutions of the modern period. Studies on traditional Shia Muslim communities living in the Middle East, South Asia, and other regions, as well as new Shia communities in the United States and other countries, are divided into three parts: the establishment of modern nation-states, the rise of Islamic revival movements, and the challenges and opportunities of the 21st century. The book systematically analyzes the fate of Shia in contemporary society and its relationship with modern nation-states. It also looks at the complex relationship between Islam and politics from the perspective of Shia, aiming to expand our understanding of the relationship between Islam and modern

---

[18] Li Fuquan, "Commentary on the Study of Islamic Shia in China over the Past Three Decades," Journal of Jiangnan Social College, Issue 1, No. 4, 35–39, 2009. (李福泉，"30年来国内伊斯兰教什叶派研究述评，《江南社会学院学报》，2009年第11期第4号、35-39页)

5. RESEARCH IN RELIGION—WORLD ISLAMIC STUDIES   115

nation states, and providing yet another path for contemplating the relationship between religion and politics.[19]

Sufism is the most unique among the Islamic sects. Islamic mysticism is famous for Sufism, which originated in the 8th century as a protest against luxury fashion and the power struggle within Islam. It is a departure from the "rational" system of religion and is characterized by advocacy for morality and abstinence. By the 9th century, the theory and practice of Sufism began to take shape and conflicts with the upper religious class became increasingly acute. After the 11th century, Ansari made Sufism an organic component of his ideology, promoting the convergence of Sufism and orthodoxy among scholars. By the second half of the 12th century, as Sufi rituals and activities became more organized, various Sufi groups rapidly developed in the Islamic world, especially in marginalized areas, and reached their peak in the 16th and 18th centuries. Overall, Sufism has been an important aspect of Islamic religious life for five centuries. The Sufi order is referred to as a "religion within the religion," and in some regions is equated to Islam. In the contemporary Islamic world, Sufism is undergoing a quiet revival among the people, becoming an issue that cannot be ignored.

Chinese research on Sufism has just begun. Sufism not only injected important spiritual vitality into the development of Islam but also had a lasting impact on its internal ideology and history. Therefore, Sufism sits alongside Islamic law as two of the most fundamental topics in Islamic research; it can also be said that without understanding Sufism, one cannot understand Islam. Sufism research, whether data collection or on-site investigation, is difficult, partly because research in foreign academic circles started later than other topics related to Islam. At the beginning of the 20th century, the collation, translation, and annotation of some Sufi works allowed scholars to begin to explore Sufi mysticism. In recent decades, some in-depth and comprehensive academic works have emerged, but overall, the study of Sufism is

---

[19] Wang Yujie, Religion and the State: A Study of Contemporary Islamic Shia, Social Science Literature Press, 2006. (王宇洁，《宗教与国家：当代伊斯兰教什叶派研究》，社会科学文献出版社，2006 年, 目录（335 页））

116 ISLAM IN CHINA AND THE ISLAMIC WORLD

still a field with few experts and few academic monographs in the Chinese academic community.

Chinese scholarly research on Sufism has just started with only a few works being published in the past thirty years. It was first discussed in *Introduction to Islam*, edited by Jin Yijiu, under the topic of sects in Chinese Islam. Some scholars also carried out research on mysticism alongside their translation of Sufi works in Arabic and Persian. One of the most foundational works of Chinese scholarship in this area is Jin Yijiu's book, *Islamic Sufi Mysticism*.

> Jin Yijiu, Islamic Sufi Mysticism, China Social Sciences Press, 1995. (金宜久, 《伊斯兰教苏菲神秘主义》, 中国社会科学出版社, 1995 年)

This book is a comprehensive and systematic discussion of the origin and development of the Sufi sect, its mystical system and path of work, and the differences between the Sufi, Sunni, and Shia sects. [20] Many of its contents are the result of years of dedicated research, all of which have a high academic level. Additional Chinese volumes on Sufism include:

> Li Chen, *Modern Arab Literature and Mysticism*, Social Science Literature Press, 2000. (李琛, 《阿拉伯现代文学与神秘主义》, 社会科学文献出版社, 2000 年)

> (Iran) Fildochi Sadi, translated by Yuan Wenqi, *Persian Classic Library*, Hunan Literature and Art Publishing House, 2001. (（伊朗）菲尔多西·萨迪 著 元文琪 译, 《波斯经典文库》, 湖南文艺出版社, 2001 年)

> Tang Mengsheng, *The Sufism in India and Its Historical Role* (Economic Daily Press, 2002. (唐孟生, 《印度苏菲派及其历史作用》, 经济日报出版社, 2002 年)

> Zhang Wende, *History of Sufism in Central Asia*, China Social Sciences Press, 2002. (张文德, 《中亚苏菲主义史》, 中国社会科学出版社, 2002 年)

---

[20] Jin Yiu, Islamic Sufi Mysticism, China Social Sciences Press, 1995. (金宜久, 《伊斯兰教苏菲神秘主义》, 中国社会科学出版社, 1995 年。)

5. RESEARCH IN RELIGION—WORLD ISLAMIC STUDIES   117

In *Modern Arab Literature and Mysticism*, Li Chen uses case studies to illuminate the relationship between modern Arab literature and mysticism, examining a large number of written works and other research materials, experiencing Arab society to better understand Islamic cultural traditions, and interviewing relevant writers and critics. [21] The book has sections and chapters dedicated to Eastern and Western mysticism; Gibran, who had the mission of prophecy; The hermit writer Nuema of Shehrub; Hakim, an intellectual monk guided by the Theory of Equilibrium; Misadi, who portrays Sufi anthropology in art; the Mahafuz that promotes a positive life; the white elegant staircase embodying the meaning of life; Shabul, who interprets poetry with mysticism; and Using the Fage Sea of Sufi mythology.

Persian Classic Library, translated by Yuan Wenqi, is a compendium of classic works of ancient Persian literature. The complete eighteen volumes are divided into Orchard (one volume), Rose Garden (one volume), Lubai (one volume), Rudaki Poetry Collection (one volume), Complete Works of Kings (six volumes), Complete Works of Masnavi (six volumes), and The Complete Collection of Hafez Lyrics (two volumes). [22]

Zhang Wende's *History of Sufism in Central Asia* discusses the relationship between the three major Sufi groups in Central Asia and the nomads or local governments of different periods and regions, and analyzes the influence of Sufism on social politics, ideology, and culture in Central Asia. [23]

In summary, Li Chen's book is a masterpiece that studies the influence of Sufism on contemporary Arab literature and is highly regarded as a reference work. The translations by Yuan Wenqi and others provide raw materials for the study of Sufi mystical

---

[21] Li Chen, *Modern Arab Literature and Mysticism*, Social Science Literature Press, 2000. （李琛，《阿拉伯现代文学与神秘主义》，社会科学文献出版社，2000 年）

[22] (Iran) Fildochi Sadi, translated by Yuan Wenqi, *Persian Classic Library*, Hunan Literature and Art Publishing House, 2001. （（伊朗）菲尔多西·萨迪 著 元文琪 译：《波斯经典文库》（湖南文艺出版社，2001 年）

[23] Zhang Wende, History of Sufism in Central Asia, China Social Sciences Press, 2002. （张文德，《中亚苏菲主义史》，中国社会科学出版社，2002 年）

poetry, and the works of Tang Mengsheng and Zhang Wende are both breakthroughs in this academic field. A more recent representative of Sufi research is the National Social Fund project led by Zhou Xiefan:

Zhou Xiefan, *The Way of Sufism: A Study of Islamic Mysticism*, China Social Sciences Press, 2012. (周燮藩, 《苏非之道：伊斯兰教神秘主义研究》, 中国社会科学出版社，2012 年)

The Way of Sufism focuses on the history and ideology of Sufism, as well as the development of Neo-Sufism. It contributes a detailed exploration of Chinese Islamic Sufism, including the spread of Sufism in China and the Yichan sect in Xinjiang, and comprehensively lays out the history, ideology, ritual, organization, and influence of Sufism from multiple perspectives. This study provides a solid foundation for Chinese scholars who research Sufism[24] and includes information on such topics as the origin and early development of Sufism, the formation of the Sufi order, Sufi theosophy and its developments, important Sufi figures, and the characteristics of Sufism in various places.

The above publications demonstrate that there is ongoing research on Shia Islam and Sufism in China. However, the field of sectarian studies still in its initial stages of academic research and needs to be strengthened. Shia Islam and Sufism are attracting more and more scholars' attention, and it appears that Shia and Sufi studies will become important areas of Islamic research in China.

---

[24] Zhou Xiefan, *The Way of Sufism: A Study of Islamic Mysticism*, China Social Sciences Press, 2012. 周燮藩, 《苏非之道：伊斯兰教神秘主义研究》, 中国社会科学出版社、2012 年、目录（472 页）

PART SIX.
RESEARCH IN THE FIELD OF PHILOSOPHY

1 RESEARCH ON PHILOSOPHICAL THOUGHT AND HUI CONFUCIANISM

In its earlier periods, Islamic society in China was composed of Arab, Persian, Turkic, and Central Asian Muslim immigrants, but that changed during the Ming and Qing dynasties when a long period of Sinicization and localization prompted a critical period of development in Chinese Islamic consciousness and cultural ideology. During this period, intellectuals who were proficient in both Islamic scriptures and Confucianism emerged in the Islamic community of China. It is precisely they who, on the basis of Islamic philosophy and under the influence of Chinese Confucianism, created a new theoretical system in China— Chinese Islamic Studies. The establishment of Chinese Islamism is not only a contribution to Chinese Islam but also to Chinese civilization. In a special sense, it also proves the close relationship between Confucianism and Islam.

Representative figures of this movement include Muslim scholars such as Wang Daiyu, Zhang Zhong, Wu Zunqi, Ma Zhu, Liu Zhi, Ma Dexin, and Ma Lianyuan who carried out a significant historical enlightenment movement in Chinese Islamic thought. Wang Daiyu and Liu Zhi in particular made founding contributions to the Islamic system in China. Wang Daiyu was the pioneer of this academic system and creatively explored the purpose, task, content, form, and path of the enlightenment movement. Liu Zhi's ideas always combined Islamic teachings with Chinese Confucianism, following the path opened by Wang Daiyu, and further standardized and refined such ideas. Wang Daiyu's and Liu Zhi's ideas were informed by Islam, Islamic theology, Islamic philosophy, Islamic ethics, and Islamic political science, and by critically absorbing Confucianism, especially the Neo-Confucianism of the Song and Ming dynasties.[1]

Since the 1980s, some Chinese researchers have dedicated themselves to the study of Chinese Islamic literature and produced in-depth publications. For example:

Yu Zhengui, "On the Characteristics of Wang Daiyu's Religious and Philosophical Thought from the Perspective of 'Qingzhen Daxue'," *Gansu Ethnic Studies*, 1982, Issue 4. （余振贵， "从 '清真大学'试论王岱舆宗教哲学思想的特点，"《甘肃民族研究》，1982 年第 4 期）
Feng Jinyuan, "Analysis of 'Lai Fu Ming'," Journal of World Religious Studies, Vol. 4, 1984. (Records of Selected Works of Feng Jinyuan's Religious Academic Works in Sanyuan Collection, Ningxia People's Publishing House, 1985, May 5-77 pages) 冯今源， "'来复铭'析，"《世界宗教研究》一九八四年第四期。（记载《三元集冯今源宗教学术论著文选》宁夏人民出版社、一九八五年、五五－七七页）
Jin Yijiu, "On Liu Zhi's Thought of 'Return'", *World Religious Studies*, 1990, Issue 1.（金宜久， "论刘智的 '复归' 思想，"《世界宗教研究》，1990 年第 1 期）
Wu Yiye, "Enlightenment and Reflection on Wang Daiyu to Liu Zhi: Islamic Thought in 17th Century China", *Research on the Hui Ethnic Group in China*, 1991, Issue 1.（伍贻业， "王岱舆到刘智的启示和反思—17 世纪中国伊斯兰教思潮，"《中国回族研究》，1991 年第 1 期）
Luo Wanshou, "Analysis of the 'True One' Theory of Islamic Philosophy in China," *Northwest Ethnic Studies*, 1996, Issue 1.

---

[1] Sun Zhenyu, *"Biography of Wang Daiyu and Liu Zhi,"* Nanjing University Press, 2006, Key Page (506 pages).（孙振玉， 《王岱舆 刘智评传》, 南京大学出版社, 2006 年、要旨页（506 页））

6. RESEARCH IN PHILOSOPHY

121

> （罗万寿，"试析中国伊斯兰哲学的 '真一'说，"《西北民族研究》，1996 年第 1 期.）

Feng Jinyuan's article, "Analysis of 'Lai Fu Ming'," discusses the Lai Fu Ming, a Chinese Islamic inscription that dates to the seventh year of the Ming Jiajing reign (1528) and was at the Mosque of Nanda in Jinan, Shandong. The first half of the inscription states that Allah's "giving orders to our people" equates to His "coming," while the second half states that people's "serving their heavens" is equivalent to "restoring," hence the inscription is sometimes referred to as "coming and restoring inscription." It consists of 155 characters and has a four-character rhyming style. It does not mention Islamic doctrine but draws a connection between Confucianism and Islamic practice. The first part of the inscription utilizes Zhou Dunyi's concept of "Tai Chi Tu Shuo" in Song and Ming Neo-Confucianism and Zhang Zai's philosophical ideas, implying and elucidating Islam's theory of the primordial essence of Allah and the "great power" of creating all things. The latter part clarifies that by using the theory of mind and nature, as well as the lessons of careful cultivation and respect, one can achieve the realization of Allah and then "become a disciple of creation." Feng Jinyuan's article is the first work by a Chinese Muslim scholar to explain the teachings of Islam and Neo-Confucianism during the Song and Ming Dynasties, which prompted academic interest in the relationship between Islamic and Confucian cultures.[2]

Wu Yiye's article, "Enlightenment and Reflection on Wang Daiyu to Liu Zhi: Islamic Thought in 17th Century China," argues that social thought in China during the 17th century or the Qing Dynasty has always been a hot topic of academic discussion. Indeed, in the past century or so, traditional Chinese society has undergone unprecedented and profound changes in politics,

---

[2] Feng Jinyuan, "Analysis of 'Lai Fu Ming'," *Journal of World Religious Studies*, Vol. 4, 1984. (Records of Selected Works of *Feng Jinyuan's Religious Academic Works in Sanyuan Collection*, Ningxia People's Publishing House, 1985, 5–77 pages).（冯今源，"'来复铭'析"《世界宗教研究》1984 年第 4 期.（记载《3 元集冯今源宗教学术论著文选》宁夏人民出版社、1985 年、55－77 页））

economy, culture, and science. On the one hand, "Western learning" entered China through introductions by Matteo Ricci, Tang Ruowang, Xu Guangqi, Li Zhizuo, and others, as part of a larger trend of Western learning spreading eastward. On the other hand, major changes have also taken place in Confucianism with thinkers such as Gu Yanwu, Huang Zongxi, Wang Fuzhi, Tang Zhen, and others critically analyzing traditional Chinese society and feudal despotism. It is no wonder some say this era is similar to the Renaissance in Europe.[3]

In the turbulent years, scholars seem to have overlooked certain trends and changes in Islam in China. Islamic thought of 17th century China is quite distinctive and deserving of its own investigation. Representative monographs in this regard include:

Jin Yijiu, *Exploring Islam in China: A Study of Liu Zhi*, Renmin University of China Press, 1999. （金宜久，《中国伊斯兰探秘—刘智研究》，中国人民大学出版社，1999 年）

Sha Zongping, *Chinese Tianfangxue: A Study of Liu Zhi's Philosophy*, Peking University Press, 2004. （沙宗平，《中国天方学—刘智哲学研究》，北京大学出版社，2004 年）

Yang Guiping, *Research on Ma Dexin's Thought*, Religious Culture Press, 2004. （杨桂萍，《马德新思想研究》，宗教文化出版社，2004 年.）

Wu Yandong, *Commentary on Chinese Hui Thinkers*, Religious Culture Press, 2004. （吴艳冬，《中国回族思想家评述》，宗教文化出版社，2004 年）

Liang Xiangming, *Research on Liu Zhi and Islamic Thought*, published and distributed by Lanzhou University in 2004. （梁向明，《刘智及伊斯兰思想研究》，兰州大学出版发行，2004 年）

---

[3] Wu Yiye, "Enlightenment and Reflection on Wang Daiyu to Liu Zhi: Islamic Thought in 17th Century China," *Research on the Hui Ethnic Group in China*, 1991, Issue 1. （伍 贻业， "王岱舆到刘智的启示和反思—17 世纪中国伊斯兰教思潮" 《中国回族研究》，1991 年第 1 期）

6. RESEARCH IN PHILOSOPHY

Sun Zhenyu, *Research on Wang Daiyu and His Islamic Thought*, Lanzhou University Press, 2000. (孙振玉，《王岱舆及其伊斯兰思想研究》，兰州大学出版社，2000 年)

Sun Zhenyu, *Research on Ma Dexin and His Islamic Thought*, Lanzhou University Press, 2002. (孙振玉，《马德新及其伊斯兰思想研究》，兰州大学出版社，2002 年)

Sun Zhenyu, *Commentary on Wang Daiyu and Liu Zhi*, Nanjing University Press, 2006. (孙振玉，《王岱舆 刘智评传》，南京大学出版社，2006 年)

Liu Yihong, *Dialogue between Hui and Confucianism - The Classic of Heaven and the Way of Confucius and Mencius*, Religious Culture Press, 2006. (刘一虹，《 回儒对话－天方之经与孔孟之道》，宗教文化出版社 2006 年)

Liu Yihong, "*Dialogue between Hui and Confucianism – A Study of Chinese Islamic Philosophical Thoughts in the Ming and Qing Dynasties,*" *Chinese philosophy*, Issue 9, 2005. (刘一虹，"回儒对话—明清时期中国伊斯兰哲学思想研究，"《中国哲学》，2005 年第 9 期)

Liu Yihong, "*Dialogue between Hui and Confucianism - The Classic of Heaven and Confucius and Mencius,*" Philosophical Dynamics, Issue 8, 2006. (刘一虹，"回儒对话—天方之经与孔孟之，"《哲学动态》，2006 年第 8 期)

Jin Yijiu, *Research on Wang Daiyu's Thought*, Ethnic Publishing House, 2008. (金宜久，《王岱舆思想研究》，民族出版社，2008 年)

In *Exploring Islam in China: A Study of Liu Zhi*, Jin Yijiu systematically presents the life, works, and thoughts of famous Chinese Hui scholar Liu Zhi (c. 1660–1730), and proposes that Liu Zhi's religious philosophy is neither a reproduction of Islamic thought nor a restatement of Confucianism, Buddhism, and Taoism. The book covers topics such as Liu Zhi's life, works, and ideological origins before delving into his theories of truth, light, human nature, world, cognition, Four Unifications, and reversion.

This is the core of the book, although there are other chapters on related topics, such as religion and ethics. [4]

Yang Guiping's *Research on Ma Dexin's Thought* is a revised doctoral thesis and the first academic monograph to systematically study Ma Dexin's thought. Yusuf Ma Dexin (1794–1874) was a famous leader of Islam and the Hui ethnic group in Yunnan in the late Qing Dynasty, as well as a renowned scholar with significant impact. Ma Dexin moved between academia and politics throughout his life. On the academic side, he devoted himself to research and wrote several profound theoretical works that promote the integration of Islam and Confucianism in order to enrich and develop Chinese Islamic culture. On the political side, he was born into a turbulent and chaotic society, passively involved in the fierce political struggles and ethnic conflicts in Yunnan, and faced the practical contradictions of politics, ethnicity, religion, and culture. He struggled through an exceptionally tortuous and dangerous life that ended in tragedy, constantly exploring the themes of justice, peace, and rationality in turbulent times. It is not easy to accurately describe a historical figure with such complex experiences, diverse identities, and rich thoughts. [5]

Wu Yandong's *Commentary on Chinese Hui Thinkers* is an exposition of several famous Hui thinkers in Chinese history and their religious, philosophical, social, political, and ethical views, exploring the trajectory of Hui ideology and its representative figures. The book covers the history and characteristics of ancient Chinese Hui thought and details the lives and thoughts of influential Hui thinkers from the Yuan, Ming, and Qing dynasties.

Critical Biography of Wang Daiyu and Liu Zhi by Sun Zhenyu details the lives and thoughts of two Islamic scholars who made founding contributions to the academic study of Islam in relation to Confucianism. Wang Daiyu pioneered this academic

---

[4] Jin Yijiu, *Exploring Islam in China: A Study of Liu Zhi*, Renmin University of China Press, 1999. (金宜久，《中国伊斯兰探秘—刘智研究》，中国人民大学出版社，1999 年，目录，（349 页））

[5] Yang Guiping, *Research on Ma Dexin's Thought*, Religious Culture Press, 2004. (杨桂萍，《马德新思想研究》，宗教文化出版社，2004 年，目录（225 页））

6. Research in Philosophy

125

specialization and creatively explored the purpose, task, content, and form of translation, while Liu Zhijin standardized and refined it, making translation more thoughtful and discriminative. This book provides a systematic review of the lives, thoughts, and contributions of these historical figures from the Hui ethnic group and uses them as case studies to explore the positive significance of various aspects of Hui Neo-Confucianism. The book introduces Ming and Qing Hui Neo-Confucianism then discusses the lives, academic contributions, and lasting influence of Wang Daiyu and Liu Zhi.[6]

Liu Yihong's *Dialogue Between Hui and Confucianism – The Classic of Heaven and the Way of Confucius and Mencius* is dedicated to the study of Chinese Muslims who, under the cultural background of Confucianism, used ancient Chinese philosophical ideas to distinguish between Islamic ideas from Arab countries and traditional philosophical theories in China in attempts to highlight their differences, affirm their commonalities, and find complementary elements between the two. In the book, Liu Yihong discusses the ideological systems of scholars such as Wang Daiyu, Wu Zunqi, Ma Zhu, Liu Zhi, and Ma Dexin. It also includes chapters on the theoretical achievements of Chinese translations, the characteristics of Chinese Sufi thought, the religious nature of Confucianism and Chinese Islamic thought, and comparative philosophical research methods.[7]

In Jin Yijiu's book, *Research on Wang Daiyu's Thought*, the author proposes that Chinese Islamic thought since the Ming and Qing dynasties is an integral part of Chinese cultural thought, and Wang Daiyu holds a pioneering position in establishing Islamic religious philosophy with unique Chinese characteristics. However, his ideas have not received due attention or been fully

---

[6] Sun Zhenyu, *Critical biography of Wang Daiyu and Liu Zhi*, Nanjing University Press, 2006. (孙振玉,《王岱舆 刘智评传》, 南京大学出版社, 2006 年, 目录（506 页）)

[7] Liu Yihong, *Dialogue between Hui and Confucianism – The Classic of Heaven and the Way of Confucius and Mencius*, Religious Culture Press, 2006. (刘 1 虹,《 回儒对话－天方之经与孔孟之道》, 宗教文化出版社, 2006 年, 目录（246 页）)

incorporated into the cultural and ideological heritage of China.[8] Jin Yijiu conducts a systematic study of Wang Daiyu's ideological system, paying attention to the historical background of Wang Daiyu's academic activities, his life and mentorships, and his works and ideology, including the influence of Islamic thought on his ideas.

There are many other works on Wang Daiyu and Liu Zhi. Looking at the number of journal articles dedicated to the ideas of Wang Daiyu and Liu Zhi, there has been an increase in publications on this topic since 2000:

Jin Yijiu, "Sufism and Chinese Islamic Writings," included in the Collected Works of *the Islamic Research Academic Society of the Five Northwest Provinces*. （金宜久， "苏菲派与汉文伊斯兰教著述，" 载入《西北五省伊斯兰研究学术会论集》）
Li Xinghua, "Religious Studies in Chinese Translation of Islam," *Journal of Qinghai University for Nationalities*, 1997, Issue 3. （李兴华， "汉文伊斯兰教译著的宗教学，"《青海民族大学学报》，1997 年第 3 期）
Liang Xiangming, "Liu Zhi's Islamic Theory of Human Nature," *Chinese Muslims*, Issue 5, 2002.（梁向明， "刘智的伊斯兰人性论，"《中国穆斯林》，2002 年第五期）
Sha Zongping, "Maximizing the Cycle, Ending the End, and Returning to the Beginning: A Preliminary Exploration of the Philosophical Outlook of Liu Zhi, a Hui Thinker in the Early Qing Dynasty," *Hui Studies*, Issue 2, 2002. （沙宗平， "大化循环，尽终返始-清初回族思想家刘智哲学观初探，"《回族研究》，2002 年第 2 期）

In "Religious Studies in Chinese Translation of Islam," Li Xinghua illustrates that Hui Muslim scholars in the Ming and Qing dynasties espoused rich religious ideas in their Chinese Islamic translations, which fall primarily into one of three categories: religious composition, religious purpose, and religious discrimination. This paper makes a systematic exposition of this

---

[8] Jin Yijiu, *Research on Wang Daiyu's Thought*, Ethnic Publishing House, 2008. （金宜久，《王岱舆思想研究》，民族出版社，2008 年，目录（448 页））

6. RESEARCH IN PHILOSOPHY

127

and argues that the emergence of this religious system is the result of the influence of traditional Chinese thought and the need to adapt to social values.[9]

In the article "Maximizing the Cycle, Ending the End, and Returning to the Beginning: A Preliminary Exploration of the Philosophical Outlook of Liu Zhi, a Hui Thinker in the Early Qing Dynasty," Sha Zongping explores how Liu Zhi absorbed and transformed traditional Chinese Confucian thought in the process of creating China's Islamic academic system. It is believed that Liu Zhi, with his sacred mission to promote Islamic doctrine in China using his profound traditional Chinese cultural education and systematic research on Islamic doctrine, absorbs the work of Hui sages such as Wang Daiyu and others, resulting in a broad and profound Chinese Islamic philosophy based on "truth theory" and with "human theory" as its main content.[10]

In recent years, foreign scholars have begun to include the works of representative figures of the Muslim "Chinese Translation" movement, such as Liu Zhi and Wang Daiyu, in their research. As a result of the integration of Chinese traditional culture and Islamic culture, Chinese Islamic literature and classics have received more and more attention. Some scholars have proposed that, given the contribution of Chinese Islamic literature to diverse Islamic thought, it should enjoy the same status and attention as the literature of other languages. For example, in *Chinese Gleams of Sufi Light: Wang Tai Yu's Great Learning of the Pure and Real and Liu Chi's Displaying the Concept of the Real* and *The Sage Learning of Liu Zhi: Islamic Thought in Confucian Terms,* co-authored by Sachiko Murata, William C. Chittick, and Tu Weiming, the basic viewpoint is that many Chinese scholars do not view the teachings of Hui Confucianism as being in line with

---

[9] Li Xinghua, religious studies in Chinese Translation of Islam, *Journal of Qinghai University for Nationalities*, 1997, Issue 3. (李兴华，"汉文伊斯兰教译著的宗教学"《青海民族大学学报》，1997 年第 3 期，1—8 页）

[10] Sha Zongping, "Maximizing the Cycle, Ending the End, and Returning to the Beginning: A Preliminary Exploration of the Philosophical Outlook of Liu Zhi, a Hui Thinker in the Early Qing Dynasty," Hui Studies, Issue 2, 2002. (沙宗平，"大化循环，尽终返始--清初回族思想家刘智哲学观初探"《回族研究》，2002 年第 2 期，78—87 页）

mainstream Islam. The main reason for this may be the pauses and gaps in the dissemination of Hui Confucianism caused by the events of the 20th century. Due to the disappearance of systematic education related to Islam, Chinese Muslims must relearn their own religious and ideological traditions and cultural customs, and most of them rely on external sources, especially the works of Western historians.

The Theory of Natural Nature by Liu Zhi, the most outstanding Muslim philosopher in China, laid out a systematic and meticulous paradigm for the worldview of Hui Confucianism. The book concisely discusses its basic principles and explains some of the detailed deductions derived from these principles. Liu Zhi's brilliant way of elucidating his philosophical insights is unmatched among Hui Confucian authors. In fact, in portraying the multiple dimensions of Islamic thought and practice in such a systematic, concise, and comprehensive manner, I doubt whether there is a philosophical work in Islamic language that can rival it. So, what exactly is the Hui Confucian worldview? Simply put, it is consistent with the ideas elaborated in many works by great Muslim mentors, theologians, and Sufis. In theoretical terms, this worldview is most succinctly expressed as the fundamental principles of three Islamic ideologies: unity, prophecy, and return. [11]

2 The Study of Islamic Philosophy Abroad

Chinese academics have achieved certain optimistic results in the field of Islamic philosophy in China. As early as the 1930s and 40s, Ma Jian had already translated:

(Egypt) Muhammad Abdul, *Islamic Philosophy*, published and distributed by the Commercial Press in 1934（（埃及）穆罕默德 • 阿布笃 著《回教哲学》, 商务印书馆出版发行，1934 年）

---

[11] 参考, アリムトヘテイ,『日本におけるイスラーム研究史ー中国篇』, 春風社、2019 年、310 页(《日本的伊斯兰研究史——中国篇》, 春风社, 2009 年，310 页. (*History of Islamic Studies in Japan - China Chapter*, Chunfeng Society, 2009, pp. 310)

6. Research in Philosophy

129

> (Germany) D. Bohr, "History of Islamic Philosophy," Zhonghua Book Company Press, 1958.（（德国）第·博尔 著《伊斯兰教哲学史》,中华书局出版社，1958 年）

The original author of *Islamic Philosophy* was Muhammad Abdul, a renowned modern Islamic scholar in Egypt. This book was originally a handout during his teaching at the Royal School of Beirut, but he later published it as a volume. In Cairo, Egypt, in 1933, Ma Jian translated the entire book into Chinese and published it after revising his original manuscript. *The Islamic Philosophy* systematically discusses the fundamental issues of Islamic doctrine from a Sunni perspective, using philosophy to discuss basic beliefs and doctrines in order to maintain the purity of Islam, oppose various heretical doctrines, and propose a complete set of concepts, categories, and principles. It also provides a general introduction to various viewpoints in the study of Islamic monotheism, "indicating the differences of various doctrines from a distance" without further analysis and evaluation. [12] However, from the perspective of Islamic philosophy, the publication of this book has promoted the study of Islamic monotheism and had a wide impact. It is an important resource for Chinese Muslims who seek to understand Islamic philosophy.

After the 1950s, the study of Arab philosophy did not stop. Regarding the relationship between Islamic and Arab philosophy, Ma Jian states: "Islamic philosophy is Arab philosophy. These philosophers grew up under the Islamic regime, and the vast majority believe in Islam. Therefore, some people call them Islamic philosophers. These philosophers are subjects of the Arab Empire, and their philosophical papers are written in Arabic. Islamic philosophy and Arab philosophy are synonymous."[13] This

---

[12] 参考 (Egypt) Muhammad Abdul, *Islamic Philosophy*, published and distributed by the Commercial Press in 1934)（（埃及）穆罕默德·阿布笃 著, 马坚 译《回教哲学》,商务印书馆出版发行，1934 年）

[13] (Egypt) Muhammad Abdul, *Islamic Philosophy*, published and distributed by the Commercial Press in 1934)（（埃及）穆罕默德·阿布笃 著, 马坚 译《回教哲学》,商务印书馆出版发行，1934 年）

is also the mainstream opinion in the international academic community. Reform and development, especially since the 1990s, have emerged one after another. The first works translated into Chinese include:

(United States) Majid Fahri, *History of Islamic Philosophy*, translated by Chen Zhongyao, Shanghai Foreign Education Press, 1992. （（美国）马吉德·法赫里，《伊斯兰哲学史》，陈中耀译，上海外国教育出版社，1992 年版）

(Japan) Toshihiko Ino, *The Course of Islamic Thought - Keram mysticism Philosophy*, translated by Qin Huibin, China Today Press, 1992. （（日本）井筒俊彦，《伊斯兰思想历程—凯拉姆·神秘主义·哲学》，秦惠彬译，今日中国出版社，1992 年）

Mousavi, *Arab Philosophy - From Kendai to Ibn Rashid,* translated by Tsai Degui and Zhong Dinkun, Commercial Press, 1997. （穆萨维，《阿拉伯哲学—从铿达到伊本·鲁世德》，著蔡德贵、仲蚧昆 译，商务印书馆，1997 年）

These works include contributions to academic conversations on the definition of philosophy, philosophical theories, philosophical research topics, the meaning of philosophy, who first uses the term "philosophy," the working methods of philosophers, the conditions for becoming philosophers, and so on.

The publications authored by Chinese scholars include:

Cai Degui, *History of Arab Philosophy*, Shandong University Press, 1992.（蔡德贵，《阿拉伯哲学史》，山东大学出版社，1992 年）

Qin Huibin, *Questions on Islamic Philosophy*, Today China Publishing House, 1994. （秦惠彬，《伊斯兰哲学百问》，今日中国出版社，1994 年）

Li Zhenzhong and Wang Jiaying, *History of Arab Philosophy*, Beijing Language and Culture University Press, 1995. （李振中、王家瑛，《阿拉伯哲学史》，北京语言文化大学出版社，1995 年）

Chen Zhongyao, *Arabic Philosophy*, Shanghai Foreign Language Education Press, 1995. （陈中耀，《阿拉伯哲学》，上海外语教育出版社，1995 年）

6. RESEARCH IN PHILOSOPHY

Cai Degui (editor), *Research on Arab Modern Philosophy*, People's Publishing House, Shandong, 1996. (蔡德贵主编，《阿拉伯近现代哲学研究》，山东人民出版社，1996 年)

Cai Degui, *Research on Contemporary Islamic Arab Philosophy*, People's Publishing House, 2001. (蔡德贵主编，《当代伊斯兰阿拉伯哲学研究》，人民出版社，2001 年)

Liu Yihong, *Contemporary Arab Philosophical Trends*, Contemporary China Publishing House, 2001. (刘一虹，《当代阿拉伯哲学思潮》，当代中国出版社，2001 年)

Wang Jiaying, *History of Islamic Religious Philosophy*, Ethnic Publishing House, 2003. (王家瑛，《伊斯兰宗教哲学史》，民族出版社，2003 年)

Zhang Bingmin, *A Concise History of Islamic Philosophy*, Ningxia People's Publishing House, 2007. (张秉民主编，《简明伊斯兰哲学史》，宁夏人民出版社，2007 年)

Zhang Bingmin (edited)，*The History of Islamic Philosophy*, published by Ningxia People's Publish，2007. (张秉民主编《伊斯兰哲学史》，宁夏人民出版社，2007 年)

Cai Degui's *History of Arab Philosophy* not only provides a useful exploration of Arab secular philosophy but also a systematic introduction to Islamic religious philosophy and various sects, such as the Shariah School, the Sufi School, the Murtaizilai School, the Sincere Comradeship, and the Ashiri School.[14] This is the first book in China that comprehensively and systematically discusses the origin, development, and evolution of Arab philosophy. The book is divided into eighteen chapters dealing with key philosophers such as Kendai, Razzi, Farabi, Ibn Sina, Ansari, Ibn Bajal, Ibn Tufeli, Ibn Russid, Ibn Heldun, and others.

After an introduction to Arab philosophy in general, Chen Zhongyao's *Arab Philosophy* mainly expounds upon scholasticism and mysticism, the Greek influence on Arab philosophers, and key topics of Arab philosophy. It covers the emergence, rise, and

---

[14] Cai Degui, *History of Arab Philosophy*, Shandong University Press, 1992. (蔡德贵，《阿拉伯哲学史》，山东大学出版社，1992, 目录（433 页）年)

decline of Arab philosophy, with attention to important movements, sects, thinkers, theories, and schools of thought.[15]

Research on Arab Modern Philosophy, edited by Cai Degui, presents the rich variety of Arab modern philosophy, which is of great value for those who wish to understand the impact of Arab culture and its status in the contemporary world.[16] *Research on Contemporary Islamic Arab Philosophy*, also edited by Cai Degui, compares the three major religions in the Arab world and other minor religions, such as Sabism, Manichaeism, and Baha'i. It includes materials on the philosophies of Islamic fundamentalism, mysticism, existentialism, positivism, rationalism, Marxism, and other trends in social thought. The volume provides a clear analysis of Arab ideology and culture from the perspectives of historical evolution, context, law, and characteristics. It also highlights the diversity of Arab philosophy and emphasizes the national and historical nature of contemporary Islamic Arab philosophy, accurately and comprehensively representing the ideological panorama that is contemporary Islamic Arab philosophy.[17]

Wang Jiaying's *History of Islamic Religious Philosophy* is the first academic work in China to detail the history of Islamic religious philosophy and is highly regarded. It is divided into major sections on the prophet Muhammad and the Quran, hadith, Islamic law, the rise of Islamic sects, Sunni schools of thought, Islamic scholasticism, Shia, historical documents of Islamic religious philosophy, fundamentalism, Illuminati, Sufi, Islamic Sufi Brotherhood, Iranian Shia, and the modern era.[18]

---

[15] Chen Zhongyao, *Arabic Philosophy*, Shanghai Foreign Language Education Press, 1995. (陈中耀，《阿拉伯哲学》，上海外语教育出版社，1995 年，目录)

[16] Cai Degui (editor), *Research on Arab Modern Philosophy*, People's Publishing House, Shandong, 1996. (蔡德贵主编，《阿拉伯近现代哲学研究》，山东人民出版社，1996 年，目录)

[17] Cai Degui, *Research on Contemporary Islamic Arab Philosophy*, People's Publishing House, 2001. (蔡德贵主编，《当代伊斯兰阿拉伯哲学研究》，人民出版社，2001 年，目录页（633 页）)

[18] Wang Jiaying, *History of Islamic Religious Philosophy*, Ethnic Publishing House, 2003. (王家瑛，《伊斯兰宗教哲学史》，民族出版社，2003 年，目录页、（1061 页）)

6. RESEARCH IN PHILOSOPHY

A Concise History of Islamic Philosophy, edited by Zhang Bingmin, recounts the history of Islamic philosophy from pre-Islamic Arabia to the present day, showcasing its rich content from multiple angles and on multiple levels. Its chapters are divided by historical period: the formation of Islamic philosophy (610–632 AD), Islamic philosophy during the Orthodox Caliphate period (632–661), Islamic philosophy during the Umayyad period (661–750), philosophical ideas during the Abbasid period (750–1258), eight chapters on Islamic philosophy in the early Ottoman Empire (1258–1798), Islamic philosophy in the later Ottoman Empire (1798–1923), and Islamic philosophy in the modern Eastern world (1923).[19]

The above-mentioned monographs and edited volumes have sorted and evaluated Arab Islamic philosophy, each with their own unique features. Among them, Wang Jiaying's *History of Islamic Religious Philosophy* is an academic work that elaborates on the history of Islamic religious philosophy in China. It is highly regarded in academic circles and fills a gap in the research of Islamic religious philosophy in the Chinese academic community.

In recent years, domestic scholars have recognized the importance of studying the history of religious thought and have begun to use primary literature to conduct in-depth thematic research on important figures in the history of thought.

> Wang Junrong, *Unity of Heaven and Man, Truthfulness of Things and Me: A Preliminary Exploration of Ibn Arabi's Existentialism*, Religious Culture Press, 2006. （王俊荣，《天人合一、物我还真—伊本·阿拉比存在论初探》, 宗教文化出版社，2006 年）

Wang Junrong's work on Ibn Arabi's existentialism relies directly on his seminal work, "The Revelation of Mecca," and Abdul Kailim Giri's authoritative Arabic original, "Opening the Door of Mystery." On this basis, the achievements of western scholars, of ancient Chinese philosophy, and of Hui Muslim scholars during China's Ming and Qing dynasties are compared with Sufi

---

[19] Zhang Bingmin, *A Concise History of Islamic Philosophy*, Ningxia People's Publishing House, 2007. （张秉民主编，《简明伊斯兰哲学史》, 宁夏人民出版社，2007 年，目录页（363 页））

mysticism so as to gain insight from the works of ancient and modern Chinese and foreign philosophers and so that the research is based on a solid academic foundation. The reliance on primary materials and their comparison is a new research method in the field of Islamic studies in China, reflecting the author's solid foundation in Arabic language and academic rigor. The author accumulated much information and used this new method to enrich and develop the scientific research on Ibn Arabi through systematic argumentation, which constitutes a breakthrough in the research of Ibn Arabi in Chinese academic circles. The theories, methods, and comments elaborated in the author's publications on this topic have important theoretical significance.[20]

Taken together, the volumes on Islamic philosophy highlighted here showcase a broad and complex definition of Islamic philosophy, breaking through the existing framework and posing numerous challenges and opportunities for future research.

---

[20] Wang Junrong, *Unity of Heaven and Man, Truthfulness of Things and Me: A Preliminary Exploration of Ibn Arabi's Existentialism*, Religious Culture Press, 2006. （王俊荣，《天人合一物我还真—伊本·阿拉比存在论初探》，宗教文化出版社，2006 年.）

PART SEVEN.
RESEARCH IN POLITICAL AND SOCIAL FIELDS

Islam has a profound connection with people's lives, especially in contemporary social and political life. In the Islamic world and regions, the relationship between Islam and social politics is even closer. Contemporary scholars even refer to it as "political Islam," "political Islamization," "Islamic politicization," and so on. In the 20th century, three major schools of Islamic politics emerged: nationalism, modernism, and fundamentalism. Nationalists regard modern nationalist countries and social views as their political cornerstone, Islam as their ideological belief, and the de facto separation of politics and religion as their fundamental national policy. Modernists use the political traditions of early Islam as a model, advocating political principles such as ethnicity, freedom, and equality. Fundamentalists believe that the aggressive expansion of Western powers has been the root cause of the political decline of the Muslim nation since modern times. Only by reviving Islamic traditions, including their political principles, ideological concepts, and ethical norms, can Muslim countries achieve peace and stability. Many of these political views are based on the Quran and the social practices of the Orthodox Caliph period.

Research in the field of contemporary Islam involves examining different countries and nations along with their economic and political conditions. Therefore, it is an interdisciplinary area of study that involves much more than religion. At present, many events that occur in Islamic regions are related to Islam in some way, but not all events are influenced solely by Islam, nor are they necessarily religious phenomena. Most often, these theories and events are directly related to world politics and utilization issues. There are ten ethnic groups in China who ascribe to Islam, and their religious issues inevitably affect the country's politics, society, and other areas of life. International Islamic turmoil also naturally affects Chinese Muslim society.

From an academic perspective, Islamic politics and social issues have attracted the attention of scholars both inside and outside the mosque. Recent decades have seen an increase in publications on the relationship between Islam and current international political life, as well as the social trends and movements of Islam.

1 RESEARCH ON ISLAMIC REVIVAL OR "FUNDAMENTALISM"

In the late 1980s, the following collection of papers was released through internal distribution:

> Liu Jing (chief editor), *Collection of Islamic Revival Movement*, Institute of West Asia and Africa, Chinese Academy of Social Sciences (internal distribution), 1989. （刘竟 主编，《伊斯兰复兴运动论集》，中国社会科学院西亚非洲研究所（内部发行），1989 年）

This volume contains important papers by representative scholars that indicate the main views at that time. After the 1990s, there was a significant increase in papers, monographs, and research reports by Chinese scholars on the issue of Islamic revival.

> Wu Yungui, *The Awakening of the Muslim Nation: The Modern Islamic Movement*, China Social Sciences Press, 1994. （吴云贵，《穆斯林民族的觉醒：近代伊斯兰运动》，中国社会科学出版社，1994 年）

> Xiao Xian, *The Return of Tradition: The Contemporary Islamic Revival Movement*, China Social Sciences Press, 1994. （肖宪，《传统的回归：当代伊斯兰复兴运动》，中国社会科学出版社，1994 年）

> Jin Yiji (Editor in Chief), *Contemporary Islam*, Eastern Publishing House, 1995. （金宜久 主编，《当代伊斯兰教》，东方出版社，1995 年）

7. RESEARCH IN POLITICAL AND SOCIAL FIELDS 137

> Peng Shuzhi (Edited), *Islam and the Modernization Process in the Middle East*, Northwestern University Press, 1997. (彭树智 主编，《伊斯兰教和中东现代化进程》，西北大学出版社，1997 年)

> Zhang Ming, *Islamic Revival Movement in the Perspective of Modernization*, Chinese Social Science Press, 1999. (张铭，《现代化视野中的伊斯兰复兴运动》，中国社会科学出版，1999 年)

Wu Yungui's *The Awakening of the Muslim Nation: The Modern Islamic Movement* takes the colonial expansion of the modern West as the historical background upon which the author briefly introduces the heroic struggle of the world's Muslim nations to revive their faith and strive for national independence, including the purification of faith movement, the jihad movement, the new prophet movement, and the Islamic modernism movement. The book includes discussions of the following movements and their sub-units: the Wahhabi Movement, Jihad Movement, Senucid Movement, Mahdi Movement in Sudan, Babu Movement in Iran, Ahmadiya Movement, Pan Islamic Movement, Islamic Modernism Movement, and others.[1]

Xiao Xian's *The Return of Tradition: The Contemporary Islamic Revival Movement* chronicles the development of the Islamic Revival Movement since the Islamic Revolution in Iran in the late 1980s. It swept the entire Muslim world and attracted the attention of the international community, especially political, press, academic and religious circles. In this book, the author systematically discusses the origin, nature, forms, developments, and other issues of the contemporary Islamic Revival Movement.[2]

In contemporary international political life, Islam's role and influence can be easily felt. There have been major international political events that appear to be related to Islam but, in fact, have nothing to do with it. *Contemporary Islam*, edited by Jin Yijiu, provides a theoretical explanation. Its contributors include

---

[1] Wu Yungui, *The Awakening of the Muslim Nation: Modern Islamic Movement*, China Social Sciences Press, 1994. (吴云贵，《穆斯林民族的觉醒：近代伊斯兰运动》，中国社会科学出版社，1994 年，目录（118 页））

[2] Xiao Xian, *The Return of Tradition: Contemporary Islamic Revival Movement*, China Social Sciences Press, 1994. (肖宪，《传统的回归：当代伊斯兰复兴运动》，中国社会科学出版社，1994 年, 目录（128 页））

discussions of the spread of Islam in various regions of the world, Islam and politics, official policies and civil movements, the development and evolution of Islam in contemporary society, Islam and legal system reform, Islam and the economy, Islam and culture, and the "emerging sects" of Islam (e.g., Ahmadism, Islamic nation, Baha'ism). There are also chapters on contemporary Islam in China, including the spread of Islam in China, the current situation of Islam in China, and the relationship between Islam and modernization in China.[3]

Zhang Ming's *Islamic Revival Movement in the Perspective of Modernization* left a deep impression on the international political stage of the post-Cold War world, with the violent, tragic, and somewhat cruel appearance of the Islamic fundamentalist movement. Some Muslims have now turned to the Islamic Revival Movement as a source of identity, meaning, stability, legitimacy, development, strength, and hope. The Islamic Revival Movement has had a huge impact on today's world. This book provides cutting-edge theoretical thinking on the ups and downs of the Islamic Revival Movement in the modernization process and its interpretation of modernization, as well as issues such as the conflict between Eastern and Western civilizations and international political interaction.[4]

These works respectively discuss the religious revival trends and movements of modern times. Chinese scholars emphasize that the Islamic Revival Movement is an international, multi-centered, and diverse political and social movement that incorporates many lived experiences.

There are also many publications on fundamentalism in Islamic politics. For example:

> Xiao Xian, *Contemporary International Islamic Tide*, World Knowledge Press, 1997. (肖宪, 《当代国际伊斯兰潮》, 世界知识出版社, 1997 年)

---

[3] Jin Yiji (Editor in Chief), *Contemporary Islam*, Eastern Publishing House, 1995. (金宜久 主编, 《当代伊斯兰教》, 东方出版社, 1995 年、401 页)

[4] Zhang Ming, *Islamic Revival Movement in the Perspective of Modernization*, Chinese Social Science Press, 1999. (张铭, 《现代化视野中的伊斯兰复兴运动》, 中国社会科学出版, 1999 年, 目录 (315 页))

7. Research in Political and Social Fields 139

> Chen Jiahou (editor), *Modern Islamism*, Economic Daily Press, 1998. (陈嘉厚主编，《现代伊斯兰主义》，经济日报出版社，1998 年）
>
> Qu Hong, *Contemporary Political Islam in the Middle East: Observation and Reflection*, China Social Sciences Press, 2001. (曲洪，《当代中东政治伊斯兰：观察与思考》，中国社会科学出版社，2001 年）

Xiao Xian's *Contemporary International Islamic Tide* introduces the concept, development, and formation of Islam, as well as the situation of the contemporary Islamic movement, and enhances Chinese people's understanding of the Islamic world.[5]

Chapter fourteen of *Modern Islamism* (edited by Chen Jiahou) provides a comprehensive introduction and analysis of the causes, organization, nature, social foundation, theoretical perspectives, strategies, and prospects of Islamism. There are also chapters on hot-button issues, groups, and nations related directly to the movement, such as Iran, Sudan, Afghanistan, Algeria, the Egyptian Muslim Brotherhood, Hamas, Hezbollah in Lebanon, Wahhabism in Saudi Arabia, and the Middle East peace process. The geographic center of the modern Islamist movement is the Middle East, yet it is a strong international religious and political social reform movement that has shocked the world, attracting close attention from governments and people of various countries. This book is the first monograph in China to systematically study what the West calls "Islamic fundamentalism," starting from 610 AD and ending with 1996.[6]

Qu Hong's *Contemporary Political Islam in the Middle East: Observation and Reflection* is comprehensive, informative, well-structured, highly systematic, and theoretical in nature. It is widely available for those engaged in related research.[7] The book contains chapters on Muslim communities, traditional Islamic political systems and political theories, modern and

---

[5] Xiao Xian, *Contemporary International Islamic Tide*, World Knowledge Press, 1997. (肖宪，《当代国际伊斯兰潮》，世界知识出版社，1997 年）

[6] Chen Jiahou (editor), *Modern Islamism*, Economic Daily Press, 1998. (陈嘉厚主编，《现代伊斯兰主义》，经济日报出版社，1998 年，目录（623 页））

[7] 曲洪『当代中东政治伊斯兰：观察与思考』（当代中東政治イスラーム：観察と思考）中国社会科学出版社、2001 年、目录（382 页）

contemporary Islamic trends, religion and politics in the history of various countries (e.g., Egypt, Algeria, Saudi Arabia), and Middle Eastern religious and political opposition. The chapter "Religion and Politics in History" offers a comprehensive review of historical changes in Islamic politics in the Middle East.

In the 21st century, Chinese scholars continue to explore modern political developments from both internal and external perspectives. The continuous emergence of publications marks the in-depth development of academic research in this field, with examples such as:

Wu Yungui and Zhou Xiefan (co-authored), *Modern Islamic Thought and Movement*, Social Science Literature Press, 2000. （吴云贵、周燮藩合著《近代伊斯兰教思潮和运动》，社会科学文献出版社，2000 年）
Cai Jiahe, *Contemporary Islamic Fundamentalist Movement*, Ningxia People's Publishing House, 2003. （蔡佳禾，《当代伊斯兰原教旨主义运动》，宁夏人民出版社，2003 年）
Wu Bingbing, *The Rise of Shi'ite Modern Islamism*, China Social Sciences Press, 2004. （吴冰冰，《什叶派现代伊斯兰主义的兴起》，中国社会科学出版社，2004 年）
Ma Fude, *The Pioneer of the Modern Islamic Revival Movement – A Study of Wahab and His Thoughts*, China Social Sciences Press, 2006. （马福德，《近代伊斯兰复兴运动的先驱—瓦哈卜及其思想研究》，中国社会科学出版社，2006 年）
Fan Ruolan, *Islam and the Modernization Process of Southeast Asia*, China Social Sciences Press, 2009. （范若兰，《伊斯兰教与东南亚现代化进程》，中国社会科学出版社、2009 年）

In today's world, the connections between Islam and international hot topics increasingly arouse widespread interest, while the number of related works is limited. In order to meet the academic needs of this phenomenon, Wu Yungui and Zhou Xiefan co-authored *Modern Islamic Thought and Movement* in which they combine history and theory in their research on various social trends and movements in the modern Islamic world, such as pan-Islamism, Islamic modernism, nationalism, socialism, funda-

7. RESEARCH IN POLITICAL AND SOCIAL FIELDS 141

mentalism, and so on.[8] The content of this book is divided into: introduction, reform and revival at the beginning of modern times, Islamic modernism, and the Revival Movement. This book not only follows the "pre-history" of modern Islamic movements from a new and unique perspective, but also comprehensively sorts and summarizes the complex relationships between various contemporary ideological trends and movements. The perspective is quite broad, the information is rich and accurate, and the arguments are objective and fair.

Cai Jiahe's *Contemporary Islamic Fundamentalist Movement* documents the movement as a contemporary international political force that quickly caught the attention of the world with the success of the Islamic Revolution in Iran. From the late 1970s to the present, this movement called for the revival of Islam and has not only surpassed Iran's borders, but also Muslim countries around the world, becoming an important political force in contemporary international relations, and has had a profound impact on the political, economic, security, and cultural development of many regions and countries. This book analyzes the Islamic fundamentalist movement from different perspectives.[9]

Wu Bingbing's *The Rise of Shi'ite Modern Islamism* discusses several major issues, including the history, beliefs, and systems of the Shia faction, the evolution of modern Shia political ideology and movements, the development of modern Shia Islamism, and the political activities and ideas of key figures such as Khomeini, Muhammad Bakir Sadr, and Moussa Sadr.[10]

---

[8] Wu Yungui and Zhou Xiefan (co-authored), *Modern Islamic Thought and Movement*, Social Science Literature Press, 2000. （吴云贵、周燮藩合著《近代伊斯兰教思潮和运动》，社会科学文献出版社，2000 年，目录（391 页））

[9] Cai Jiahe, *Contemporary Islamic Fundamentalist Movement*, Ningxia People's Publishing House, 2003. （蔡佳禾，《当代伊斯兰原教旨主义运动》，宁夏人民出版社，2003 年，目录（301 页））

[10] Wu Bingbing, *The Rise of Shi'ite Modern Islamism*, China Social Sciences Press, 2004. （吴冰冰，《什叶派现代伊斯兰主义的兴起》，中国社会科学出版社，2004 年，目录（370 页））

Maford's *The Pioneer of the Modern Islamic Revival Movement—A Study of Wahhab and His Thoughts* demonstrates that a thorough study of Muhammad ibn 'Abd al-Wahhab (c. 1703–1792) is helpful for understanding trends in contemporary Islamic revival and makes a fair evaluation of them. The subject of this book, the ideology of Wahhab, the pioneer of the modern Islamic revival movement, is considered one of the foundation stones of contemporary Islamic fundamentalism. This book examines the historical and social background of the rise of Wahhab's reformation thought and uses the theoretical methods of history, religious studies, sociology, and politics to conduct a complete presentation, in-depth analysis, and summary of his thought and its impact. There are also useful appendices on translations of Wahhab's works and letters.[11]

In *Islam and the Modernization Process of Southeast Asia*, Fan Ruolan focuses on six countries in Southeast Asia—Malaysia, Indonesia, Brunei, Thailand, the Philippines, and Singapore—and systematically analyzes the relationship between Islam and political, economic, and legal modernization, as well as its role in ethnic relations. Among them, Malaysia, Indonesia, and Brunei have majority Muslim populations, and Islam holds an important position in their development and ethnic relations. The Malays of Thailand, the Moro people of the Philippines, and the Malays of Singapore—all Muslim minorities—have played an important role in the modernization process of their respective countries. The author of the book believes that the modernization process has had a profound impact on Islam from content to form. Faced with the impact of modernization, Islam needs to adapt its doctrines, systems, and laws, yet Islam has not declined in the face of the challenges modernization presents. On the contrary, it

---

[11] Ma Fude, *The Pioneer of the Modern Islamic Revival Movement – A Study of Wahab and His Thoughts*, China Social Sciences Press, 2006. (马福德, 《近代伊斯兰复兴运动的先驱—瓦哈卜及其思想研究》, 中国社会科学出版社, 2006 年, 目录（218 页））

7. Research in Political and Social Fields   143

is growing stronger, and the Islamic Revival Movement is a positive response to modernization.[12]

2 Islam and International Politics

Some scholars believe that the study of Islamic fundamentalism should entail not only the study of extremists who are passionate about terrorist activities but also the study of moderate mainstream factions, as moderate factions that strive to integrate into mainstream society may represent the best future direction. However, the activities of extremist factions will continue to be a topic of social attention and thus a fruitful area of academic research.

The China Social Science Literature Press has continuously published monographs on Islam and politics for several years, such as:

> Jin Yijiu, *Islam and World Politics*, China Social Science Literature Press, 1996. (金宜久，《伊斯兰教与世界政治》，中国社会科学文献出版社，1996 年)
>
> Dongfang Xiao (Editor), *Islam and the World after the Cold War*, China Social Science Literature Press, 1999. (东方晓主编，《伊斯兰与冷战后的世界》，中国社会科学文献出版社，1999 年)
>
> Liu Jinghua and Zhang Xiaodong (co-authored), *Modern Politics and Islam,* China Social Science Literature Press, 2000. (刘靖华 张晓东 合著，《现代政治与伊斯兰教》，中国社会科学文献出版社，2000 年)
>
> Chen Decheng (Edited), *Political Modernization in the Middle East: Exploration of Theory and Historical Experience*, China Social Science Literature Press, 2000. (陈德成 主编，《中东政治现代化--理论和历史经验的探索》，中国社会科学文献出版社，2000 年)

After World War II, Islam not only consolidated and developed in its traditional popular regions—West Asia, North Africa, South

---

[12] Fan Ruolan, *Islam and the Modernization Process of Southeast Asia*, China Social Sciences Press, 2009. (范若兰，《伊斯兰教与东南亚现代化进程》，中国社会科学出版社、2009 年, 目录（458 页）)

144   ISLAM IN CHINA AND THE ISLAMIC WORLD

Africa, Southeast Asia, and Central Asia—but also gained corresponding dissemination and development in sub–Saharan Africa, Western Europe, North America, and other regions. Jin Yijiu's *Islam and World Politics* looks at the geographical regions that have been influenced by Islam and focuses on its relationship to their politics. It includes sections on the relationship between Islam and politics in history, Islam and nation, democratic revolution, Islam and modern reform, Islam and socialism, pan-Islamism, and the Islamic Revival Movement.[13]

Islam and the World after the Cold War, edited by Dongfang Xiao, presents the overarching argument that the end of the Cold War was marked by a series of historical events, including the democratization of Eastern Europe, the outbreak of overseas wars, and the disintegration of the Soviet Union. In the Muslim world, especially in the Middle East, the prospect of this change is far from what people think. Without external influence, some contradictions and conflicts tend to ease. The political changes and economic restructuring of certain Muslim countries have activated many political forces that have intervened in various ways and even tried to enter the political process, thus challenging the structure of Muslim countries. The book examines the internal and external factors that influence change in the Islamic world, including the threats and challenges it currently faces.[14]

Liu Jinghua and Zhang Xiaodong co-authored *Modern Politics and Islam*. The content of this book is divided into: New Synthesis of Theory, Islam and Political Tradition, Islam and Political Culture, Political Ideology under Islam, Islam and Political Legitimacy, Islam and Political System, Islam and Political Authority, Islam and Political Participation, Contemporary Islamic Revival—Analysis from a Cultural Perspective Contemporary Islamic Fundamentalism—Analysis from the

---

[13] Jin Yijiu, *Islam and World Politics*, China Social Science Literature Press, 1996. （金宜久, 《伊斯兰教与世界政治》, 中国社会科学文献出版社, 1996 年）

[14] Dongfang Xiao (Editor), *Islam and the World after the Cold War*, China Social Science Literature Press, 1999. （东方晓主编, 《伊斯兰与冷战后的世界》, 中国社会科学文献出版社, 1999 年, 目录（309 页））

7. RESEARCH IN POLITICAL AND SOCIAL FIELDS 145

Perspective of Political Science. The author of the book focuses on the relationship between modern politics and Islam.[15]

In the book *Political Modernization in the Middle East – Exploration of Theory and Historical Experience*, edited by Chen Decheng, contributors offer detailed discussions of the political modernization theories of scholars such as Turabi and Erbakan. After focusing on the influence of Islam on the process of political modernization in the Middle East, the volume then switches to case studies on Turkey, Egypt, Iran, Saudi Arabia, Algeria, Syria, and Iraq.[16]

Due to the end of the Cold War, the global political landscape has undergone drastic changes since the 1990s. Many regional conflicts that were long concealed have erupted one after another, while religious extremism and ethnic separatism, under the indulgence and exploitation of external forces, have fueled various conflicts and disputes around the world. In response, relevant departments and research institutions in China have held multiple seminars on this topic, conducted extensive academic exchanges and policy consultations, and organized many research projects and topics. Of course, these must be based on previous academic publications and basic theories in contemporary Islamic research. In 2000, the research report "Islam in International Politics in the 1990s" by Jin Yijiu and Wu Yungui was published. This report provides a systematic analysis of regional issues related to Islam, analyzes the causes and consequences of hot topic issues, and makes a fair evaluation.[17]

---

[15] Liu Jinghua and Zhang Xiaodong (co-authored), Modern Politics and Islam, China Social Science Literature Press, 2000. (刘靖华 张晓东 合著, 《现代政治与伊斯兰教》, 中国社会科学文献出版社, 2000 年, 目录（348 页））

[16] Chen Decheng (Edited), *Political Modernization in the Middle East: Exploration of Theory and Historical Experience*, China Social Science Literature Press, 2000. (陈德成 主编, 《中东政治现代化--理论和历史经验的探索》, 中国社会科学文献出版社, 2000 年, 目录（528 页）

[17] Jin Yijiu, Wu Yungui, "Islam in International Politics in the 1990s' (research report), the research group of "Research on Islam and International Political Relations" of the Institute of World Religions, Chinese Academy of Social Sciences, and the "Ninth Five Year Plan" key project of the National Social Science Foundation, completed in April

146   ISLAM IN CHINA AND THE ISLAMIC WORLD

Other important works on Islam and international politics include:

Yang Haocheng, Zhu Kerou, editors, *Historical Exploration of Contemporary Middle East Hot Issues: Religion and Secularity*, People's Publishing House, 2000.（杨灏城、朱克柔 主编《当代中东热点问题的历史探索—宗教与世俗》，人民出版社，2000 年）
Jin Yijiu and Wu Yungui co-authored, *Islam and International Hotspots*, Eastern Publishing House, 2001.（金宜久 吴云贵 合著，《伊斯兰与国际热点》，东方出版社，2001 年）
Wang Yizhou, *Tracing the Origin of Terrorism*, Social Science Literature Press, 2002.（王逸舟，《恐怖主义溯源》，社会科学文献出版社，2002 年）

Yang Haocheng and Zhu Kerou edited *Historical Exploration of Contemporary Middle East Hot Issues: Religion and Secularity*, which has become a distinctive academic work due to the authors' perspective on world history.[18]

Jin Yijiu and Wu Yungui co-authored *Islam and International Hotspots* in which they selected thirteen representative countries in the Islamic world to discuss their political and religious relations. This includes the spread of Islam in these countries, the revival of Islam in various countries since the late 1960s and early 70s, and the issue of political and religious relations in the 1980s and 90s. It also analyzes regional conflicts and wars during the Cold War, specifically in the Islamic world, and discusses the often-tense relationships between Islamic countries and the United States, on one hand, and the Soviet Union, on the other. Finally, Jin Yijiu and Wu Yungui discuss the Islamic world after the Cold War from different perspectives, addressing the disintegration of the Soviet Union, the drastic changes in Eastern

---

2000.（金宜久、吴云贵：《20 世纪 90 年代国际政治中的伊斯兰》（研究报告），中国社会科学院世界宗教研究所《伊斯兰教与国际政治关系研究》课题组，国家社会科学基金"95"重点项目，2000 年 4 月完稿）

[18] Yang Haocheng, Zhu Kerou, *Historical Exploration of Contemporary Middle East Hot Issues: Religion and Secularity*, People's Publishing House, 2000.（杨灏城、朱克柔 主编《当代中东热点问题的历史探索—宗教与世俗》，人民出版社，2000 年（457 页））

7. RESEARCH IN POLITICAL AND SOCIAL FIELDS 147

Europe, and the development and evolution of international politics towards multipolarity. Finally, the book provides a summary of the Islamic factors in contemporary international politics.[19]

Tracing the Origin of Terrorism by Wang Yizhou presents evidence that international terrorism has become a major challenge facing all countries in the information age, calling its organizers masters of logic and psychoanalysis. Terrorists are neither "cold-blooded animals," nor "guerrilla fighters" or "anti-violence martyrs" but have cruelty, extreme secrecy, and clear political goals. The phenomenon of international terrorism reflects certain deep-seated and structural contradictions in international politics, and its high incidence areas are closely related to the international trends after the end of the Cold War. The eradication of international terrorism is a comprehensive governance approach that cannot be solved through quick combat and requires completely different security strategies. This book offers a comprehensive view of terrorism, including its roots, variations, relations to other powers, and issues it aims to address.[20]

Similarly, there is also:

> Zhou Xiefan, "Terrorism and Religious Issues," West Asia and Africa, Issue 1, 2002. （周燮藩，"恐怖主义与宗教问题，"《西亚非洲》，2002 年第 1 期）

Since the 9/11 terrorist attack on the United States in 2001, phrases such as "religious terrorism" and "Islamic terrorism" have become quite popular. However, there is no inevitable connection between terrorism and religion historically. In contemporary international terrorism, those with religious connotations or under the guise of religion can be divided into three categories: terrorism combined with ethnic separatism, terrorism dominated

---

[19] Jin Yijiu and Wu Yungui co-authored, *Islam and International Hotspots*, Eastern Publishing House, 2001. （金宜久 吴云贵 合著，《伊斯兰与国际热点》，东方出版社，2001 年，目录（650 页））

[20] Wang Yizhou, *Tracing the Origin of Terrorism*, Social Science Literature Press, 2002. （王逸舟，《恐怖主义溯源》，社会科学文献出版社，2002 年，目录（296 页））

by religious extremism, and terrorism of worship groups. The root cause is the conflict between political and economic interests. From the perspective of Islamic research, the achievements of the above aspects, namely the study of the Islamic Revival Movement, Islamism or "Islamic Fundamentalism," Islam and international politics, and Islam and international hotspots, all focus on the study of contemporary Islam and Islamism. At present, some people believe that Islamism has failed, or that the entire Islamic Revival Movement is at a low point. How will the situation develop in the future? As Wang Yujie has said, "where political Islam will go in the 21st century depends on the different political Islamic organizations themselves, as well as the country and social environment they are in. The factor that determines the future direction of political Islam is politics, not religion itself. Moreover, once the political and social situation changes, religious forms, trends, and functions will also change."[21]

---

[21] Wang Yujie, "The Trend of Political Islam in the 21st Century," Research on World Religions, Issue 1, 2001, pp. 19–25. (王宇潔, "21世纪政治伊斯兰的走向"《世界宗教研究》2001 年第 1 期、19－25 页.)

PART EIGHT. RESEARCH IN CULTURE AND OTHER FIELDS

1 RESEARCH ON THE RELATIONSHIP BETWEEN ISLAM AND CHINESE CULTURE

In the history of Chinese civilization, religious culture not only played a role in the spiritual life of believers but also had an impact on the spiritual and cultural life of society. Since China's reform and development, under the influence of the global religious and cultural boom, Chinese scholars have paid attention to the study of Islamic culture and related fields, and many important representative works have appeared. These include the following:

The Islamic Research Office of the World Religion Research Institute of the Chinese Academy of Social Sciences, *Aspects of Islamic Culture,* Qilu Press, 1991. （中国社会科学院世界宗教研究所伊斯兰教研究室合编，《伊斯兰教文化面面观》，齐鲁出版社，1991 年）
Nazhong Zhu Kai, *Tradition and Blending: Arab Culture,* People's Publishing House,1993. （纳忠 朱凯 合著，《传统与交融：阿拉伯文化》，浙江人民出版社，1993 年）
Qin Huibin (editor), *Series of World Civilizations: Islamic Civilization,* China Social Sciences Press, 1999. （秦惠彬主编，《世界文明大系：伊斯兰文明》，中国社会科学出版社，1999 年）

Ma Mingliang, *New Comments on Islamic Culture*, Ningxia People's Publishing House, 1999. （马明良，《伊斯兰文化新论》，宁夏人民出版社，1999 年）
Ma Mingliang, *Collection of Frontier Studies on Islamic Culture,* China Social Sciences Press, 2006. （马明良，《伊斯兰文化前沿研究论集》，中国社会科学出版社，2006 年）

The book *Aspects of Islamic Culture* was edited by important scholars from the Islamic Research Office of the Chinese Academy of Sciences, including Wang Junrong, Feng Jinyuan, Wu Yungui, Sha Qiuzhen, Li Xinghua, Jin Yijiu, Zhou Xiefan, and Qin Huibin. Like most religions, Islam has extremely close connections with people's social life, and the relationship between Islam and social politics is unavoidable. This book offers a brief introduction to issues related to Islam and current international political life, as well as modern social trends and movements within Islam. In terms of geography, this book focuses on South and Central Asia with a significant amount of content on China, including the origin of Islam in China, famous scholars of Islam, famous mosques, the relationship between Islam and traditional Chinese culture, the official, Taoist, and sectarian aspects of Islam in China, and the contributions of Islam to China's technology, culture, and other fields. This book is divided into four major topics: the history of Islam, Islamic culture, Islamic science, and the contributions of Islam to society.[1]

Tradition and Blending: Arab Culture, co-authored by Nazhong and Zhu Kai, elaborates on the Arab culture of the Abbasid dynasty centered around Baghdad, explaining its historical conditions, the reasons for its formation, important aspects of its culture, and its impact on the Eastern and Western worlds. Domestic and foreign writings on Arab culture often overlook important aspects, such as economic development, social life, and international cultural exchange. The book discusses these issues and a wide variety of others, with sections dedicated to pre-

---

[1] The Islamic Research Office of the World Religion Research Institute of the Chinese Academy of Social Sciences, *Aspects of Islamic Culture,* Qilu Press, 1991. （中国社会科学院世界宗教研究所伊斯兰教研究室合编，《伊斯兰教文化面面观》，齐鲁出版社，1991 年，目录（325 页））

8. RESEARCH IN CULTURE AND OTHER FIELDS   151

Islamic Arabia, Islamism, the Enlightenment period of Arab culture, the heyday of Arab culture, national system, economic development, social life and social relations, the Hundred Year Translation Movement, doctrine and culture, literature and art, historians and geographers, sects and philosophy, natural sciences, and the relationship between medieval China and Arabia.[2]

Qin Huibin's *Series of World Civilizations: Islamic Civilization* draws from the latest publications of scholars in China and abroad to put forth a comprehensive exploration of Islamic civilization. With an interest in both theory and religious practice, the author discusses the rise of Islamic civilization, the spread and development of Islam, Islam after the dissolution of the traditional caliphate system, modern Islamic civilization, and Islamic politics, economy, society, feminism, literature, art, education, and science. It also includes chapters on the contributions of Islamic civilization to world civilization.[3]

Ma Mingliang's *New Comments on Islamic Culture* comprehensively applies the theories of culturology, religious studies, sociology, and philosophy to set Islamic culture against the broad background of human culture. The result is a unique perspective, novel method, and distinct academic style. It addresses many aspects of Islamic culture, such as religion, ethics, law, politics, economics, science, technology, ecology, marriage and family, sex, education, clothing, food, housing, transportation, festivals, entertainment, funeral culture, mosque culture, and human needs.[4]

Ma Mingliang's *Collection of Frontier Studies on Islamic Culture* is a collection of papers that focuses on cutting-edge

---

[2] Nazhong Zhu Kai, *Tradition and Blending: Arab Culture,* People's Publishing House, 1993. (纳忠 朱凯 合著, 《传统与交融: 阿拉伯文化》, 浙江人民出版社, 1993 年, 目录)

[3] Qin Huibin (editor), *Series of World Civilizations: Islamic Civilization,* China Social Sciences Press, 1999. (秦惠彬主编, 《世界文明大系: 伊斯兰文明》, 中国社会科学出版社, 1999 年, 目录（436 页）)

[4] Ma Mingliang, *Collection of Frontier Studies on Islamic culture,* China Social Sciences Press, 2006. (马明良, 《伊斯兰文化前沿研究论集》, 中国社会科学出版社, 2006 年)

achievements in the field of Chinese Islamic studies in the first few years of the 21st century. Most of the papers have been published in public venues and scattered in various Chinese academic journals. Contributors to this volume mainly come from Northwest University for Nationalities, but there are also papers from scholars at other domestic universities and research institutes such as Beijing and Shanghai. This collection of essays is a valuable contribution to the academic study of religion because it promotes the field, makes theoretical contributions, and expands the boundaries of scholarship, while also displaying religion's role in promoting social harmony.

There is also a growing body of publications on the historical evolution of Islamic culture in China, that is, the relationship between Islamic culture and Chinese traditional culture. For example:

Ye Haya Linsong, *Hui History and Islamic culture*, China Today Press, 1992. （叶哈雅 林松，《回回历史和伊斯兰文化》，今日中国出版社，1992 年）

Yang Huaizhong and Yu Zhengui (co-authored), *Islam and Chinese Culture,* Ningxia People's Publishing House, 1995. （杨怀中、余振贵（合著），《伊斯兰与中国文化》，宁夏人民出版社，1995 年）

Qin Huibin, *Islam and Traditional Culture in China* ,China Social Sciences Press, 1995. （秦惠彬《中国伊斯兰教与传统文化》，中国社会科学出版社，1995 年）

Ma Tong, *Muslim Culture on the Silk Road* , Ningxia People's Publishing House, 2000. （马通，《丝绸之路上的穆斯林文化》，宁夏人民出版社，2000 年）

Ding Jun, *A Survey of Islamic culture*, Gansu Ethnic Publishing House, 2002. （丁俊，《伊斯兰文化巡礼》，甘肃民族出版社，2002 年）

Ma Mingliang, *The Exchange Course and Prospects of Islamic Civilization and Chinese Civilization,* China Social Sciences Press, 2006. （马明良，《伊斯兰文明与中华文明的交流历程和前景》，中国社会科学出版社，2006 年）

8. RESEARCH IN CULTURE AND OTHER FIELDS   153

In *Islam and Chinese Culture*, Yang Huaizhong and Yu Zhengui propose that the Hui nationality was a sophisticated culture from its very beginning. It introduced Islamic culture into China and continues to be its carrier, but on the winding and bumpy historical path, it gradually fell from the height of culture. During the Xiantong period in the late Qing Dynasty, the Hui uprising failed, and the agricultural and economic foundations of the Hui ethnic groups in the southwest and northwest were severely damaged. Economic poverty accelerated the decline of culture, and the unique knowledge of the Hui, such as astronomy and medicine, was neglected. Islamic religious leaders who were proficient in Arabic and could write elegantly were rare, such as those who wrote poems to Ma in the early Qing Dynasty's "Halal Guide." This historical downturn is explained by the relationship between Islamic culture and Chinese culture at that time. To give a few examples of topics covered, *Islam and Chinese Culture* covers the economic and cultural exchanges between the Arab empires, on one hand, and the Tang and Song Dynasties, on the other; the Mongolian army's westward expedition and the Hui people's eastward arrival; the four climaxes of Islamic culture in Chinese history; the impact of Islamic astronomy and medicine; Chinese Islamic scripture education and translation activities, including the translation of the Quran; and the defining characteristics of Chinese Islamic culture.[5]

In his book *Islam and Traditional Culture in China*, Qin Huibin argues that 'Islam' does not refer specifically to religion but is endowed with multiple layers of meaning. It simultaneously refers to a social system, lifestyle, cultural form, and even the characteristics of the times, permeating all fields of Muslim life as the "Islamic spirit." This Islamic spirit relates to important aspects of the tradition's origins in Arabia, such as nomadism, desert, and commerce. Under the guidance of this spirit, various Chinese ethnic groups that believe in Islam have created brilliant Islamic civilizations that take into account the unique heritage of Chinese

---

[5] Yang Huaizhong and Yu Zhengui (co-authored), *Islam and Chinese Culture,* Ningxia People's Publishing House, 1995. (杨怀中、余振贵（合著），《伊斯兰与中国文化》, 宁夏人民出版社，1995 年, 目录（633 页））

Islam and its relationship to traditional culture. With full and accurate materials and fluent language, this book systematically introduces Islam's influence on Chinese culture and the process of its integration into China in the Tang, Song, Yuan, Ming, and Qing dynasties, and vividly represents the spirit of Islamic culture and Chinese culture.[6]

Ma Tong's book *Muslim Culture on the Silk Road* documents Muslim culture along the ancient trade route connecting East Asia, West Asia, and the Mediterranean, which played an indelible role in world trade history. Ma Tong describes the two main roads of the Silk Road, the commercial and cultural exchanges between sea and land routes, and the various aspects of Muslim culture involved, such as Muslim commerce, coins, sects, and Sufism schools. This book provides a detailed record of the widespread influence of Muslim culture on ethnic minorities along the route, including Tajik Muslims in Tashkurgan, Kazakh Muslims in the Altyn Mountains, Kirgiz Muslims in Kizilsu, the Dongxiang, Bao'an, and Salar Muslims in the Hehuang region, Uyghur Muslims in the north and south Tianshan Mountains, the Uzbek and Tatar Muslims on the Silk Road, and the Donggan Muslims of the Kyrgyz grasslands. In summary, the author provides a detailed introduction to the profound impact of Muslim culture on the architecture, culture, education, and communities of the Silk Road. The content is comprehensive, the analysis is thorough, and it is of great academic value.[7]

Ding Jun's *A Survey of Islamic Culture* is precisely that. After the introduction, it focuses on the Quran, hadith, doctrines and dogmatics, teaching methods and pedagogy, and the relationship between Islamic, Chinese, and world cultures.

Ma Mingliang's *The Exchange Course and Prospects of Islamic Civilization and Chinese Civilization* focuses on the historical trajectory and practical trends of Islamic civilization in China,

---

[6] Qin Huibin, *Islam and Traditional Culture in China*, China Social Sciences Press, 1995. (秦惠彬《中国伊斯兰教与传统文化》, 中国社会科学出版社, 1995 年, 目录（136 页）)

[7] Ma Tong, *Muslim Culture on the Silk Road,* Ningxia People's Publishing House, 2000. (马通, 《丝绸之路上的穆斯林文化》, 宁夏人民出版社, 2000 年, 目录（227 页）)

8. Research in Culture and Other Fields 155

and the process and prospects of communication between Islamic and Chinese civilizations. Both Islamic civilization and Chinese civilization are vast and profound, with long histories, rich ideologies, meaningful cultural heritage, and long-lasting vitality. Over the past 1,300 years of historical development, the two have established a foundation of mutual exchange. In the wake of globalization, both are increasingly showing their unique charm and facing similar challenges. Only by interacting, exchanging, and learning from each other can they benefit from and complement each other's strengths, achieve common prosperity, and contribute to multiculturalism and the development of human civilization in the context of globalization. This book explores the history of the multi-faceted relationship between Islam and China before turning to issues of globalization and three "areas of dialogue" identified by the book's authors: ecological environment issues, world peace, and global ethical issues. [8]

Among the many publications on Islamic culture, there are also important book series from Baiwen publications that deserve our attention. For example:

Chen Guangyuan, Feng Jinyuan, et al.'s, *Questions on the Quran,* published by Today's China Publishing House, 1994. (陈广元、冯今源《古兰经百问》, 今日中国出版社出版的图书, 1994 年)

Feng Jinyuan et al., *Questions on Islam,* published by Today's China Publishing House, 1992. (冯今源（等编著）《伊斯兰教百问》, 今日中国出版社出版的图书, 1992 年)

Liu Yihong and Qi Qianjin , *Questions on Islamic Art,* published by Today's China Publishing House in 1992. (刘一虹、齐前进,《伊斯兰艺术百问》, 今日中国出版社出版的图书, 1992 年)

Wu Yungui, *Questions on Islamic Classics,* published by Today's China Publishing House in 1992. (吴云贵,《伊斯兰教典籍百问》, 今日中国出版社出版的图书, 1992 年)

---

[8] Ma Mingliang, *The Exchange Course and Prospects of Islamic Civilization and Chinese Civilization,* China Social Sciences Press, 2006. (马明良,《伊斯兰文明与中华文明的交流历程和前景》, 中国社会科学出版社, 2006 年, 311 页)

> Ma Mingliang (edited), *Islamic Culture Series,* published by Today's China Publishing House in 1992. (马明良主编《伊斯兰文化丛书》等)
>
> Wu Yungui, Zhou Xiefan, Qin Huibin (editor), *Islamic culture Series.* (吴云贵、周燮藩、秦惠彬 主编《伊斯兰文化小丛书》)

Questions on the Quran is divided into three major sections: history, culture, and the Quran. The "History" section was composed by Feng Jinyuan and Sha Qiuzhen; "Culture" was written by Feng Jinyuan and Tie Guoxi; and "Quran" was compiled by Chen Guangyuan, Feng Jinyuan, and Tie Guoxi.[9]

Wu Yungui, Zhou Xiefan, and Qin Huibin edited *Islamic Culture Series* (12 volumes). It includes: Islamic Philosophy, Islamic Sects, the Dharma of God – Islamic Shariah, Sufi mysticism of Islam, Islamic Literature, Islamic Doctrine, the Language of God: An Introduction to the Quran, Islam and Traditional Culture in China, the Awakening of the Muslim Nation – Modern Islamic Movement, the Prophet of Islam: Muhammad, and Islamic Education and Science. This set of books provides a comprehensive and systematic introduction to the Quran, Islamic law, Sufism, various schools of Islamic philosophy, and the literary and artistic achievements of Muslims. It provides a concise and complete introduction to the life of the great prophet and politician Muhammad, categorizes major sects, and briefly introduces the development of Islamic education and science. It also introduces the representative dogmatic schools and their belief systems in various periods in Arab countries, and vividly represents the spirit of Islamic culture and Chinese culture.[10]

The following is a brief introduction to the content of the *Islamic Culture Series*, a small series of 12 books edited by Wu Yungui, Zhou Xiefan and Qin Huibin:

---

[9] Chen Guangyuan, Feng Jinyuan, et al.'s, *Questions on the Quran,* published by Today's China Publishing House,1994. (陈广元、冯今源《古兰经百问》, 今日中国出版社出版的图书, 1994 年)

[10] Wu Yungui, Zhou Xiefan, Qin Huibin (editor), Islamic Culture Series. 吴云贵、周燮藩、秦惠彬 主编《伊斯兰文化小丛书》

8. RESEARCH IN CULTURE AND OTHER FIELDS 157

Jin Yijiu, *Islamic Sufi mysticism*, Chinese Academy of Social Sciences, 1995.

This book is the first popular book in China that systematically discusses Sufism. A brief introduction was given to the origins, historical evolution, development trends, basic doctrines, dogmatic propositions, organizational forms of religious organizations, internal cultivation methods, important representatives and their works of Sufism.

《伊斯兰的苏非神秘主义》

本书是中国第一部较系统论述苏非主义的通俗读物。简要介绍了苏非主义的超源、历史沿革、发展趋势、基本教义、教理主张、教团组织形式、内部功修方式、重要代表人物及其著作。

Wang Huaide, *Islamic Sects*, Chinese Academy of Social Sciences, 1994.

Based on detailed historical materials and scientific classification, this book introduces the historical evolution, religious beliefs, organizational methods, customs, and practical influences of various major denominations, including Sunni, Shia, Hawalighis, Sufi, Sufi, Wahhabi, and others.

《伊斯兰教教派》

以翔实的史料、科学的分类为基础，分门别类地介绍各主要教派的历史沿革、教义主张、组织方式、礼俗习尚、现实影响等，涉及逊尼派、什叶派、哈瓦利吉派、苏非派、苏非教团、瓦哈比派等。

Sha Zongping, *Islamic Philosophy*, Chinese Academy of Social Sciences, 1995.

Using accurate information, this book introduces the origins, main philosophical ideas, representative figures and their works, and historical influences of various schools of Islamic philosophy from a historical perspective. It has important reference value for understanding Islamic cosmology and epistemology.

《伊斯兰哲学》

以准确的资料，从历史的角度逐次介绍了伊斯兰哲学各流派的起源、主要哲学思想、代表人物及其著作、历史影响等。对了解伊斯兰宇宙观、认识论有重要参考价值。

Zhou Xiefan, *The Language of Allah*, Chinese Academy of Social Sciences,1994.

This comprehensive and systematic introduction to the classic "Explanation of Everything, Guide to Believers" is presented in terms of Muhammad and Revelation, the historical differences in the writing, arrangement, style, and text of the Quran, the evolution of the name of Revelation, annotation, translation, and research.

《真主的语言》

以穆罕默德与启示，《古兰经》的成书、编排形式、风格、经文的历史分歧，启示名称的演变，注释、翻译和研究等方面，全面、系统地介绍了这部"详解万事，向导信士"的经典。

Zhou Xiefan, *The Prophet of Islam: Muhammad*, Chinese Academy of Social Sciences,1998.

Provides a concise and complete introduction to the life of this great prophet and politician. Muhammad, in the name of the Messenger of Allah, taught a scripture to be recited, leading Arabs from tribes to nations and nations, and spreading Islam to various parts of the world. His words and actions still affect the lives of billions of Muslims to this day.

《伊斯兰教的先知:穆罕默德》

对这位先知兼政治家的伟大人物的一生作简明而完整的介绍。穆罕默德以真主使者的名义，传授一部诵读的经典，使阿拉伯人从部落走向民族和国家，把伊斯兰教传播到世界各地。他的言行至今仍在影响亿万穆斯林的生活。

Xiao Xian, *The Return of Tradition: Contemporary Islamic Revival Movement*, Chinese Academy of Social Sciences,1994.

This is the first systematic exposition of the origin, nature, manifestation, development momentum, and trend of the contemporary Islamic revival movement, using detailed information and vivid language. Since the Islamic Revolution in Iran in the late 1980s, the Islamic Revival Movement has surged and flourished, sweeping the entire Muslim world, becoming one of the international events that attracted the attention of all mankind, and arousing wide attention from the political, press, academic and religious circles.

8. RESEARCH IN CULTURE AND OTHER FIELDS 159

《传统的回归：当代伊斯兰复兴运动》

以翔实的资料、生动的语言，首次系统地论述了当代伊斯兰复兴运动的起源、性质、变现形式、发展盛况及发展趋势。自本世纪 80 年代末伊朗伊斯兰革命以来，伊斯兰教复兴运动风起云涌、蓬勃发展，席卷了整个穆斯林世界，成为全人类瞩目的国际大事之一，引起政界、新闻界、学术界、宗教界广泛的关注。

Qin Huibin, *Islam and Traditional Culture in China*, Chinese Academy of Social Sciences,1994.

With full and accurate materials and fluent language, this book systematically introduces the process of Islam's integration into China in the Tang, Song, Yuan, Ming and Qing dynasties, its influence on itself and on Chinese culture, and vividly represents the spirit of Islamic culture and Chinese culture.

《中国伊斯兰教与传统文化》

以翔实的资料，流畅的语言，较系统地介绍了伊斯兰教在唐宋元明清各个朝代融入中国的过程，对自身及对中国文化的影响，生动地再现了伊斯兰文化与中国文化的精神。

Wu Yungui, *The Awakening of the Muslim Nation: The Modern Islamic Movement*, Chinese Academy of Social Sciences,1994.

Taking the colonial expansion of modern western countries as the historical background, this book briefly introduces the heroic struggles of the world's Muslim nations to revive their beliefs and strive for national independence, including the purification of faith movement, jihad movement, the new prophet movement, the Islamic movement, and the Islamic modernism movement. The Wahhabi Movement (Wahhabi people, basic reform propositions, process and influence of the movement); Jihad Movement (Indian Jihad Movement, Indonesian Milan Badelj Movement, West African Jihad Movement); The Senucid Movement (the rise of New Sufism and an overview of the Senucid Movement); The Mahdi Movement in Sudan (the historical background of the movement, the rise of the Mahdi Movement); The Babu Movement in Iran (the rise of the Sheikh School, the beginning and end of the Babu Movement); The Ahmadiya movement (Ahmed himself, religious ideas, and influence); Pan Islamic Movement (social history background, Ottoman Sudan and Pan

Islamic Movement, Afghani and Pan Islamic Movement); Islamic modernism Movement (Ahmad Khan and Aligal Movement, Afghani and Islamic modernism, Abdul and Salafiya Movement, Iqbal and Islamic modernism) and other chapters.

《穆斯林民族的觉醒：近代伊斯兰运动》

以近代西方的殖民扩张为历史背景，简要介绍了世界穆斯林民族为复兴信仰、争取民族独立而进行的英勇斗争，其中包括净化信仰运动、圣战运动、新先知运动及伊斯兰运动、伊斯兰现代主义运动等。瓦哈比运动（瓦哈布其人、基本改革主张、运动的过程和影响）；圣战运动（印度的圣战者运动、印尼的巴德利运动、西非的圣战运动）；赛奴西运动（新苏非主义的兴起、赛奴西运动的概况）；苏丹的马赫迪运动（运动的历史背景、马赫迪运动的兴起）；伊朗的巴布运动（谢赫学派的兴起、巴布运动的始末）；阿赫默迪亚运动（阿赫默德其人、宗教思想和影响）；泛伊斯兰运动（ 社会历史背景、奥斯曼苏丹与泛伊斯兰运动、阿富汗尼与泛伊斯兰运动）；伊斯兰现代主义运动（阿赫默德汗与阿利加尔运动、阿富汗尼与伊斯兰现代主义、阿布杜与沙拉非叶运动、伊克巴尔与伊斯兰现代主义）等章节。

Wu Yungui, *Islamic Doctrine*, Chinese Academy of Social Sciences, 1994.

It is the first book in China to systematically discuss Islamic theology. It takes historical development as a clue, and briefly introduces the representative religious schools and their belief systems in various periods of Arab countries. The text is simple, clear, and full of freshness.

《伊斯兰教义学》

是中国第一部系统论述伊斯兰教义学的著作，它以历史发展为线索，扼要介绍了阿拉伯国家各个时期有代表性的教义学派及其信仰体系。文字通俗，条理清晰，富有新鲜感。

Wu Yungui, *The Dharma of Allah: Islamic Law*, Chinese Academy of Social Sciences,1994.

In concise language, this article introduces the origin of Islamic law, the content of legal provisions such as civil law, commercial law, criminal law, marriage and family, and inheritance, as well as the legal theoretical viewpoints of different sects and schools, as well as the trend and content of modern legal reform.

8. RESEARCH IN CULTURE AND OTHER FIELDS   161

《真主的法度：伊斯兰教法》

以简明的语言，介绍了伊斯兰法的起源，民法、商法、刑法、婚姻家庭、遗产继承等法律规定的内容，不同教派、学派的法学理论观点，以及现代法制改革的趋向和内容。

Yuan Wenqi, *Islamic Literature*, Chinese Academy of Social Sciences, 1995.

This book briefly introduces the literary and artistic achievements of Muslims in Arab, Persian, Indian, Türkiye and other countries or regions with rich materials and vivid and fluent language, including artistic treasures such as novels, poems and essays, as well as the literary and artistic thoughts, traumatic styles of representative writers and their influence on later generations.

《伊斯兰文学》

以丰富的资料，生动、流畅的语言简要地介绍了阿拉伯、波斯、印度、土耳其等国家或地区穆斯林的文学艺术成果，内容包括了小说、诗歌、散文等艺术珍品，以及有代表性的文学家的文艺思想、创伤风格与其对后世的影响。

Islamic Education and Science

This book briefly introduces the grand development of Islamic education and science in vivid language, which has important reference value for comprehensive understanding of Islamic culture. In history, Islam has created a developed religious education system centered on temple education. Muslim people of all ethnic groups have made great contributions in mathematics, medicine, astronomy, physics, geography, biology and other fields.

《伊斯兰教育与科学》

以生动的语言，简略地介绍了伊斯兰教育与科学的发展盛况，它对全面理解伊斯兰文化有重要参考价值。
历史上伊斯兰教创建了以寺院教育为中心的、发达的宗教教育体系，穆斯林各族人民曾在数学、医学、天文学、物理学、地理学、生物学等领域做出过巨大贡献。[11]

---

[11] Wu Yungui, Zhou Xiefan, Qin Huibin (editor), Islamic culture Series (12 sets), China Social Sciences Press, 1994. (吴云贵、周燮藩、秦惠彬主编《伊斯兰文化小丛书》（12 本套装），中国社会科学出版社，1994 年)

The content of these volumes is comprehensive and systematic, with novel discussions that make them valuable assets to researchers in their respective areas.

The distinct characteristics of Islamic architecture and residential culture have always attracted the attention of scholars. Representative works in this field should be promoted:

Ma Ping, Lai Cunli, *Chinese Muslim Residential Culture*, Ningxia People's Publishing House, 1995. （马平、赖存理，《中国穆斯林民居文化》，宁夏人民出版社，1995 年）

Liu Zhiping, *Chinese Islamic Architecture*, Xinjiang People's Publishing House, 1985. （刘致平，《中国伊斯兰教建筑》，新疆人民出版社，1985 年）

Wesen, Abduriyim, *Islamic Architecture Art,* Xinjiang People's Publishing House, 1989. （艾山、阿布都热衣布，《伊斯兰教建筑艺术》，新疆人民出版社，1989 年）

Ma Ping and Lai Cunli's *Chinese Muslim Residential Culture* examines the dwellings of ten different Muslim ethnic groups in China, then explores the natural environment, social background, cultural characteristics, and religious regulations of Islam that arise from these special dwellings. Starting with residential buildings, we delve into the elements of their construction, layout, and decoration. After extensive and meticulous investigation by the authors, they present a cultural model of Chinese Muslim dwellings, completing their novel research assignment and contributing to many other topics as well. Specifically, they discuss the ethnic types of Chinese Muslim dwellings, the relationship between Chinese Muslim dwellings, geographical climate, and natural environment, the economic and social background of Chinese Muslim residential culture, the taboos and rituals of ethnic, religious, and folk life in Chinese Muslim dwellings, and the structural types, materials, and construction of Chinese Muslim dwellings, including their spatial layout, colors, patterns, and decorative arts.[12]

---

[12] Ma Ping, Lai Cunli, *Chinese Muslim residential culture*, Ningxia People's Publishing House, 1995. （马平、赖存理，《中国穆斯林民居文化》，宁夏人民出版社，1995 年）

8. Research in Culture and Other Fields 163

Liu Zhiping's *Chinese Islamic Architecture* is divided into two parts: architectural examples and a comprehensive review of architectural practices. It includes chapters on the architecture of mosques, scripture halls, Daotang, tombs, general layouts, and various architectural systems and practices. Due to religious needs, the mosque is generally composed of a chapel (prayer hall), a wake-up building (Baike building), a bathroom, a dean's office, a school, a gate, and other buildings. The worship hall must be built along the east-west axis so that believers can face Mecca to the west during worship. The decoration inside the temple does not use animal themes but geometric shapes, plant patterns, and Arabic calligraphy. Islamic architecture in the Xinjiang region uses the traditional structure of wooden columns, dense beams, flat roofs, adobe arches, and dome roofs, but also draws on certain techniques from Central Asia to create a regional ethnic style with a free and flexible layout, rich decoration, and color. In the Central Asia mosque, the Awakening Tower is the name of the minaret, a tower-shaped building known in Persian as a Bangke Tower. Its function is to call people to worship, and it has become a unique symbol of Islam.[13]

Since the 1990s, the number of papers related to Islamic culture has increased significantly, and new progress has been made in research fields and methods. Not only are there articles that discuss the attributes and characteristics of Islamic culture from the perspective of world history and culture, there are also many others that discuss specific aspects of Islamic culture:

Lu Peiyong, "Islamic Culture and Its Relationship with Civilization," *The Arab World*, 1989, Issue 1. (陆培勇，"伊斯兰文化及与文明关系，"《阿拉伯世界》，1989 年第 1 期)
Liu Jinghua, "Revival and Transcendence of Islamic Traditional Values," *West Asia and Africa*, 1989, Issue 4. (刘靖华，"伊斯兰传统价值的复兴与超越"《西亚非洲》，1989 年第 4 期)

---

[13] Liu Zhiping, Chinese Islamic Architecture, Xinjiang People's Publishing House, 1985. (刘致平，《中国伊斯兰教建筑》，新疆人民出版社，1985 年)

Ma Qicheng, "On the Attribute of Islamic Culture in China," *Journal of the Central Institute for Nationalities*, 1992, Issue 6. （马启成，"论中国伊斯兰大文化属性"《中央民族学院学报》，1992 年第 6 期）
Ge Zhi, "Islam and Traditional Chinese Culture," *Exploration and Contention*, Issue 3, 1992. （葛状，"伊斯兰教和中国传统文化"《探索与争鸣》，1992 年第 3 期）
Wu Yungui, "The Generality and Individuality of Islamic Culture," World Religious Culture, Spring 1996, Issue 5. （吴云贵，"伊斯兰文化的共性与个性"《世界宗教文化》，1996 年第 5 期）
Ma Ping, "On the Ethnic Emotions and Rationality of the Hui Ethnic Group," Hui Studies, Issue 3, 2000. （马平，"论回族的民族情感与民族理性"《回族研究》，2000 年第 3 期）

The exact meaning of "culture" in "Islamic Culture and Its Relationship with Civilization" is quite difficult to grasp. According to relevant dictionaries, this word can be divided into broad and narrow senses, representing many different meanings. From a cultural perspective, there are over 160 definitions of "culture" as a scientific term. Therefore, the concept of culture discussed in this article can only be based on a general definition that is recognized by most Chinese and foreign scholars. Sir Edward B. Tylor (1832–1917), the founder of British cultural anthropology, briefly defined culture as "the sum of the entire way of life." This article analyzes Islam from the perspectives of cultural studies and civilization studies.[14]

In the article "Revival and Transcendence of Islamic Traditional Values," Islam is a special religion with multifaceted characteristics. Islam, as a religion and a culture, has its own philosophy, ideology, way of life, social behavior, moral and ethical norms, and legal system. For many centuries, it has experienced both the glory of a prosperous era and the humiliation of a declining era. However, to this day, Islamic

---

[14] Lu Peiyong, "Islamic Culture and Its Relationship with Civilization," *The Arab World*, 1989, Issue 1. （陆培勇，"伊斯兰文化及与文明关系,"《阿拉伯世界》，1989 年第 1 期）

8. RESEARCH IN CULTURE AND OTHER FIELDS 165

traditional values continue to experience revival and transcendence as an ideology.[15]

In the article "On the Attributes of Islamic Culture in China," Ma Qicheng centers on the fact that Islam has been passed down for a long time in Chinese history and, through mutual influence and integration with China's long-standing cultural traditions, has developed into a version of Islam with Chinese characteristics. As a cultural phenomenon accumulated in history, Chinese Islam encompasses a wide range of contents, including belief systems, social consciousness, moral norms, values, folk customs, language, writing, and scientific and cultural achievements. Taking a comprehensive view of the basic characteristics of Chinese Islamic culture, we can say that there are four attributes, namely, the attributes of culture, religion, folk custom, and lifestyle, in addition to its blending with the national community.[16]

In the article "Islam and Traditional Chinese Culture," Ge Zhi argues that when discussing the development, evolution, and coverage of traditional Chinese culture, people often characterize it as the integration of Confucianism, Buddhism, and Taoism, while neglecting the integration of Islam after its introduction in the early Tang Dynasty. The influence of Islamic culture in the composition of traditional Chinese culture is also discussed and must be taken seriously when considering China's precious cultural heritage.[17]

In the article "The Generality and Individuality of Islamic Culture," Wu Yungui presents the perspective that religious belief systems are always based on a certain cultural way. Without a foundation in a specific culture, religious belief is like water

---

[15] Liu Jinghua, "Revival and Transcendence of Islamic Traditional Values," *West Asia and Africa*, 1989, Issue 4. (刘靖华，"伊斯兰传统价值的复兴与超越"《西亚非洲》，1989 年第 4 期)

[16] Ma Qicheng, "On the Attribute of Islamic Culture in China," *Journal of the Central Institute for Nationalities*, 1992, Issue 6. (马启成，"论中国伊斯兰大文化属性"《中央民族学院学报》，1992 年第 6 期)

[17] Ge Zhi, "Islam and Traditional Chinese Culture," *Exploration and Contention*, Issue 3, 1992. (葛状，"伊斯兰教和中国传统文化"《探索与争鸣》，1992 年第 3 期)

without a source or a tree without roots. Therefore, the study of religious culture attaches particular importance to the position and role of religion in human culture, as well as the relationship between religious culture and secular culture. Wu Yungui's study of Islam in this regard displays both the commonness and individuality of Islamic culture.[18]

In the article "On the Ethnic Emotions and Rationality of the Hui Ethnic Group," Ma Ping discusses the emotional and rational characteristics of the Hui ethnic group based on a deep analysis of ethnic emotions and rationality. Ma Ping argues that the ethnic emotions of the Hui should be further linked to the common ethnic emotions of the Chinese nation, and modern rationality and scientific elements should be included to enhance the ethnic rationality of the Hui ethnic group and continuously improve their quality of life.[19]

These are quite distinctive articles. It is a dazzling array, involving a variety of fields such as diet, marriage, clothing, ethics, literature, philosophy, and cultural psychology. Papers in the area of Islamic culture cover almost all of its aspects, at least at an introductory level, which is of great significance for people wanting to re-examine it from different perspectives. Looking at trends in future development, although the religious culture craze will certainly encourage some scholars to continue to engage in the study of Islamic culture, I am afraid that research in this area will remain incomplete for some time.

2 RESEARCH IN FIELDS SUCH AS DIALOGUE AMONG CIVILIZATIONS

Samuel P. Huntington (1927–2008) was a famous contemporary American international political theorist known for his article "The Clash of Civilizations?" published in *Foreign Affairs* magazine in 1993, which he then developed into an influential

---

[18] Wu Yungui, "The Generality and Individuality of Islamic culture," World Religious Culture, Spring 1996, Issue 5. (吴云贵，"伊斯兰文化的共性与个性"《世界宗教文化》，1996 年第 5 期)

[19] Ma Ping, "On the Ethnic Emotions and Rationality of the Hui Ethnic Group," Hui Studies, Issue 3, 2000. (马平，"论回族的民族情感与民族理性"《回族研究》，2000 年第 3 期)

8. Research in Culture and Other Fields 167

book, *The Clash of Civilizations and the Reconstruction of World Order* (1996). The book was translated into thirty-nine languages, causing many reactions worldwide. However, the 9/11 incident forced people to revisit four of Huntington's key ideas: first, the root causes of international conflicts in the future world will be mainly cultural, not ideological or economic. The main conflicts in global politics will take place between countries and groups of different civilizations. These conflicts will dominate global politics, and the (geopolitical) fracture zone between civilizations will become the future front line. Second, the clash of civilizations is the greatest threat to future world peace, and a world order based on civility is the most reliable guarantee to avoid world war. Therefore, crossing boundaries between different civilizations is very important, and respecting and recognizing each other's boundaries is equally important. Third, for the first time in history, multipolar and multicultural global politics have emerged. Countries with different cultures are more likely to have distant and indifferent relationships with each other or even highly hostile relationships, while differing civilizations are more likely to have competitive coexistence, as seen in the Cold War. Huntington also stated that racial conflicts will also be widespread due to this political environment. Fourth, by "clash of civilizations," Huntington mainly refers to the seven major civilizations currently in the world.

Huntington's viewpoint was surprising and unacceptable to many Chinese people, as well as international experts: according to Huntington, the main source of future instability and the possibility of war come from the revival of Islam and the rise of East Asian society, especially China. The relationship between the West and these challenging civilizations may be extremely difficult, with the relationship to the United States being the most dangerous. Some scholars criticize Huntington's viewpoint, arguing that "civilization conflict" was by no means the mainstream idea of cultural development in the world today. Huntington's cultural understanding is one-sided, standing on a narrow political standpoint that reflects the unhealthy mentality of a minority within North American society after the end of the Cold War. Although the theory of "clash of civilizations" has had a considerable impact on political thought and is still developing, its influence will become increasingly weak in the future because of its questionable rationale. Now, we are faced with the 21st century, which calls for increased dialogue between different ethnic groups and civilization systems both regionally and across the globe.

Under the influence of academic research trends such those prompted by Huntington's work, research on dialogue between Chinese Islamic civilization and other civilizations has been fruitful. Multiple academic conferences have been held in China, including the "International Symposium on Dialogue between Civilizations," which focused mainly on Hui Confucianism, and the international symposium "Life and Death: Hui Buddha Dialogue" held in Beijing. At the same time, there have been publications on the mutual influence of and integration between Islamic and Chinese civilizations, especially as it pertains to Confucianism, such as:

Liu Yihong, *Dialogue between Hui Confucianism: The Classic of Heaven and the Way of Confucius and Mencius*, Religious Culture Press, 2006. （刘一虹，《回儒对话：天方之经与孔孟之道》，宗教文化出版社，2006 年）
Ma Mingliang, *The Exchange Course and Prospects of Islamic Civilization and Chinese Civilization*, China Social Sciences Press, 2006. （马明良，《伊斯兰文明与中华文明的交流历程和前景》，中国社会科学出版社，2006 年）

In the book *Dialogue between Hui Confucianism: The Classic of Heaven and the Way of Confucius and Mencius*, Liu Yihong explains that the so-called "Hui Confucianism Dialogue" refers to Chinese Muslims who speak Chinese and use the concepts of Confucianism and the Dao as the basis for understanding Islam while at the same time distinguishing between Islamic ideas from Arab countries and the traditional philosophical theories of China. This ideological activity of highlighting their differences while affirming their commonalities lasted for over a thousand years and ultimately determined the shape of Chinese Islamic philosophy. This book provides many historical examples of this phenomenon woven together to present a coherent narrative of the Hui Confucianism dialogue.[20]

In *The Exchange Course and Prospects of Islamic Civilization and Chinese Civilization*, Ma Mingliang begins with the basic observation that both Islamic civilization and Chinese civilization have rich ideological systems, profound cultural heritage, and long-lasting vitality. Over the past 1,300 years of historical development, the two have established a foundation of mutual exchange. In the wake of globalization, both are increasingly showing their unique charm and facing similar challenges. Only by interacting, exchanging, and learning from each other can they benefit from and complement each other's strengths, achieve common prosperity, and contribute to multiculturalism and the development of human civilization in the context of globalization. This book explores the history of the multifaceted relationship between Islam and China before turning to issues of globalization and three "areas of dialogue" identified by the book's authors: ecological environment issues, world peace, and global ethical issues.[21]

The dialogue between Islamic civilization and other civilizations, as well as the dialogue between Islam and other religions, has become a trend in recent years. As we know, both cultural conflicts and religious dialogues are rooted in a fundamental background, namely the flourishing of religious pluralism in the 20th century. Therefore, it is undeniable that a closely related issue is the study of religious pluralism.

Editor in Chief Jin Yijiu and Vice Editor in Chief Wu Yungui, *Contemporary Religion and Extremism*, China Social Sciences Press, 2008.（金宜久主编、吴云贵副主编，《当代宗教与极端主义》，中国社会科学出版社，2008 年）

---

[20] Liu Yihong, *Dialogue between Hui Confucianism: The Classic of Heaven and the Way of Confucius and Mencius*, Religious Culture Press, 2006. （刘1虹，《回儒对话：天方之经与孔孟之道》，宗教文化出版社，2006 年）

[21] Ma Mingliang, *The Exchange Course and Prospects of Islamic Civilization and Chinese Civilization*, China Social Sciences Press, 2006. （马明良，《伊斯兰文明与中华文明的交流历程和前景》，中国社会科学出版社，2006 年）

> Ding Ke Jia, "Reconstruction, Dialogue, Cultural Enlightenment – Historical Types and Ideal Pursuits of Chinese Muslim Intellectuals," *Hui Studies*, 2000, Issue 3. (丁克家，"重构·对话·文化启蒙--中国回族穆斯林知识分子的历史类型与理想追求，"《回族研究》，2000 年第 3 期)

According to the overarching narrative of the edited volume *Contemporary Religion and Extremism*, edited by Jin Yijiu and Wu Yungui, the relationship between contemporary religion and politics is extremely close. An important trend in the development of religion in contemporary society is the evolution toward non-religion, that is, the transformation of religion. Due to extreme belief and fanatical behavior, especially the politicization and organization of religions, contemporary religions inevitably degenerate into religious extremism. This book theoretically analyzes the relationship between religion and religious extremism based on many examples and social phenomena. On the one hand, religious extremism maintains a certain connection with its religion of origin, and it is "religious" extremism; on the other hand, it is fundamentally different from the religion it originates from, hence the term "extremism." This book helps readers gain an overall understanding of the development and spread of religious extremism worldwide, as well as the trends of Islamic extremist forces in various countries and its impact on the individuals who live there. It also discusses the trends of contemporary religion, how religion transforms into religious extremism, and the impact these issues have had on Buddhism, Hinduism, Sikhism, Catholicism, Eastern Orthodoxy, Protestantism, Judaism, and Shintoism.[22]

Ding Kejia's "Reconstruction, Dialogue, Cultural Enlightenment - The Historical Types and Ideal Pursuits of Chinese Muslim Intellectuals" proposes that generations of Hui Muslim intellectuals have made unremitting efforts and significant contributions to the development of Chinese Hui culture. From

---

[22] Editor in Chief Jin Yijiu and Vice Editor in Chief Wu Yungui, *Contemporary Religion and Extremism*, China Social Sciences Press, 2008. (金宜久主编、吴云贵副主编，《当代宗教与极端主义》，中国社会科学出版社，2008 年）

the founder, inheritors, and Chinese translators of scripture education to the active representatives of Hui Muslim intellectuals in the modern New Culture Movement, all reflect a distinct sense of the times and richness of Hui culture from which we can see the historical trajectory of its development.[23]

Throughout the literature on dialogue among civilizations, new viewpoints have been proposed to address related issues, and there have been theoretical innovations in certain areas. For example, most researchers adhere to the perspective of "differentiated treatment" and oppose conflating international terrorism with universal religions. Thus, they make clear distinctions between Islamic religious extremism and Islam, radical religious organizations, and international or regional terrorist organizations.

---

[23] Ding Ke Jia, "Reconstruction, Dialogue, Cultural Enlightenment – Historical Types and Ideal Pursuits of Chinese Muslim Intellectuals," *Hui Studies,* 2000, Issue 3. (丁克家，"重构·对话·文化启蒙--中国回族穆斯林知识分子的历史类型与理想追求"《回族研究》, 2000 年第 3 期)

SUMMARY.
ISLAMIC STUDIES IN CHINA

By way of conclusion, I offer a summary of my findings on the academic history of the study of Islam in China, looking first at the overarching characteristics of the topic then at each of the book's chapters.

1. The history of academic research of Islam in China can be characterized in the following ways:

1.1. Definition of the research object. Islam spread from Arabia to China in the middle of the 7th century, and, in the course of its transmission and development, Chinese language (Hui and other) and Turkic language (Uyghur) communities of Muslims were formed. Islam has shaped the character of the Chinese nation throughout history and is one of China's five major religions today. Because of the historically and geographically diverse nature of China's Islam, its study requires a variety of research methods.

1.2. Academic history of Islam in China. This phrase not only refers to the academic history of Chinese scholars' research on Chinese Islam, but also includes the studies and achievements of Chinese scholars studying foreign Islam and Muslims. This includes but is not limited to the study of the Quran, hadith, and other classics, history, religion, philosophy, politics, society, and culture. Islam and Muslims in different regions abroad have different characteristics, and these are accounted for by a scholar's research method.

1.3. On the beginning of academic history. The academic study of Islam in China in the contemporary sense began at the

174 ISLAM IN CHINA AND THE ISLAMIC WORLD

dawn of the 20th century. As Western learning spread to the East, along with modern academic research methods, it impacted the study of Islam in China. There were four imams with high academic standing: Ha Decheng, Wang Jingzhai, Da Pusheng, and Ma Songtin. There are also Chen Hanzhang, Chen Yuan, and other non-Muslim scholars who have joined the ranks of Islamic researchers.

1.4. Stages of academic history. In terms of the stages of the academic history of the study of Islam in China, the year 2000 can be regarded as the dividing line, with the beginning of the 20th century and the founding of new China as the early period. During the first century of Islamic research in China, Islamic academic history and many other fields encountered setbacks due to various political movements and historical reasons, but the period from reform and development to 2000 can be regarded as a prosperous period of Islamic academic research in contemporary China. The study of Islam is not only the task of religious studies but also belongs to the fields of political science, sociology, economy, and even information science. From 2001 to now, the discipline has become clear and the research methods diverse. Many industries and scholars actively participate in this research field by systematically studying the historical, political, economic, and cultural phenomena of Islam and Muslims using the theories and methods of religious studies, ethnology, anthropology, sociology, history, philosophy, linguistics, culture, political science, and other disciplines. Thus, the work of the 20th and current centuries provides a foundation for the continued development of China's Islamic research.

2. The research findings of each of this book's chapters may be summarized as follows:

2.1. "People, Institutions, Journals, and Academic Conferences" demonstrates that early scholars, through unremitting efforts, strengthened the theoretical and practical foundation of various research institutions and paved the way for many excellent scholars after China's reform and opening up. Institutions such as the Islam Research Office of the Chinese Academy of Social Sciences and Ningxia Institute of Social Sciences are just two examples of organizations that play an

SUMMARY. ISLAMIC STUDIES IN CHINA

extremely important role in academic history. The important publications of this period came in the form of books and journals, such as *Hui Research* and *World Religion Research* issued by research institutions.

2.2. 1979 marks the beginning of the National Religious Research Planning Conference organized by the Institute of World Religions. Since then, domestic and international academic conferences have been held in China and play an important role in promoting the cause of Islamic research.

2.3. The chapter "Collation and Publication of Reference Books and Historical Materials" supports the claim one outstanding achievement in the study of Islam in China in recent years is the collection and organization of historical materials. This work advances in two aspects simultaneously. On the one hand, it is the collection and organization of rare historical materials on Islam in China from a global perspective; on the other hand, it is the compilation of local Islamic historical materials. The organization and rescue of information on Islam in China are increasingly receiving attention from scholars. This is the content of the investigation report on the Tenth Five Year Plan of Religious Discipline, which was highly praised by the religious discipline planning review team of the National Philosophy and Social Science Planning Office.

2.4. With the reform and opening up of China, research and publication on Chinese Islam and Muslim history have expanded. The chapter "Research in the Field of History" looks at the history of academic research at home and abroad from the vantage points of general, special, national, and regional history. In this area, scholars such as Jin Yijiu, Li Xinghua, Qin Huibin, Zhou Guoli, Sha Qiuzhen, Zhou Xiefan, Wu Yungui, and Yang Huaizhong have made the most outstanding achievements.

2.5. Most scholars agree that doctrinal studies did not start until the 20th century and, even then, it was discussed only within the framework of religion and philosophy. Since 2000, there have been advances in doctrinal research, particularly in the areas of theory and method. Since China's reform and development, research on sharia law has been influenced by traditional Islamic jurists and modern western Islamic law researchers, and gradually formed a contemporary Chinese Islamic law research system with its own style. The main goal of this chapter was to compare the publications of western scholars, ancient Chinese philosophical thinkers, and Hui Muslim scholars during the Ming and Qing Dynasties so as to better understand the works of philosophical and ideological masters at home and abroad in a variety of historical periods.

2.6. According to political and social research, modern Islamic politics evolved into three schools in the 20th century: nationalism, modernism, and fundamentalism. Research on contemporary Islam involves many different countries, nationalities, economic systems, and political conditions, and thus requires an interdisciplinary approach that attracts both Muslim and non-Muslim scholars. In recent decades, there have been many problems related to Islam in international political life, as well as a proliferation of Islamic social thought and movements.

2.7. In the history of Chinese civilization, religious culture has played an important role in traditional culture and the spiritual life of believers, as well as the spiritual and cultural life of society. Since China's reform and development, and under the influence of the upsurge of world religious culture, China has also paid attention to the study of Islamic culture and related fields, resulting in many important publications. Samuel Huntington put forward a far-reaching theory of the conflict of civilizations that was rejected by many Chinese experts and scholars, and some put forward a theory of dialogue among civilizations in response, resulting in a new area of study and publication.

Throughout the chapters summarized above, the author analyzes the evolution of China's modern Islamic academic history by stages and presents key publications.

Finally, the prospects for this topic: as we all know, in today's era of English language hegemony, works in English have a special position in the world academic community, which affects the academic community's understanding of Chinese Islam to a great extent. The study of Islam and Muslims in China by western academic circles such as those in France, Russia, Germany, Japan, Britain, and the United States are important in the construction of China's Islamic research and should be of concern to Chinese scholars. However, except for a few papers, no scholar has yet systematically collected and sorted western research literature. In future research, the author will try to fill this gap in the field of academic history and thus make his own contribution to the history of Islamic research.

APPENDIX 1.
SUMMARY: CHINESE ISLAMIC STUDIES IN THE WEST

Western studies on Islam and Muslims in mainland China can be divided into two categories according to geographical and linguistic boundaries:

(1) English publications from Britain and the United States, and

(2) publications written in French, Russian, and German.

The main purpose of this appendix is to comment on key publications in each period of the academic history of the study of Islam in the West with a focus on Islamic Chinese literature. Generally, foreign scholarly research on Islam and Muslims in mainland China includes the Uyghur and other Turkic language groups, as well as the Hui. Due to the different histories, languages, and cultures of these groups, research results and methods vary.

The study of Chinese Islam in Western academic circles can be roughly divided into four stages, which will be discussed in chronological order.

BEFORE THE 20TH CENTURY

Before the 19th century, there was no academic research in today's sense. In the 19th century, the continued development of the natural sciences and the ongoing impact of the Enlightenment gradually gave birth to social science in modern Europe. As Europe opened the door to China in the middle of the 19th century, Western academia began to pay attention to China, and

Western theories and methods progressively entered China and found acceptance among Chinese scholars.

During this period, those who studied Islam and Muslims in China could be divided into two categories.

(1) Religious people, including Christian missionaries, and

(2) scholars, including Orientalists.

Some Christian missionaries and Orientalists completed serious studies of Islam in China and published corresponding works. The missionaries' attention to Islam in China derived from the needs of missionary work as they were familiar with Islam and regarded it as an important competitor to Christianity. Russian Orthodox missionaries were the first to collect information about Chinese Islam. When Western missionaries entered China, they found more Muslim groups than anticipated and began to study them for the sake of organizing missionary work. Although this missionary activity proved unsuccessful in terms of the number of converts to Christianity, it maintains a certain significance regarding religious and cultural exchange, and cross-civilization interaction.

Documents recording the encounters between Christianity and Islam in China in modern times are scattered in journals such as *Chinese Repository* "中国丛报," *The Chinese Recorder* "教务杂志," *Friends of Moslems* "穆斯林之友," *The Moslem World* "穆斯林世界," and *China's Millions* "亿万华民."

Due to the nature of their work and travels, missionaries are often credited with starting what we now know of as the field of anthropology because their missions required the study of local societies and cultures. Russian Orthodox missionaries provide an example: In the 19th century, as one of the three major Christian factions at the time and the first to gain the privilege of preaching in China, the Russian Orthodox mission made considerable achievements in the study of Chinese Islam. This early group of scholars includes outstanding sinologists who laid a solid foundation for the development of modern sinology in China. Among them are Hyacinth Yakovlevich Bichurin (尼基塔·雅科夫列维奇·比丘林斯基), Vasili P. Vasilev（瓦西里·帕夫洛维奇·瓦西里耶夫）, and Archimandrite Palladusu (彼得·伊凡诺维奇·卡法罗夫).

APPENDIX 1. CHINESE ISLAMIC STUDIES IN THE WEST   181

After the turn of the 20th century, British and American missionaries also paid attention to Islam in China.

French Jesuit missionaries and Orientalists also made great achievements regarding the study of Chinese Islam. The research of Jesuit missionaries was intended to enable the European upper class to learn more about China—then a remote country—and, in turn, support their missionary activities. Considering the setbacks of previous missionary activities and China's great civilizational history, the flexible approach of Jesuit missionaries proved favorable. This afforded them great access to the local communities and customs of China, which enabled the translation of Chinese works. In this way, the missionary activities of Jesuits were not only an opportunity for China to understand the West but also a great opportunity for the West to learn from the East.

The establishment of the French academic study of sinology can be traced back 1814 when the first European sinology chair was set up at Collège de France. In 1889, the École Pratique des Hautes Études established a position as chair of "Far East and Indian American Religion." The establishment of both positions greatly facilitated resource sharing and academic mobility. These institutions also conducted academic research on traditional Chinese religions, including Buddhism, Taoism, and Confucianism, among others. Scholars like Dabry de Thiersant (梯尔桑) and Gabriel Devéria (德韦理亚) are representative Orientalist scholars of Islam and Muslims in China. One of the most valuable contributions of the French scholars of this time is the collection of Chinese mosque inscriptions, including Arabic rubbings and photos, which vividly describe the life of Chinese Muslims.[1]

In the first half of the 20th century, the missionary work of western Christian churches reached a climax in China. The China Inland Mission (CIM) was founded by English missionaries in 1865 but was transnational in scope, with missionaries from Britain, the United States, Canada, New Zealand, Germany,

---

[1] For an overview of these publications, see Alimu Tuoheti, *Islam in China: A History of European and American Scholarship*, Gorgias Press, 2021.

182   ISLAM IN CHINA AND THE ISLAMIC WORLD

Austria, and Northern Europe. CIM asked missionaries to devote themselves, regardless of payment, and to undergo Chinization. As a result, they became the vanguard of missionaries in mainland China. Every time they arrived, they set up missionary stations then expanded rapidly to the most remote areas. By the end of the 19th century, CIM had about 650 missionaries, 270 missions, and 5,000 believers, making CIM converts the largest Protestant group in China. In this context, missionaries began to investigate and study Islam in China from the perspective of missionary work. At the same time, the contributions of British and American missionaries to the field of Islam in China reached a peak.

Many research papers on Chinese Islam and Muslims were published in *The Chinese Recorder and Missionary Journal*, which was the leading publication for the English language missionary community in China; hence, the relationship between this journal and the study of Chinese Islam requires exploring. Protestant missionaries in China founded this journal in 1867, and it ran for seventy-five years. The first to write about Muslims in *The Chinese Recorder* was J. Edkins (艾约瑟), a famous missionary and sinologist who visited the mosque in Beijing and published "Notes on Mahommedanism in Peking" in 1868. This paper introduced the layout of the mosque, worship, Muslim customs, the Imam's duties, and so on.[2]

With the deepening of missionary activities in the mainland, the missionaries' understandings of different regions gradually emerged. Some missionaries introduced Muslims to Christianity during the uprising of the Hui Muslim people in the northwest. The missionaries in Nanjing found that they and Muslims could maintain good relationships, as missionaries often visited mosques to discuss matters with imams and the relationships were relatively harmonious. In the eyes of Guangdong missionaries, Chinese Muslims were another scene. Missionaries in areas where Muslims were highly concentrated, in the central and western regions, seemed to pay more attention to analyzing their characteristics. For example, missionaries found that many

---

[2] J. Edkins. Notes on Mahommedanism in Peking. *Chinese Recorder and Missionary Journal* Vol.1, No.1, 1869.

APPENDIX 1. CHINESE ISLAMIC STUDIES IN THE WEST   183

of the Muslims in Henan were leaders and businessmen who were more receptive to Christianity and that some of the indigenous mullahs in Gansu could read Arabic. However, the villagers were considered more ignorant, which was regarded as an opportunity for preaching.

By the second half of the 19th century, Western academics had begun to contact and take note of Islam and Muslims in mainland China. In this period, missionaries and Orientalists completed a lot of data collection, although some materials were not published and thus did not have a vital impact. However, its pioneering value should be recognized because there had not been any academic studies of Islam in China before that time. Indeed, there are many articles from this period that relate to the Muslim uprising in the late Qing Dynasty, but other than that, the Western study of Islam in China related to the study of China as a whole.

THE FIRST 50 YEARS OF THE 20TH CENTURY

In the first half of the 20th century, the study of Islam and Muslims in mainland China by Anglo-American missionaries reached its peak. The two most important milestones of this period are:

(1) The establishment of important academic journals and associations, and

(2) The publication of the first important research works.

One of the most important symbols of progress in the field is *The Moslem World* (《伊斯兰世界》), a publication founded by Christians in 1911 that would become the longest lasting and most influential publication among Muslim missionary journals. In the introduction to the first issue of the journal, editor Samuel M. Zwemer summarized the state of publication on Islam: "In recent secular and religious publishing houses, no matter in terms of history or philosophy, there is no lack of written materials about Muslims, let alone concern about the political situation of the Muslim world, the expansion and collapse of Islam, its cultural value or defect, and the inner uneasiness of all Muslims."[3] *The Moslem World* focused on Muslims in the Arabic-speaking

---

[3] S. M. Zwemer. Editorial, *The Moslem World*, Vol.1, p.1, 1911.

184   ISLAM IN CHINA AND THE ISLAMIC WORLD

world, mainly West Asia, North Africa, and Southeast Asia. Indeed, China was also a focus area. Notably, the first article of the first issue surveys the Muslim population in China and was written by Marshall Broomhall, who was active in Chinese Muslim public relations.[4] In *The Moslem World*, about 133 articles relate to China. From 1916 to 1920 and from 1934 to 1936, there were about forty-nine Chinese-focused articles. In 1918, the publication ran a special issue on Chinese Muslims with many articles, an intensive project inspired by Zwemer's own 1917 visit to China.

The Society of the Friends of Moslems in China was founded on May 10, 1927 and dissolved in 1951 when missionaries began to leave China. It was a cross-sectarian organization established by Protestant missionaries to Chinese Muslims specifically, and its establishment brought about the climax of the Protestant missionary movement in China.

In January 1927, the preparatory committee chaired by H. J. Molony (麦乐义) was held in Shanghai. The committee had eleven members, including Isaac Mason (梅益盛), H. J. Molony (麦乐义), Claude L. Pickens and Mrs. Pickens (比敬士和夫人), J. Hodgkin (窦乐安), Zia Sung-Kao (谢颂羔), W. J. Drummond (董文德), H. T. Hodgkin (霍德进), Ma Feng-po (马逢伯), Hsiung Hung-Chih, and C. K. Li. The committee decided to hold a founding conference in Shanghai in May through which they announced the establishment of the Society and planned to publish the proceedings of the conference later that year. Molony was elected chairman, Pickens as secretary, and Mrs. Pickens as journal editor. The committee went on to hold annual meetings in Shanghai.

In May 1928, at the second annual meeting held in Shanghai, the articles of the Society of the Friends of Moslems in China were submitted and adopted. The constitution further emphasized the purpose of the Society, required Christians to establish friendly relations with Muslims, and called on Chinese and foreign workers to help evangelize Muslims.

---

[4] Marshall Broomhall, "The Mohammedan Population of China," *The Moslem world,* Vol.1, p.32, 1911.

APPENDIX 1. CHINESE ISLAMIC STUDIES IN THE WEST   185

In addition to spreading the gospel, the Society of the Friends of Moslems in China was also responsible for the study of Islam in China. In 1933, Samuel M. Zwemer, a missionary with rich working experience among Muslims and editor of *The Moslem World*, was invited by the Muslim People's Association to visit China. He delivered speeches on various aspects of Islam in different regions of China and aroused interest in the study of Islam in China. The Society gradually formed many study groups. Before the Sino-Japanese War, the Muslim People's Association set up a library, which made it easier to study Islamic issues in China.

A seminal publication from this period was *Islam in China: A Neglected Problem* by George Findlay Andrew (安献令, 1887–1971), a missionary who paid close attention to the Muslim groups in China since arriving in the country. After studying at Oxford, Andrew was appointed by British Inland Mission as a preacher. In 1920, he compiled a report on Chinese Muslims and presented it at the annual meeting of the Inland Mission of London, and in 1921, he published his first book, *The Crescent in North-West China*. From 1922 to 1924, Andrew assisted Swedish geologist, archaeologist, and prehistoric researcher Johan Gunnar Anderson (1874–1960), who traveled to China for research and data collection in the fields of prehistory and archaeology. In 1933, Andrew went to the border of Gansu and Tibet for research. In the same year, he returned to England temporarily and displayed in London two volumes of the Quran with a history of more than 630 years in the Salar region of Qinghai Province. He left China on the eve of the liberation of Shanghai in 1949.

Marshall Broomhall, whose Chinese name is 海思波 (Hai Sibo), was a missionary of the British Inland Church. He was born in London in 1866 and his father worked as a secretary at the Inland Missionary for more than twenty years. In 1890, after graduating from Cambridge University, Broomhall began working in the London office of the Mainland Association and was sent to China for missionary work that same year. He was impressed by various aspects of Chinese Muslim culture, including a mosque at

186 ISLAM IN CHINA AND THE ISLAMIC WORLD

the junction of the Henan（河南）and Anhui（安徽）provinces.[5] After being sent to Taiyuan, Shanxi Province, for propaganda, he oversaw the missionary work around Shanxi starting in 1896. In 1900, Broomhall returned to London to serve as a secretary for the next twenty-seven years, while also teaching Chinese to missionaries headed for China. In 1910, he was invited to participate in the Edinburgh Missionary Conference, where Broomhall actively promoted missionary work in China. That same year, he published *Islam in China: A Neglected Problem*, which soon became a necessary work for Western scholars studying Islam in China. The Chinese title of the book is 《清真教》(Qingzhen Jiao). After the 1911 Revolution, he paid a short visit to China and began writing many works and articles.

From a historian's point of view, these publications focus on the relationship between Chinese Islamic regions and ethnic groups, on one hand, and Arab, Persian, Turkic, and other Islamic regions and ethnic groups, on the other hand. They also devote much attention to the earliest Muslims to the mainland, Chinese and Arabic inscriptions, the late Qing Dynasty Yunnan and Northwest Hui uprising, and the meaning of Hui. From the perspective of current affairs and practices, they describe visits to mosques, population estimation, social and religious conditions, and how to preach the gospel to Muslims. These monographs are significant because they are the first important works about Islam in China written by Westerners. As such, they share certain characteristics.

(1) Extensive reference to previous research and publications. For example, although a certain number of papers were published before Broomhall's book, there were no English-language works published in this field. Among the small number of works in French, German, Russian, and Turkish, the most important contributions were in French, particularly those of the above mentioned 德弗瑞 (Devéria) and 和梯尔桑 (de Thiersant). In Broomhall's bibliography, he lists all his references. In this way,

---

[5] Marshall Broomhall, *Islam in China: A Neglected Problem* [M]. London: DARF Publishers Limited, 1987. Xi.

APPENDIX 1. CHINESE ISLAMIC STUDIES IN THE WEST   187

Broomhall's work is sometimes considered a summary of Islamic studies in China through the mid-19th century.

(2) Authors collected primary research materials through first-hand field work, correspondence, and surveys of missionaries, diplomats, and local people.

(3) A lot of materials were preserved that are hard to discern now, especially photos and rubbings of inscriptions. As one of the earliest published works on Islam, its main value lies in the collection and preservation of many important materials.[6] After 100 years, it is difficult to make out the mosques and inscriptions listed in the book. Nevertheless, the mullahs in the photos are obviously in the traditional attire and appearance of the Uyghur people. Such snapshots are important records of the communities they document because, after the Republic of China was formed, these Uyghurs became integrated with the Hui people.

(4) These publications present a comprehensive introduction to the history and current realities of Islam and Muslims in mainland China and have high academic standing for their rigor and contributions to the field.

Before 1949, Western scholars also collected and studied Islamic books and documents in Chinese and published bibliographies and introductions. However, with the Japanese invasion of China, Western activities in China declined. In the 1930s and 40s, Japanese research on Chinese Islam reached a climax, but this is beyond the scope of this appendix.

THE 50 YEARS AFTER THE FOUNDING OF NEW CHINA

The academic research of this half-century can be divided into two periods: before and after the 1980s. Before the 1980s, it was a "low tide" period. After the founding of the People's Republic of China in 1949, all Western entities were forced to leave China, regardless of whether they were missionaries or Orientalists. After the Second World War and independence of colonial countries, Western disciplines such as Orientalism and anthropology gradually lost prestige, and Western research on Chinese Islam

---

[6] For a survey of this scholarship, see Alimu Tuoheti, *Islam in China: A History of European and American Scholarship*, Gorgias Press, 2021.

188   ISLAM IN CHINA AND THE ISLAMIC WORLD

continued to decline under the influence of the Cold War. This low tide persisted until the 1960s, when some studies slowly began anew. Looking at anthropology, for example, it was this era that prompted its academic turn because only after the 1960s did structuralist anthropology emerge.

In the academic field of Islamic Studies in China, a similar shift took place with literary research as the emerging focus. The sociological and anthropological study of Islam in China also became dominant during this time. Important works of this era include:

(1) Claude L. Pickens's *Annotated Bibliography of Literature on Islam in China*, which is the best bibliography published during this period. [7]

(2) Rudolf Loewenthal's paper, "Russian Materials on Islam in China: A Preliminary Bibliography," which lists 142 Russian documents. [8]

(3) Ludmilla Panskaya and Donald Daniel Leslie's paper, "Introduction to Palladii's Chinese Literature of the Muslims," which describes the situation of the Beijing mission of the Russian Orthodox Church and introduces the biography and works of Russian missionary Baladi. [9]

(4) Rudolf Loewenthal's 1960 translation of Vasilij Pavlovich Vasil've's *Islam in China*.[10] The original version of this book, written in Russian, was commissioned by proclamation of Archimandrite Palladius, Head of the Russian Orthodox Mission in Beijing, in 1862.

---

[7] Claude L Pickens, "*Annotated Bibliography of Literature on Islam in China*," Published by Society of Friends of the Moslems in China, 1950.

[8] Rudolf Loewenthal, "Russian Materials on Islam in China: A Preliminary Bibliography," *Monumenta Serica Journal of Oriental Studies*, Vol.16, No.1/2, pp 449–479, 1957.

[9] Ludmilla Panskaya and Donald Daniel Leslie, "*Introduction to Palladii's Chinese Literature of the Muslims* ," Faculty of Asian Studies, Australian National University Press (Oriental Monographs Series No.20) 1977, 106pp—Book Reviews.

[10] Vasilij Pavlovich Vasil've (Translated from the Russian) by Rudolf Loewenthal, "*Islam in China*" (Central Asian Collectanea, No.3), Published by Washington, D.C (1960), 37 pages.

APPENDIX 1. CHINESE ISLAMIC STUDIES IN THE WEST   189

(5) Another important work of the same name, *Islam in China*, was written by M. Rafiq Khan.[11]

(6) *Cohesion and Cleavage in a Chinese Muslim Minority*[12] by American scholar Barbara Pillsbury.

(7) *Muslim Peoples*, which is about ethnographic survey.[13] The book also comments on Hui, Uyghur, Kazak, Kyrgyz, Tajik, Tatar, Uzbek, and other ethnic minorities who ascribe to Islam in China. This is convenient reference book.

(8) *China's Forty Million: Minority Nationalities and National Integration in the People's Republic of China.*[14] While studying Hui and other ethnic minorities in China, the author introduces her own beliefs, some of which may not be correct.

(9) The work of Raphael Israeli. After the 1970s, his works on Chinese Muslims were published continuously and had great influence on Western academia. In addition to several monographs, Israeli published more than twenty papers on Chinese Muslims and Islam, with his crowning achievement being *Muslims in China: A Study in Cultural Confrontation.*[15] This book uses sociological methods to analyze the relationship between ethnic minorities who ascribe to Islam and the Han nationality, the main ethnic group in China. Simultaneously, it puts Chinese Islam against the backdrop of global Islam. Widely recognized by the academic community, it is regarded as one of the most foundational works published between the 1950s and 70s.

---

[11] M. Rafiq Khan, "*Islam in China*," Delhi: National Academy (1963), 144pages.and Map.Rs.5.

[12] Barbara L. K. Pillsbury, "*Cohesion and Cleavage in a Chinese Muslim Minority*," Columbia University, 1973.

[13] Richard V. Weekes, "*Muslim Peoples: A World Ethnographic Survey*," Greenwood Press: Westport, Connecticut,1978.

[14] June Teufel Dreyer, *China's Forty Millions: Minority Nationalities and National Integration in the People's Republic of China*, Harvard University Press, 1976.

[15] Raphael Israeli "*Muslims in China: A Study in Cultural Confrontation*," London: Curzon Press,1979. Book Reviews.

With the change of China's national policy in the 1980s, Western scholars have been able to carry out fieldwork in mainland China, even more so since the 1990s. With the continuous expansion and exchange of academic ideas between China and the international community, the Western study of Hui Islam in China has entered a new stage with considerable advances in theory, research method, and practical concerns. Compared to past eras, the disciplines and research paradigms are now more diversified. Not only is there traditional historical and religious research, but there are also contributions from anthropology, political science, gender studies, and other disciplines in recent development.

The research of this period is also more reflective. For example, among the many Western studies of Chinese Islam in the middle and inland areas, Du Lei, a famous American anthropologist, has conducted field research in Northwest China numerous times. Furthermore, he has written five monographs with great academic weight and value, such as *Muslim Chinese: Ethnic Nationalism in The People's Republic*. [16] Not only has Lei advanced our understanding of ethnic group theory, he also pioneered the study of Chinese ethnic minorities and Chinese Muslims.

An important characteristic of this period is that research focused mainly on Islamic and Muslim literature. Examples of scholars proficient in this area include, but are not limited to:

(1) With a rich knowledge of language and historical background, Joseph Fletcher translated select Islamic works by Wang Daiyu (王岱輿), Liu Zhi (刘智), Ma Zhu (马注) and Ma Dexin (马德新) into English and briefly introduced their academic works and thoughts as well as.

(2) Jonathan N. Lipman inherited and developed Joseph Fletcher's research. In his doctoral dissertation, *The Border World of Gansu, 1895–1935*, he used many

---

[16] Dru C. Gladney (Du Lei), *Muslim Chinese: Ethnic Nationalism in The People's Republic*, Harvard University Press, 1990, 473.

original Chinese materials and performed unique research on the relationship between the local and central government, Hui nationality, and the legal application of the feudal system to Hui nationality. He published the book *Familiar Strangers: A History of Muslims in Northwest China.* [17] Lipman transcends Fletcher in that he expands his literary research to include theory. In the era of post-modern deconstruction, Lipman researches the Hui nationality of the northwest using the academic discourse of race theory, which allows him to make a specific, in-depth analysis of select historical events and figures in place of a grand narrative of Hui history.

(3) Donald Daniel Leslie also has profound language skills and the ability to sort out historical materials. In 1981, he published *Islamic Literature in Chinese Late Ming and Early Qing: Books, Authors, and Associates.* [18]

(4) In 1996, Michael Dillon of France published a brief book called *China's Muslims* that examines each of the country's ten Muslim groups. He sketches the history of Islam's arrival in China, explains its languages and customs, and describes the work and daily life of its members. Dillon includes portraits of the most important Muslim centers, from Hui towns of the Ningxia region to the Uyghur city of Kashghar near China's western boundary. [19]

AFTER THE 20TH CENTURY

Under the impact of the *Clash of Civilizations* and "Dialogue of Civilizations" debate, previously mentioned, research on the dialogue between Chinese Islamic civilization and other

---

[17] Jonathan N, Lipman, *Familiar Strangers: A History of Muslims in Northwest China,* University of Washington Press, 1997.
[18] Donald Daniel Leslie, *Islamic Literature in Chinese Late Ming and Early Qing: Books, Authors, and Associates,* Canberra College of Advanced Education, 1981.
[19] Michael Dillon, *"China's Muslims (Images of Asia),"* New York: Oxford University Press, 1996.

civilizations has made considerable progress. Tu Weiming, a professor at Harvard University, has worked closely with Nanjing University, Yunnan University, Ningxia Academy of Social Sciences, and other institutions to carry out a series of research projects and publish many achievements. There have also been many academic conferences that address different levels of dialogue in China, as well as achievements in the study of the interaction between Islamic and Chinese civilizations, especially between Islam and Confucianism.

This is directly related to the study of Chinese Islamic studies. Islamic teaching can be defined as the academic attribute of religious teaching in Islam. In a broad sense, "Islamic teaching" can include the study of classic literature, pedagogy, dogmatics, sectarianism, and so on. Dogmatism is a traditional Islamic discipline formed through rational and speculative interpretation of the faith. Islamic dogmatism has always been of great importance to Chinese Muslims and has been the focus of scripture education and Chinese translation since the Ming and Qing dynasties. Islamic law is also an important part of Islamic teaching. The study of Islamic law in contemporary China has resulted in a discipline that focuses on its unique Chinese characteristics and practical dimensions. At present, it is facing the question of how to use the study of Islamic law in the modern era. Influenced by both traditional and modern Western Islamic jurists, there are two academic traditions in this field, namely "traditionalists" and "academics."

Since the start of the 21st century, new areas of research have emerged. Regarding Muslim-Confucian studies, in recent years, some foreign scholars have taken an interest in the Chinese Muslim Han Kitabu movement. Chinese Islamic literature and records have also attracted more attention due to the intersection of Chinese traditional culture and Islamic culture, and increasing numbers of scholars, such as Sachiko Murata (村田幸子) and Willam C. Chittick, have proposed that Chinese Islamic literature should enjoy the same high status and attention as other literatures because of its contributions to the diversity of Islamic thought.

APPENDIX 1. CHINESE ISLAMIC STUDIES IN THE WEST 193

In respect to academic publications based on fieldwork, students of Dru C. Gladney have furthered his work and methods through numerous projects. For example, American scholar Maris Boyd Gillette published her research on Xi'an Huifang in 2000: *Between Mecca and Beijing: Modernization and Consumption Among Urban Chinese Muslims.*[20] This book is an exemplary anthropological work of Western scholarship studying the Muslim community in China after Gladney's *Muslim Chinese: Ethnic Nationalism in The People's Republic* (1991). Following Gladney, Gillette expanded the research of Hui nationality, yet again.

Another scholar with research based on fieldwork is Professor Maria Jaschok of Oxford University, who focuses on female Chinese Muslims. Jaschok's research is in the areas of religion, gender, and agency, including gendered constructions of memory, feminist ethnographic practice, and marginality and identity in contemporary China. She is involved in ongoing collaborative research projects in central China, addressing issues of religious and secular identity, and the implications of growing female membership in both officially sanctioned religions and local cults for women's participation in civic society.[21]

The study of sects and menhuan plays an important role in the study of Chinese Islamic religion, ethnicity, and culture. The first proponent of China's Muslim religious education system was Hu Dengzhou, a Confucian teacher in Shaanxi Province during the Ming Dynasty, and it has lasted more than 400 years from its early development to today. Historically, Jingtang education has constantly improved and adapted to the times. However, this has not been the case since the 20th century, especially in the northwest; indeed, it has difficulty being accepted by the mainstream education system because of its medieval status. In the history of Chinese civilization, it is an important part of Chinese traditional culture as religious culture not only plays a role in the spiritual life of believers but also impacts the spiritual and cultural life of society.

---

[20] Maris Boyd Gillette, *Between Mecca and Beijing: Modernization and Consumption Among Urban Chinese Muslims* (Stanford: Stanford University Press, 2000.

[21] http://www.ox.ac.uk/news-and-events/find-an-expert/dr-maria-jaschok

Since the 1990s, there has been a significant increase in papers related to Islamic culture and related fields, and new progress has been made in research methods. This includes work on Islam in world history and culture in general, and specific topics that explore various aspects of Islamic culture in-depth.

Regarding research in the political field, China's One Belt, One Road initiative has been of interest to the academic community as it is China's major development strategy. Islam is an important factor surrounding One Belt, One Road and the stability of Xinjiang's social development. We should fully understand and consider its influence, then we can give full play to its advantages, prevent risks, promote regional development, and maintain social prosperity and stability. The Silk Road Economic Belt and the 21st Century Maritime Silk Road Initiative have also been studied frequently in recent years.

Islam has a deep connection with its adherents' lives, especially in the contemporary social and political life of China's Xinjiang, Gansu, Ningxia, and other Islamic regions. Contemporary scholars even call it "the Islam of politics," "the Islamization of politics," or "the politicization of Islam." 20th century Islamic politics are generally divided into three major schools: nationalism, modernism, and fundamentalism, and the evolution of these schools in the 21st century is more evident. Nationalists regard the nation to be the political cornerstone, Islam as ideological belief, and separation of politics and religion as basic state policy. Modernists consider early Islamic political tradition as an example and advocate the political principles of nationality, freedom, and equality. Fundamentalists believe that the invasion and expansion of Western powers has caused the decline of Muslim national politics in modern times, and it is only by reviving Islamic tradition, including its political principles, ideas, and ethical norms, that Muslim countries can enjoy peace and stability.

The study of Islam and Muslims in China by foreign scholars involves interdisciplinary research into diverse ethnic groups and economic and political conditions. At present, many events in China's Islamic regions are related to Islam, but not all events are Islamic, nor religious in nature. Ten ethnic groups in China ascribe to Islam, and their Islamic religious problems inevitably affect the country's political and social life. International Islamic unrest also impacts Chinese Muslim society.

From the perspective of academic research, these situations have aroused the attention of scholars both at home and abroad on the Islamic political and social issues in China.

APPENDIX 2.
SUMMARY: CHINESE ISLAMIC STUDIES IN JAPAN

Outside of China, Chinese Islamic studies consists of two schools: Western and Japanese. With the opening of China in the latter half of the 19th century, Western missionaries, ambassadors, and merchants entered the inner China region and encountered Chinese Muslim society and culture. Regarding the Japanese study of Chinese Islam, I have listed four stages of academic development with representative figures, achievements, and traits for each stage. I give detailed comments so as to provide a full understanding of the development of the academic study of Islam and Muslims in China conducted by Japanese scholars, and to contribute a useful reference for cultural exchange and worldwide scholarship.

BACKGROUND

In December 2012, I published a literature review titled, "Research on Chinese Islamic Studies in Pre-1945 Japan."[1] As Akira Haneda (羽田明) explains, "Research on Chinese Islamic Studies in Japan was started in the year 1911–12 (Meiji 44-First year of Taisho era/明治四四年－大正元年) by both Endo Sazayoshi (遠藤佐々喜) and Jitsuzo Kuwabara (桑原隲蔵), especially by Dr.

---

[1] Alimu Tuoheti, ""Research on Chinese Islamic Studies in Pre-1945 Japan," Journal of Beifang University of Nationalities, Vol.6, 2012, pp.78–84. (阿里木 托和提《1945 前日本的中国伊斯兰研究》，《北方民族大学学报》，2012 年第 6 期，78-84 页。)

Kuwabara."[2] I also discuss research by Jitsuzo Kuwabara and Tasaka Kohmichi（田坂興道）, and briefly analyze wartime investigative reports for the first time. As Haneda concludes, "I cannot help but feel that, on the whole, research on Chinese Islamic studies has not been fully explored."[3] Kazutada Kataoka（片岡一忠) divided the history of Chinese Islamic studies in Japan into three phases, namely, the first period (before 1930), the second period (1930-1945), and the third period (after 1945), and gave a brief overview of key publications from 1910 to 1980.[4] Hirofumi Tanada's (店田廣文) research pertained to documents in the Waseda University library (referred to as "Islamic Bunko" /イスラム文庫, within the university) related to the Dai Nippon Kaikyo Kyokai (大日本回教協会), or Greater Japan Muslim League, which was established in 1937 and dissolved in 1945. This allowed him to evaluate Islamic studies in Japan during the war period.[5] Additionally, articles such as Hiroshi Osawa's (大澤広嗣) "Islamic Studies in the Early Showa Period-Kaikyoken-Kenkyujo (Institute of Islamic Area Studies) and Okubo Koji"[6] and

---

[2] Akira Haneda, "Islamic Studies in Japan (1) — Volume on China," *Southwest Asian Studies*, Vol. 3, 1958, pp.1-5.（羽田明「わが国における イスラーム研究（1）－中国篇」『西南アジア研究』第 3 号、1958 年、 1－5 頁。）

[3] Akira Haneda, "Islamic Studies in Japan (1) — Volume on China," *Southwest Asian Studies*, Vol. 3, 1958, pp.1-5.

[4] Kazutada Kataoka, "A Brief History of Chinese Islamic Studies in Japan," *Memoirs of Osaka Kyoiku University* II, vol. 29, No. 1,1980, pp.21-42.（片岡 1 忠「日本における中国イスラーム研究小史」『大阪教育大学 紀要』第 2 部門第 29 巻第 1 号、1980 年、21－42 頁。）

[5] Hirofumi Tanada, *Research Results and Evaluation of Islamic Studies in Japan during the War Period—An Analysis of the Waseda University <Islamic Bunko>* (Research Report, 2003–2004, Grants-in-Aid for Scientific Research KAKENHI C, Number 15530347), 2005, p123.（店田 廣文『戦中期日本におけるイスラーム研究の成果と評価－早稲田大学「イスラム文庫」の分析』研究成果報告書（平成 15 年度－平成 16 年度科 学費補助金基盤研究 C 課題番 15530347 ）、2005 年、123 頁。）

[6] Hiroshi Osawa, "Islamic Studies in the Early Showa Period-Kaikyoken-Kenkyujo (Institute of Islamic Area Studies) and Okubo Koji," *Journal of Religious Studies*, Vol. 78, No. 2, 2004, pp. 493-516.（大澤広嗣「昭和前 期におけるイスラーム研究－回教圏研究所と大久保幸次」『宗教研究』 第 78 巻第 2 号、2004 年、493－516 頁。）

Yoshinobu Nakata's (中田吉信) "Literature on the Hui People"[7] are also discussed.

I then expanded the results of my article into a book, *History of Islamic Studies in Japan—Volume on China*,[8] in which I clarify the conditions for researching Islamic studies in China during Japan's foundational post-war period and evaluate how each example of research was received. This study attempted to compensate for insufficient research on the academic history of Islamic studies in Japan and to provide a novel research perspective.

The study is comprised of four chapters: Chapter 1 "Early Period (before 1931)," Chapter 2 "The Tense War Period (1931–1945)," Chapter 3 "Post-war Period of Reform (Transformation) (1945–1979)," and Chapter 4 "The Period of Reconstruction (1979-present)." Chinese Islamic studies garnered attention in Japan starting in the 20th century. The Meiji government, influenced by Europe and the United States, recognized that an understanding of the Islamic world was indispensable and that a specific interest in Islam in China had to be nurtured. However, Japan's interest was in neither Islamic culture nor the Muslim faith. The following is a synopsis of the characteristics of each period.

EARLY PERIOD (BEFORE 1931)

In Japan before the 19th century, little information was available about Chinese Islam and the concerns of Muslims. It was not until the 20th century that Chinese Islam garnered attention in Japan. At the end of the Meiji era (1868–1912) and under Western influence, Japan was urged to recognize the utility of understanding the Islamic world and developed various

---

[7] Yoshinobu Nakata, "Literature on the Hui People" (in the Institute of Asian Economic Affairs "*A Comprehensive Study of Modern Islam*" [Showa 44 Interim Report (II)], 1970. （中田吉信「回回民族に関する文献」（アジア経済研究所所内資料『現代イスラームの総合研究』〔昭和 44 年度中間報告（II ）〕所収、1970 年。）

[8] Alimu Tuoheti, *History of Islamic Studies in Japan—Volume on China*, Shumpusha Publishing, 2018, p. 310. （アリムトヘテイ『日本におけるイスラーム研究史－中国篇』春風社、2018 年 2 月、310 頁。）

initiatives to learn about Muslims in regions such as Central Asia, West Asia, and North Africa, including Muslims in the Chinese region. Due to the aggressive overseas expansion of the Meiji period, at first Japan was interested in learning only about the politics and economies of the Islamic countries, not Islamic culture or Muslim religious life.

The history of Chinese Islamic studies in Japan is closely related to the history of Sino-Japanese relations. After the Meiji Restoration, Japan began to invade China, and in 1931, the "Manchurian incident" (満洲事変) occurred. In 1932, Fugi (溥儀, the last Emperor of the Qing Dynasty) established the "Manchukuo" or "State of Manchuria" (満洲国). This event increased the Japanese people's interest in the northern region of mainland China and made them aware that the Hui people who lived there were directly connected to the religiously distant regions of the Steppes of Central Asia and the Arabian Desert, and this served as the impetus that finally led to the earnest study of the religion of Islam in Japan. Thus, 1931 was a notable year in the history of Chinese Islamic studies in Japan.

In 1906, the first Japanese paper on Chinese Islam and the concerns of Muslims, Hirondo Tomizu's (戸水寛人) "Muslims among the Beijing Zhangjiakou,"[9] was published. However, I assert that Sasaki Endo's (遠藤佐々喜) "On China's Muslims,"[10] published in 1911, marks the true beginning of the history of academic research in this field. Most of the literature from this period on Chinese Muslims, especially Huizu Muslims, was undertaken by private organizations unaffiliated with political and military activities. However, the motivation and purpose were, understandably, closely related to Sino-Japanese relations at that time. Two research reports, namely, "Problems of Chinese

---

[9] Hirondo Tomizu, "Muslims among the Beijing Zhangjiakou," *Diplomacy Times*, Vol. 6, 1906, pp. 14–15. (戸水寛人「北京張家口間の回々教徒」『外交時報』第 61 号、1906 年、14－15 頁。)

[10] Endo Sasaki, "On China's Muslims," *The Oriental Library*, Vol. 1, No.3, 1911, pp. 417–421. (遠藤佐々喜「支那の回回教に就て」『東洋学報』第 1 巻第 3 号、1911 年、417－421 頁。)

APPENDIX 2. CHINESE ISLAMIC STUDIES IN JAPAN   201

Muslims" [11] and "Mantetsu Chosa Shiryo (South Manchuria Railway Research Documents) Volume 26—Research on Chinese Muslims," [12] are especially important resources from this period. These reports are systematically organized historical sources on Chinese Islam and the concerns of Muslims from a sociological and anthropological perspective. Rokuro Kuwata (桑田六郎) was a major researcher of Chinese Islamic classics and had a great influence on Chinese scholars, especially his 1925 paper "Minmatsu Shinsho no Kaiju (Chinese Muslim scholars from the End of the Ming Period to the Early Qing Period)." [13] Additionally, the research achievements of Japanese Muslims who converted to Islam comprise a notable portion of the Japanese research on Chinese Islam and Muslims. According to Fujio Komura's (小村不二男) "History of Islam in Japan," [14] Muslims in the early period referred to researchers on Chinese Islamic studies, including Bunhachiro Ariga (有賀文八郎), Kotaro Yamaoka (山岡光太郎), Torajiro Yamada (山田寅次郎), Ryouichi Mita (三田了一), Teijiro Sakuma (佐久間貞次郎), Ippei Tanaka (田中逸平), and Kyodo Kawamura (川村狂堂).

Field research on Chinese Islam and Muslims in 1920s and 30s Japan was politically related to the history of Japan's invasion of China; however, from an academic perspective, they have great value and significance.

---

[11] Kazuyuki Omura, *Problems of Chinese Muslims*, Qingdao Defense Forces Staff, 1922, p. 90.（大村一之『支那の回教問題』青島守備軍 3 謀部、1922 年、9 十页。）

[12] Matususaburo Dazai, *Mantetsu Chosa Shiryo* (South Manchuria Railway Research Documents) Volume 26-Research on Chinese Muslims. Minamimanzu Railway Co., Ltd., General Affairs Department Research Division, 1924.（太宰松 3 郎『満鉄調査資料第 2 十 6 篇ーー支那回教徒の研究』、南満洲鉄道株式会社　庶務部調査課、1924 年）

[13] Rokuro Kuwata, "Minmatsu Shinsho no Kaiju (Chinese Muslim scholars from the End of the Ming Period to the Early Qing Period)," *Haku Doctor 60th Anniversary Memorial Oriental Paper*, 1925, pp. 377–386.（桑田 6 郎「明末清初の回儒」『白博士還暦記念東洋論冊』1925 年、377－386 页。）

[14] Fujio Komura, *History of Islam in Japan*, Japan Islamic Friendship Federation, 1988, p. 554.（小村不 2 男『日本イスラーム史』、日本イスラーム友好連盟、1988 年、554 页。）

THE TENSE WAR PERIOD (1931–45)

The 1930s was a period when military tyranny advanced, with some of the most famous examples of military activity being the Manchurian Incident (満洲事変) of 1931, the Shanghai Incident (上海事変), the establishment of Manchukuo (満洲国建国), the May 15 Incident (五・一五事件) of 1932, the February 26 Incident of 1936, the 1937 Marco Polo Bridge Incident (盧溝橋事件), the outbreak of the Second Sino-Japanese War (日華事変), and Japan's imperialistic expansionism. Most notably, 1932 through the end of World War II was a period of great progress in developing Japanese interest in Islam. First, the Dai Nihon Kaikyo Kyokai (大日本回教協会/Greater Japan Muslim League) was established; next, the Islam Bunka Kyokai (イスラーム文化協会/Association of Islamic Culture), Kaikyoken-Kenkyujo (回教圏研究所/Institute of Islamic Area Studies), East Asiatic Economic Investigation Bureau of the South Manchurian Railways Company Islam Division (満鉄東亜経済調査局回教班), and Ministry of Foreign Affairs Research Department Islam Division (外務省調査部回教班) were established, and historical materials on Islam and Islamic culture (イスラム（回教文化）), the Islamic world (回教世界), Islamic area studies (回教圏), Islamic affairs (回教事情), and the New Asia (新亜細亜) were published. As evaluated by Hirofumi Tanada in "The First Boom of Islamic Studies in Japan,"[15] in this period, research, pedagogy, and awareness programs on Islam were actively conducted, and researchers—which included Japanese Muslims, foreign Muslims residing in Japan, and military personnel—also participated in these activities. These Islamic research institutes were founded because of the urgency imbedded in the national policies of the time and possessed diverse characteristics.

The Association of Islamic Culture was established to study, research, and introduce an "accurate understanding of Islamic culture and facts about its people," and its primary purpose was to conduct research on Islam in China and the concerns of

---

[15] Hirofumi Tanada, *Research Results and Evaluation of Islamic Studies in Japan during the War Period—An Analysis of the Waseda University <Islamic Bunko>* (Research Report, 2003–2004, Grants-in-Aid for Scientific Research KAKENHI C, Number 15530347), 2005, p. 123.

APPENDIX 2. CHINESE ISLAMIC STUDIES IN JAPAN   203

Muslims. The number of papers on Chinese Islamic studies and concerns of Muslims published in magazines was one-third the total number of papers, and I observed that these areas were regarded as important.

The Institute of Islamic Area Studies and the magazine *Islamic Area Studies* were developed to facilitate and publish research related to Islam in China, including the following works: "On the Daido Kiyozane Temple's 'Mikotonori Ken Kiyozane Temple Monument Records'" (Tazaka Kodo), [16] "Some Considerations on the Dungan People" (Eiichiro Ishida), [17] and "Muslim Merchants of Beijing and Friendly Relations" (Noboru Niida). [18] However, the majority of the research papers and materials introduced were on the theme of northwest Chinese Muslims and ethnic problems. In addition, the magazine actively introduced information on northwestern Islamic organizations and the circumstances of the Muslim people.

The research objective of the Greater Japan Muslim League was to explain the conditions of Islam in China and the concerns of Muslims, and to increase awareness of the importance of research in Islamic regions, including Central Asia, Turkey, Iran, and various countries of Africa. For the institute's magazine, *Kaikyu Seikai* (*The Islamic World*), publishing research on Islam and Muslims in China was the most important objective, and studies were categorized into overseas research (e.g., "The Muslim People in China" by Bai Jinyu[19]), philological methods

---

[16] Kodo Tazaka, "On the Daido Kiyozane Temple's 'Mikotonori Ken Kiyozane Temple Monument Records'," *Islamic Area Studies,* Vol. 6, No. 2, 1942, pp. 22–32. (田坂興道「大同清真寺の「勅建清真寺碑記」に就いて」『回教圏』第 6 巻第 2 号、1942 年、22－33 頁。)

[17] Eiichiro Ishida, "Some Considerations on the Dungan People," *Islamic Area Studies,* Vol. 7, No. 4, 1943, pp. 9–30. (石田栄 1 郎「東干にたいする若干の考察」『回教圏』第 7 巻第 4 号、1943 年、9－30 頁。)

[18]Noboru Niida, "Muslim Merchants of Beijing and Friendly Relations" *Islamic Area Studies,* Vol. 8, No. 6, 1944, pp. 2–27. (仁井田陞「北京の回教徒商工人とその仲間的結合」『回教圏』第 8 巻第 6 号、1944 年、2－27 頁。)

[19] Bai Jinyu, "The Muslim People in China," *The Islamic World,* Vol. 2, No. 12, 1940, pp. 37–44. (白今愚「中国の回教民族」『回教世界』第 2 券第十 2 号、1940 年、37－44 頁。)

(e.g., "Arabian Records on China" by Mikinosuke Ishida[20]), and fieldwork in Japan's military-occupied areas (e.g., "Trends and Development of Various Peoples in Manchuria"[21]). The majority of these works center on the theme of Muslims and ethnic problems in China.

The Ministry of Foreign Affairs Research Department's Islam Division also conducted research on Islam in China and the concerns of Muslims. Most of what their magazine, *Islamic Affairs*, published are anonymous studies by researchers who worked for the department and that present the contemporary situation from a sociological perspective. However, no detailed analyses are shown, sources are not cited, and the content requires careful consideration when using it for research purposes. Papers can be divided into the results of overseas research, studies using philological methods, such as "The Great Learning of Islam (*Qingzhen Da Xue*) by Wang Daiyu" [22] and "Clarifying Misunderstandings about Islam (*Qing Zhenshiyi*) by Jin Tianzhu,"[23] historical research, such as "The Anti-Islam Policy of the Early Qing Period—Especially about Xinkyu Musilim Huimin,"[24] and sociological field surveys, such as "The Northwest

---

[20] Mikinosuk Ishida e, "Arabian Records on China," *The Islamic World*, Vol. 2, No. 8, 1940, pp. 47–56. (石田幹之助「支那にかんするアラビアの記録」『回教世界』大日本回教協会発行、第 2 巻第 8 号、47〜56 頁。)

[21] Editorial staff, "Trend and Development of Various Peoples in Manchuria," *The Islamic World*, Vol. 1, No .4, 1939, pp. 1–16. (編集部「満蒙に於ける諸民族の動向」『回教世界』第 1 券第 4 号、1939 年、1−6 頁。)

[22] Anonymous studies, "The Great Learning of Islam (*Qingzhen Da Xue)* by Wang Daiyu," *Islamic Affairs,* Vol. 2, No. 2, 1939, pp. 67–68. (無記名「王岱與著「清真大学」」『回教事情』、第 2 券・第 2 号、1939 年、67−68 頁。)

[23] Anonymous studies, "Clarifying Misunderstandings about Islam (*Qing Zhenshiyi*) by Jin Tianzhu," *Islamic Affairs,* Vol. 2, No. 2, 1939, pp. 59–66. (無記名「金天柱著「清真釈疑補輯」」『回教事情』、第 2 券・第 2 号、1939 年、59−66 頁。)

[24] Anonymous studies, "The Anti-Islam Policy of the Early Qing Period-Especially about Xinkyu Musilim Huimin," *Islamic Affairs,* Vol. 2, No. 4, 1939, pp. 33–53. (無記名「清初の対回教政策−特に新彊纏回について」『回教事情』、第 2 券・第 4 号、1939 年、33−53 頁。)

Han Hui Society." [25] Most of the literature and documents introduced center on the theme of Muslims and ethnic issues.

The Islam Division of the East Asiatic Economic Investigation Bureau of the South Manchurian Railways Company also conducted studies on Chinese Islam. Following the 1939 expansion of the South Manchuria Railway Research Department, the Bureau was again integrated into the South Manchurian Railways Company and came under the management of the Major Research Department and the division in charge of the domains of World of Islam, Southeast Asia, and Australia. Shumei Okawa (大川周明), who guided their research activities, was a Japanese philosopher who conducted research on Islam and authored reports, such as "Introduction to Islam." [26]

Results of studies on the Huimin in moukyu (蒙疆), conducted by Shinobu Iwamura (岩村忍), Toru Saguchi (佐口透), and Shinobu Ono (小野忍) at the *Minzoku Kenkyujo* (Institute of Ethnology), were published in 1944 as "Survey Items of the first period of research moukyu Huimin" (第一期蒙疆回民調査項目), which was jointly edited by the *Minzoku Kenkyujo* (Institute of Ethnology) and *Seihoku Kenkyujo* (Northwest Research Institute). In 1945, Iwamura published the "Social Structure of the moukyu Huimin" (蒙疆回民の社会構造)" in the *Bulletin of the Institute of Ethnology* (民族研究所紀要) based on research cards and interim reports that he compiled into two volumes after the war. [27] Post-WWII, Saguchi continued his research and asserted that his time at the Institute of Ethnology helped establish the foundations of his research.

The Toa Kenkyujo (東亜研究所/Center for East Asian Studies), established by the *Toa Shominzoku Chosa Iinkai* (東亜諸民族調査委員会/Research Committee on East Asian Peoples) in

---

[25] Anonymous studies, "The Northwest Han Hui Society," *Islamic Affairs,* Vol. 1, No. 1, 1938, pp. 84–88. (無記名「西北漢回の社会」『回教事情』、第 1 券・第 1 号、1938 年、84－88 頁。)

[26] Shumei Okawa, *Introduction to Islam*, Keio Library, 1942, p. 167. (大川周明『回教概論』、慶應書房、1942 年、167 頁。)

[27] Iwamura Shinobu, *The Structure of the Chinese Islamic Society*, Japanese review publishing, 1964. (岩村忍 『中国回教社会の構造』（上・下）」日本評論社版、1964 年。)

206 ISLAM IN CHINA AND THE ISLAMIC WORLD

1940 as the national institution of the Imperial Academy of Japan, aimed to study the ethnic groups of all East Asian regions. In 1942, the same committee dispatched Eiichiro Ishida (石田英一郎), Masayoshi Nomura (野村正良), Akiyoshi Suda (須田昭義), and others to conduct research on the Huimin of moukyu (蒙疆). The reports were destroyed by fire in the war, but an outline of the studies was published in *Reports of Research Projects on East Asian Peoples for the Years 1941 and 1942.* [28] Additionally, Ishida Eiichiro's "Some Considerations on the Dungan People," [29] published in *Islamic Area Studies*, and Masayoshi Nomura's "Records of 23 Islamic Narratives Regarding the Moukyu"[30] were based on these research results.

Regarding the research trends of this period, the translation of studies on Chinese literature and the results of Western studies were critical, and philological research was actively conducted. Historical research on the introduction of Islam to China garnered the attention of researchers in the 1920s and 30s. One representative work in this area is Kodo Tazaka's *Islam in China: Its Introduction and Development (Volumes I and II).* [31]

After 1930, Japanese researchers advanced the study of Islam and Muslims in China using sociological and ethnological perspectives. These studies differed from those of historical and philological research and focused on the range of actual societies, ethnicities, economies, and customs of Chinese Islam and Muslims. These publications provide critical reference materials

---

[28] The Toa Kenkyujo, *Reports of Research Projects on East Asian Peoples for the Years 1941 and 1942*, Center for East Asian Studies publish, 1943. (東亜研究所『昭和十 6・7 年度東亜諸民族調査事業報告』東亜研究所、1943 年。)

[29] Eiichiro Ishida, "Some Considerations on the Dungan People," *Islamic Area Studies*, Vol. 7, No. 4, 1943, pp. 9–30. (石田英 1 郎「東干に対する若干の考察」『回教圏』第 7 巻第 4 号、1943 年、9−3 十。)

[30]Masayoshi Nomura, "Records of 23 Islamic Narratives Regarding the Moukyu," *Islamic Area Studies*, Vol. 7, No. 4, 1943, pp. 58–62. (野村正良「蒙疆に於いて採録せる 23 の回教説話」『回教圏』第 7 券第 4 号、1943、58−62 頁。)

[31] Kodo Tazaka, Islam in China: Its Introduction and Development, The Oriental Library, 1964. (田坂興道『中国における回教の伝来とその弘通』（上・下）東洋文庫、1964 年。)

APPENDIX 2. CHINESE ISLAMIC STUDIES IN JAPAN 207

for research on Islam in China and the concerns of Muslims prior to the establishment of the Chinese Republic.

POST-WAR PERIOD OF REFORM (1945–79)

Studies of Islam in China gained momentum during the war, but that changed drastically after Japan's defeat in 1945. All the institutions of the South Manchurian Railways Company were requisitioned to the Soviet Union or China. In Japan, the Kaikyoken-Kenkyujo (Institute of Islamic Area Studies) had been burnt down, and various research institutions, including the Center for East Asian Studies and the Institute of Ethnology, were closed and their researchers dispersed. Their literature and research documents were either damaged or removed from official locations. However, according to Kazutada Kataoka, "one can say that although they were scattered, given that the collection of the East Asia Economic Research Bureau was seized by the United States Army and taken away to the United States, there is some comfort in that they were stored again in other research institutes and libraries in the country."[32]

Research conducted in Japan on Islam in China and the concerns of Muslims is related to the establishment of Japanese imperialism, and it was the defeat of 1945 that caused China's Islamic studies in Japan to temporarily stop. However, Hirofumi Tanada (店田廣文) has presented documents that suggest that Islamic studies in post-war Japan increased with the establishment of the Islamic Association of Japan (日本イスラーム協会), which attempted to continue the academic research of the former Greater Japan Muslim League. Tanada states, "I hesitate to affirm that the achievements of Islamic studies at the Greater Japan Muslim League disappeared after the war without being inherited, but I can neither affirm positively that the route to further development with these achievements as the foundation

---

[32] Kazutada Kataoka, "A Brief History of Chinese Islamic Studies in Japan," *Memoirs of Osaka Kyoiku University* II, vol. 29, No. 1, 1980, pp. 21–42.

has been opened."[33] The association's connections through the pre-war and post-war periods are a notable topic to explore.

Were pre-war research not related to that of the post-war period, the research trends would have been completely different after the war. As Norio Suzuki (鈴木規夫) states, "Research on Islam and the Middle East in Japan has developed with resolute steps in terms of both quality and quantity since the 60s of the 20th century."[34] Additionally, "Exchanges between the academic community in Japan and Chinese Muslims began before the war and continue till today. Naturally, it was temporarily interrupted because of the post-war Cultural Revolution, but since the start of the opening of reforms in China, the relations between both have completely recovered." [35] In other words, the cause of the stagnation in Chinese Islamic studies in Japan after the war is closely related to the political situation, including the Cultural Revolution and an increased interest in China's reform.

Post-war studies in Japan on Islam in China and Chinese Muslims encountered a variety of problems. As people involved in the study of Islam in China before and during the war shifted their focus or passed away, new researchers from the post-war generation appeared one after another. Among those who were experts on Islam, some left because of the defeat; however, there were others who did not abandon the study of Islam in China despite facing difficulties. One representative of these experts is Kodo Tasaka (田坂興道).

The most important academic journal in Japan on the Islamic world and Muslims, *The Islamic World,* was launched in 1964. However, in this period, papers on Chinese Islam were few,

---

[33] Hirofumi Tanada, *Research Results and Evaluation of Islamic Studies in Japan during the War Period—An Analysis of the Waseda University < Islamic Bunko >* (Research Report, 2003-2004, Grants-in-Aid for Scientific Research KAKENHI C, Number 15530347), 2005, p. 123.

[34] Norio Suzuki, "Review and Reflection on the Study of Islam in Japan" (Translation by Gao Mingjie), *The Journal of International Studies*, Quaternary Period, 2004, pp. 68-75.

[35] Ze Masaki, "The Study of Chinese Muslims in Japan-Focusing on the Study of Hui Nationality after 1980" (Translated by Wang Rui), *Religious Anthropology (Series III)*. Beijing: Social Science Literature Press, 2012, pp. 286–302.

APPENDIX 2. CHINESE ISLAMIC STUDIES IN JAPAN   209

and there was an indifferent attitude toward this field of study in Japan. For researchers of Islam in China, the concerns of Chinese Muslims are a notable part of the Islamic world, and an awareness that the study of Islam in China is critical for understanding the Islamic world gradually began to emerge.

Research in the post-war period was stagnant, but various studies were conducted based on pre-war resources, and some works were published. One of the characteristics of these studies is that they were conducted from a philological perspective, including the collection, organization, and analysis of pre-war research materials. In summary, because the war was over, researchers had no opportunity to conduct research and surveys in areas such as Central Asia and China, and promoting sociological and ethnographical research was difficult. However, conducting research from a philological perspective was not significantly difficult. One notable achievement of this period is Shinobu Iwamura's (岩村忍) *The Structure of Chinese Islam Society (Volume I and II, 1949–50).*[36]

After the war, Japanese researchers lost the opportunity to conduct field research in China, and certain types of studies (e.g., sociological and ethnological research), were temporarily stopped. Notably, studies based on pre-war resources progressed.

PERIOD OF RECONSTRUCTION (1979–PRESENT)

Since the 1980s, the field of Islamic and cultural studies in Japan has welcomed new research areas. Various research institutes were established, the number of researchers increased, and academic exchanges deepened. These institutions were directly related to research on Chinese Islam and Muslims. Unlike in the war period, Islam and Muslims in China came to be studied as a relevant part of the Islamic world.

From 1945 through 1980, Japanese researchers did not organize, analyze, or evaluate the history of Islam in China in pre-war Japan or in Japan during the war. However, beginning with

---

[36] Iwamura Shinobu, *The Structure of the Chinese Islamic Society*, Japanese review publishing, 1964. (岩村忍 『中国回教社会の構造』 （上・下） 』日本評論社版、1964 年。）

Kazutaka Kataoka's (片岡一忠) "Brief History of Chinese Islamic Studies in Japan"[37] published in 1980, documents pertaining to the history and achievements of pre-war research appeared one after another. Among these, Akira Usuki (臼杵陽) asserted that Islamic studies in Japan were discontinued after the defeat in 1945 and, "disintegrated both organizationally and conceptually with the collapse of the Empire of Japan," and that "one had to wait till the 1970s to the 1980s for the resurgence of Islamic studies in post-war Japan when it came to be recognized both by itself and others as an economic power."[38]

Although cultural exchange activities between Japan and China were limited to the private sector from 1945 to 1979, the passage of the "Agreement between the Japanese government and the government of the People's Republic of China for the promotion of cultural exchanges" in 1979 provided the political security to welcome a new phase. Although there is no direct relationship between the academic history of Chinese Islamic studies in China and the history of research in Japan, an ideal research environment was established by this agreement.

Under this new agreement, institutes for research on Islam were established one after another in the 1980s. The Chinese Muslim Research Association (中国ムスリム研究会) is directly related to Islamic studies in China. The main objective of this research group is to investigate the various concerns of Muslim minority groups in the People's Republic of China and those who have migrated from China to Southeast Asia, Central Asia, and West Asia, and to promote mutual cultural exchange. The members' fields of specialization include a wide range of areas, including historical studies, cultural and social anthropology, geography, sociology, education, and regional studies, and active discussions are held in regular meetings. In addition, the journal

---

[37] Kazutada Kataoka, "A Brief History of Chinese Islamic Studies in Japan," *Memoirs of Osaka Kyoiku University* II, vol. 29, No. 1, 1980, pp. 21–42.

[38] Usuki Akira, "A Legacy of Wartime Islamic Studies: As a Prototype of Islamic Area Studies in Post-war Japan," *Shiso*, Vol. 941, 2002, pp.191-204. (臼杵陽「戦時下回教研究の遺産－戦後日本のイスラーム地域研究のプロトタイプとして」『思想』第 941 号、191－204 頁、2002 年。)

Studies in Chinese Islamic Thought edited by the Association of Studies in Chinese Islamic Thought (回儒の著作研究会) features excellent research from scholars such as Takashi Aoki (青木隆), Gao Kuroiwa (黒岩高), Minoru Sato (佐藤実), Tatsuya Nakanishi (中西竜也), and Hiharu Niko (仁子寿晴).

Islamic area studies is a new field of research that aims to create a system of empirical knowledge about Islam and the Islamic civilization. For the development and promotion of this field, the National Institutes for the Humanities (NIHU) started the NIHU Program (Islamic Area Studies [IAS]) in 2006, a collaborative research network linking five academic bases: Waseda University, University of Tokyo, Sophia University, Kyoto University, and Toyo Bunko. This program combines research on Islam as a religion and a culture, including regional studies, and analyzes the relationship between Islam and the regions in a multifaceted manner, thus deepening the overall understanding of regional Islam in China.

After the war, especially after the 1980s, the ideas, social background, and research methods of Japanese studies of Islam in China underwent drastic changes compared to the pre-war period. Research during the pre-war and wartime periods was closely related to Japan's military strategy, while research in the post-war period regards Islam in China as a relevant part of the Islamic world.

Some of the research results of pre-war studies have been re-evaluated. For example, Hirofumi Tanada analyzed the historical background of the first Japanese Muslims, evaluated their research achievements, and attempted to critically examine the gap between pre-war and post-war research on Islam and the "rise of new Islamic area studies brought about as a consequence of this lack of continuity."[39] Chinese Muslims were regarded as a relevant part of Chinese culture and as part of Islamic civilization writ large. Specifically, researchers divided Islam in China and Chinese Muslims into two areas of study, namely, the Hui people

---

[39]Hirofumi Tanada, *Research Results and Evaluation of Islamic Studies in Japan during the War Period—An Analysis of the Waseda University <Islamic Bunko>.* (Research Report, 2003-2004, Grants-in-Aid for Scientific Research KAKENHI C, Number 15530347), 2005, pp. 123.

and the Gokturk language (Turk language) ethnicities, and they also divided the academic study of Islam in China into two spheres, namely, historical research and socio-ethnographic research.

COMPREHENSIVE ANALYSES OF RESEARCH CHARACTERISTICS

1) The history of Chinese Islamic studies in Japan is closely linked to the political relations between Japan and China.
2) The military and geopolitical interests of Japan were emphasized in the research of the pre-war period, and I cannot assert that sufficient research was conducted on Islam in China at that time. However, post-war studies indicate that later research did not have such a strong militaristic nature.
3) Research in the pre-war period is quite significant because it became the basis of post-war studies of Islam in China. However, the characteristics of pre-war and post-war research differ.
4) It is critical to elucidate the various concerns of the Islamic regions of the world, including Islam in China, in a basic and comprehensive manner based on historical perspectives, and to analyze and evaluate it in a more detailed manner. This involves examining Islam with respect to the areas of politics, economics, and culture, rather than religion alone.

Further, it is necessary to analyze and evaluate the academic history of this field from a historical perspective, without depending on the political background. Despite the militaristic concerns behind the research of the pre-war and wartime periods, I assert that the research results achieved during this period constitute the basis of various fields of study today and are hence of great value and significance. Although interest in Islam in the pre-war period certainly had a strong militaristic color, the research was indeed academic. In this study, I focused on the work of post-war scholars of Chinese Islamic studies in Japan and introduced their respective research conditions, including the post-war continuation of various institutions that were established during the pre-war and wartime period.

Appendix 3.
A Survey of "Uyghurs" in Nanjing—Misconduct and Correct Analysis

In modern society, the realities of China's eastern border areas are little understood, especially for the Uyghur region. In recent years, there have been "special groups" from the border areas in Nanjing, mainly Hui people from Gansu who make a living by opening "Lamian Noodles" restaurants, Han people from Qinghai who make their living by begging, and the Uyghurs. These non-native special populations from the border areas have to some extent affected the lives, work, and safety of the residents in Nanjing, resulting in mutual hostility, exclusion, and hatred between the mobile population from the border areas and local residents. In fact, these "special groups" in Nanjing are manifestations of various social problems currently existing in Chinese society.

Hui people from Gansu and other regions do business in Nanjing through "Lamian Noodles" outlets. It can be said that it is for economic purposes, but a survey has revealed that most of the children who work in "Lamian Noodles" outlets are underage. Some are just seven or eight years old, and the oldest are only teenagers. China's compulsory education law explicitly states that it is the obligation of Chinese citizens to receive education for nine years, and these children are citizens of China. This clearly illustrates the serious problems existing in the current Chinese education sector. What of the "beggar crowds" from Qinghai and other places? Their numbers are also very large. This phenomenon clearly illustrates the poverty problem in China.

What of Uyghurs in Nanjing? From July to August 2000 and from March to April 2004, I performed a social survey of Uyghurs in the southern Uyghur region. They number in the hundreds of thousands, and most of them are children, which shows the educational problems in the Uyghur region. They are very poor because they cannot find legal means of survival, not to mention that they cannot get a job in Nanjing—even work at the lowest levels can be impossible for them (due to religious beliefs, cultural levels, language barriers, age differences, etc.).

In this Appendix I will endeavor to explain the social and human rights problems existing in the Uyghur region in modern-day China.

THE INVESTIGATION OF UYGHUR "MISCONDUCT" IN NANJING

The Uyghurs from the Uyghur region in Nanjing fall mainly into two categories: those who come for learning and those who come to survive. The first type of Uyghur is one who, after graduating high school, took the college entrance examination and was admitted to Hehai University, Nanjing University, Nanjing Normal University, and other universities in Nanjing. At present, there are nearly two hundred Uyghur students at Hehai University, eighty Uyghur students at Nanjing University, and thirty Uyghur students at Nanjing Normal University. There are more than 400 Uyghur students at all the colleges and universities combined, most of which are undergraduates.

We will now turn to investigate the second category of Uyghurs in Nanjing. Although the number of Uyghurs is small compared to the population of Nanjing (perhaps less than 1% of the population), the community has attracted the attention of people from all walks of life and has impacted the public security of Nanjing. As a result, the behavior of a small number of Uyghurs has led local residents to have a low opinion of the Uyghur population as a whole.

In Nanjing, people often hear negative comments about Uyghurs, whether they are shopping in stores or communicating

APPENDIX 3. "UYGHURS" IN NANJING   215

with local people for various reasons. My classmate's mobile phone was stolen by a "Uyghur youth" in the street market, and another classmate's mother had just withdrawn 5,000 yuan from the bank only to have it also stolen by a "Uyghur youth." I have also seen many internet articles about Uyghur people stealing in the street. These simple examples illustrate the seriousness of the current situation in Nanjing.

Why do these Uyghurs come to Nanjing from such a remote place to violate the law? Through social investigation and in-depth study of the situation the Uyghurs find themselves in, we can arrive at an answer. Problems such as these are the manifestation of a series of problems in contemporary Chinese society and an expression of people's dissatisfaction with the unequal distribution of wealth between the eastern and western regions of contemporary China.

Currently, there are about several hundred Uyghurs (excluding students) from the Uyghur region in Nanjing, ranging from five to sixty years old. Uyghurs between the ages of five and twenty account for 70% of this population, those between the ages of twenty-one and forty account for 20%, and children and older adults account for 10%. The ratio of men to women is one to ten. Some Uyghurs left their hometowns and went directly to Nanjing for the purpose of earning money, while others lived in other cities for some time before arriving in Nanjing. This type of Uyghur has lived in Nanjing for a long time, some of them for over a decade. Others come to Nanjing in various ways: for example, some of the youngest children are kidnapped from rural areas and brought here. There are also people who come to Nanjing to find relatives but cannot return for various reasons. There are still others who cannot survive in the Uyghur region for various reasons and have fled to Nanjing for refuge, although this type of Uyghur has not been in Nanjing for a long time. Mostly, the Uyghurs of Nanjing live near the Nanjing Confucius Temple and the Nanjing Railway Station.

In terms of schooling, only 60% of the Uyghurs of Nanjing have been educated at the primary school level, while others have not been to school and do not know their own mother tongue. A small number of them have high school degrees, and few have college, junior college, or technical secondary school degrees. Overall, their proficiency with the Chinese language is extremely low.

I have given examples of the negative behavior of Uyghurs, but a considerable number of them rely on legal business activities to make a living. For example, there are more than a dozen Muslim restaurants in Nanjing that have been opened by Uyghurs, several with capacity for over a hundred customers and more than a dozen smaller restaurants. Since few can open restaurants, others sell mutton kebabs, raisins, sesame tangs, and other specialities on the street.

According to my survey, more than 90% of the Uyghurs in Nanjing come from rural areas in the south, and a small number come from the north and cities. Although they come from all parts of the Uyghur region, more than 60% of Uyghurs are oppressed by others, referred to as "bosses." There are some Uyghurs in Nanjing called "leaders" who have their own legal businesses (such as restaurants), and have dozens of young people working as subordinates.

I found an eleven-year-old child to understand his situation. The boy's nickname is A, a male of Uyghur nationality, born in a village near Hotan City. As I learned from my classmates who are from the same village (such children will never tell strangers their history), A had to quit primary school because of his family's poverty. Around this time, several strangers in their twenties and thirties appeared in the village, calling themselves relatives of the village. They had a good relationship with A and other children in the village and lured them by telling them many good things about the mainland, promising to take them to the mainland if they wanted to go. A told me that at that time, there was nothing to do in the village if you did not attend school, so he was very bored and, along with several of his friends, wanted to see what it was like outside the village. Several older children had already gone, and A heard that they had a good time outside. So, A and his friends left with these strangers without telling their families. In fact, they did not know they had been kidnapped until they arrived in Nanjing.

Children who have been kidnapped are under strict control. They are imprisoned in a small house, and the duration of their stay depends on the obedience of the children. Those who have been in the mainland for a long time teach the younger ones how to steal and perform other illegal activities, leading to the situation in Nanjing today.

In addition to these deceived children, there is another group of Uyghurs who are about twenty years old who also come from the Uyghur region. Each young person in this group has a unique experience of coming to Nanjing, but soon after arriving, many unknowingly enter gangs and are henceforth under their control. This is a complex process.

Through face-to-face conversation with them, I learned that every time these groups "take action," everyone must follow strict procedures. They start to steal in the street, called "playing" for short, with no more than four or five people going out to play each time. One or two of them are older and the most trusted "leaders," while the three or four young people under their command are kept at a distance (100-200m). The leader monitors the children committing crimes through a specially arranged child in the middle. The plan is to steal things, transfer them to the child in the middle, and escape. The middle child quickly sends the items to the leader. If they are not noticed after this achievement, they return to the market to play. If those children are arrested by the police or other relevant departments, the leader can escape quickly. The children who are arrested are soon released because they are not old enough to be convicted. Consequently, many of the street criminals are young.

It is difficult to conduct in-depth research on the Uyghurs in Nanjing, and there are also certain risks. This is because more than half of the Uyghurs in Nanjing already have a very tight and organized group. If such a phenomenon is found in all cities across the country, we can imagine the consequences for future research.

ANALYZE AND CORRECTLY UNDERSTAND PHENOMENA

Surveys reveal serious problems in China's border areas at present—rural issues, corruption, unemployment, poverty gaps, etc. These problems are serious in rural areas all over China but more so in border areas. The consequences are reflected in the criminal acts of urban refugees. People who do not know the actual situation in the border areas see the bad behavior of the Uyghur youth in Nanjing and do not consider the factors informing that behavior, resulting in great dissatisfaction, hostility, and hatred towards these Uyghurs. On the contrary, people who can understand them have deep sympathy for these people.

Why? It is because they are products of the morbid phenomenon existing in the contemporary Uyghur region. From the perspective of psychology, people have various needs. The most basic needs are biological needs. Food and clothing needs. Only by ensuring that these needs are met at the lowest level can we maintain social and public security. If other people live so happily in contemporary society, yet there are still people whose need for food and clothing is not met, it is conceivable that they have an "abnormal" mentality. From the perspective of criminal psychology, a person can be stimulated to commit crimes by a variety of social phenomena without feeling ashamed or wrong for their behavior.

According to my survey of the actual situation of the Uyghurs in Nanjing, more than 90% come from the countryside, and more than 70% have no education or only primary education. In their hometown, they have nothing to do and no income to support themselves. More than 70% come to Nanjing just to eat. It would be fruitful to perform a more in-depth and directed investigation of the problems of these Uyghurs and their hometowns.

It is surprising that today, when the eastern region of China is so developed, the western region still lives in extreme poverty. It can be said that they are living in a way that is more pitiful and backward than even feudal society. In the countryside, children cannot go to school, eat enough, or even afford to wear clothes. Local officials bully, squeeze, and deceive farmers. This kind of life is crueler than life in prison.

CONCLUSION

During my survey in southern Uyghur, I spoke with several farmers, and they revealed that the situation of Uyghurs in Nanjing is the same: they have no food, no opportunity to go to school in their hometown, and they are subject to various kinds of bullying and fraud. They have gone from a backward and poor place to a free, developed, and happy city—Nanjing. But they are lost and mentally unwell. Their discontent results in hatred toward the local residents. Moreover, their dissatisfaction is manifested through abnormal behavior. The criminal behavior of the Uyghurs in Nanjing is caused by the environment they grew up in—and this is a very serious social problem. If Uyghurs could eat and dress well, many would not commit immoral acts that humiliate their personal dignity.

The above exposition illustrates the current human rights issues in China. If we want to improve the criminal behavior of ethnic youth from the border, we should not only target their actual behavior, but also transform their villages of origin. That is to say, the Chinese government has said that there are three issues in rural areas—rural areas are really poor, farmers are really bitter, and agriculture is really dangerous. If some of these issues are remedied, perhaps their resulting social crises would be improved as well.

BIBLIOGRAPHY

Abdul Mutyadi, 1946, *Comparison between Islamic Inheritance Law and Other Inheritance Laws*, translated by Lin Xingzhi, Commercial Press. (阿卜杜勒·穆泰阿迪 著, 林兴智翻译《回教继承法与其他继承法之比较》, 商务印书馆, 1946 年)

Akira Haneda, 1958, "Islamic Studies in Japan (1) — Volume on China", *Southwest Asian Studies*, Vol. 3, pp. 1–5. (羽田明, "わが国におけるイスラーム研究（1）－中国篇", 《西南アジア研究》, 第 3 号, 1958 年, 1-5 頁)

Alim Tohti, 2009, *History of Islamic Studies in Japan - China Chapter*, Chunfeng Society, pp. 310. (アリムトヘテイ, 《日本におけるイスラーム研究史－中国篇》, 春風社, 2019 年, 310 頁)

Alimu Tuoheti, 2012, "Research on Chinese Islamic Studies in Pre-1945 Japan", *Journal of Beifang University of Nationalities*, Vol.6, pp. 78–84. 阿里木 托和提, 《1945 前日本的中国伊斯兰研究》, 《北方民族大学学报》, 2012 年第 6 期, 78 - 84 页

Anonymous studies, 1939, "Clarifying Misunderstandings about Islam (Qing Zhenshiyi) by Jin Tianzhu", *Islamic Affairs*, Vol.2, No.2, pp. 59–66. 無記名, "金天柱著 "清真釈疑補輯"", 《回教事情》, 第 2 券·第 2 号, 1939 年, 59 - 66 页

Anonymous studies, 1939, "The Anti-Islam Policy of the Early Qing Period-Especially about Xinkyu Musilim Huimin", *Islamic Affairs*, Vol.2, No.4, pp. 33–53. (無記名, "清初の対回教政策－特に新彊纏回について", 《回教事情》, 第 2 券·第 4 号, 1939 年, 33-53 頁)

Anonymous studies, 1939, "The Great Learning of Islam (Qingzhen Da Xue) by Wang Daiyu", *Islamic Affairs*, Vol.2, No.2, pp. 67–68. （無記名，"王岱輿著"清真大学""，《回教事情》，第 2 巻・第 2 号，1939 年，67-68 頁）

Anonymous studies,1938, "The Northwest Han Hui Society", *Islamic Affairs*, Vol.1, No.1, pp. 84–88. （無記名，"西北漢回の社会"，《回教事情》，第 1 巻・第 1 号，1938 年，84-88 頁）

Bai Jinyu, 1940, "The Muslim People in China", *The Islamic World*, Vol.2, No.12, pp. 37–44. （白今愚，"中国の回教民族"，《回教世界》，第 2 巻第十 2 号，1940 年，37-44 頁）

Bai Shouyi, 1946, "*Outline of Islamic History in China*", Chongqing: Wentong Bookstore, first edition; reprinted 1947 （白寿彝，《中国伊斯兰史纲要》，重庆文通书局，1946年初版；1947年再版）

Bai Shouyi, 1984, "Opinions on the study of the history of the Hui people", *Social Sciences in Ningxia*, Vol. 1, pp. 8–14. （白寿彝，"有关回族史工作的几点意见"，《宁夏社会科学》，1984 年第 1 期，8-14 页）

Bai Shouyi, 2000, "*Records of Hui People*" (upper and lower versions), Ningxia People's Publishing House. （白寿彝，《回族人物志》（上下本），宁夏人民出版社，2000 年）

Bai Shouyi, 2000, *A Brief History of Islam in China*, Ningxia People's Publishing House. （白寿彝，《中国回教小史》，宁夏人民出版社，2000 年）

Bai Shouyi, 2003, *History of the Chinese Hui Ethnic Group*, Zhonghua Book Company. （白寿彝，《中国回回民族史》，中華書局，2003 年）

Bai Shouyi,1943, *A Brief History of Islam in China* ,published in *Frontier Politics*; published by the Commercial Press, revised in 1944; included in *The History of Islam in China*, published by Ningxia People's Publishing House, 1982. （白寿彝，"中国回教小史"，发表于《边政公论》杂志，1943年；商务印书馆出版，1944 年修订本；收入《中国伊斯兰教史存稿》，宁夏人民出版社出版，1982 年）

BIBLIOGRAPHY 223

Barbara L. K. Pillsbury, 1973, *Cohesion and Cleavage in a Chinese Muslim Minority*, Columbia University.

Bernard Lewis (America), 1981, *The Arabs in History*, translated by Ma Zhaochun and Ma Xian, Chinese Publishing House. （（美国）伯纳德·刘易斯 著，马肇椿，马贤 译，《历史上的阿拉伯人》，华文出版社，1981 年）

Brief Annotations of the Quran, 2005, by Ma Zhonggang (Chinese translation of the Quran annotated with the Holy Sermon), Religious and Cultural Publishing House. （《古兰经简注》馬仲剛（以《圣训》注释《古兰经》的中文译本），宗教文化出版社, 2005 年）

Cai Degui (editor), 1996, *Research on Arab Modern Philosophy*, People's Publishing House, Shandong. （蔡德贵主编，《阿拉伯近现代哲学研究》，山东人民出版社，1996 年）

Cai Degui, 1992, *History of Arab Philosophy*, Shandong University Press. （蔡德贵，《阿拉伯哲学史》，山东大学出版社，1992 年，433 页）

Cai Degui, 2001, *Research on Contemporary Islamic Arab Philosophy*, People's Publishing House. （蔡德贵主编，《当代伊斯兰阿拉伯哲学研究》，人民出版社，2001 年，633 页）

Cai Jiahe, 2003, *Contemporary Islamic Fundamentalist Movement*, Ningxia People's Publishing House. （蔡佳禾，《当代伊斯兰原教旨主义运动》，宁夏人民出版社，2003 年，301 页）

Carl Brockelmann (Germany), 1980, The History of Islamic Nations and States, published by the Commercial Press. （（德国）卡尔·布罗克尔曼著，《伊斯兰教各民族与国家史》，商务印书馆出版，1980 年）

Chen Decheng (Edited), 2000, *Political Modernization in the Middle East: Exploration of Theory and Historical Experience*, China Social Science Literature Press. （陈德成 主编，《中东政治现代化--理论和历史经验的探索》，中国社会科学文献出版社，2000 年，528 页）

Chen Guangyuan, Feng Jinyuan, 1994, *Questions on the Quran*, published by Today's China Publishing House. (陈广元, 冯今源《古兰经白问》, 今日中国出版社出版的图书, 1994 年)

Chen Hanzhang, 1926, "History of Chinese Islam", *historiography and geoscience*, Vol.1, pp. 16–22.

Chen Huisheng (Chief Editor), 2000, *History of Islam in Xinjiang China*, People's Publishing House, Xinjiang. (陈慧生主编,《中国新疆地区伊斯兰教史》, 新疆人民出版社, 2000 年)

Chen Jiahou (editor),1998, *Modern Islamism*, Economic Daily Press. (陈嘉厚主编,《现代伊斯兰主义》, 经济日报出版社, 1998 年, 623 页)

Chen Yuan, 1927, "A Brief History of Hui Hui's Entry into China", initially published in the Monthly Journal of *Chinese Studies at Peking University Research Institute*, Volume 25, No. 1, titled "The Origins and Flows of Hui Hui's Entry into China", later published in the *Eastern Journal*, Volume 25, No. 1928, changed to its current name. (陈垣,《回回教入中国史略》(初载《北京大学研究所国学门月刊》1927 年第 25 卷第 1 号, 题为《回回教进中国的源流》, 后刊于《东方杂志》1928 年第 25 卷第号, 改为今名)

Chen Zhongyao, 1995, *Arabic Philosophy*, Shanghai Foreign Language Education Press. (陈中耀,《阿拉伯哲学》, 上海外语教育出版社, 1995 年)

Chief Editorial Committee of China ethnic minority area painting series, 1986, *Collection of paintings in ethnic minority areas of China*, Ethnic Publishing House.

Chinese translation of the Koran, 1920 (a line bound stone engraved version), Ji juomi was completed in 1920. The first edition in 1931 was printed and distributed by Shanghai ailiyuan guangcang Academy. (《汉译古兰经》(系线装石刻本) 姬觉弥在 1920 年完成, 1931 年的初版由上海爱丽园广仓学馆印刷并发行)

Chuan Tongxian, 1940, *History of Chinese Islam*, published by the Commercial Press. (傳统先,《中国回教史》, 商务印书馆出版, 1940 年)

BIBLIOGRAPHY 225

Claude L Pickens, 1950, *Annotated Bibliography of Literature on Islam in China*, Published by Society of Friends of the Moslems in China.

Compiled by the Editorial Committee of China Islamic encyclopedia, 1994, *China Islamic Encyclopedia*, Sichuan Dictionary Publishing House（中国伊斯兰百科全书编辑委员会编写，《中国伊斯兰百科全书》，四川辞书出版社出版，1994 年）

Coulson, 1986 ,*The History of Islamic Law*, translated by Wu Yungui, China Social Sciences Press(originally reprinted in 1964 and 1971, and published as a popular version in 1978)（库尔森 著 吴云贵 译，《伊斯兰教法律史》，中国社会科学出版社，1986 年（该书原本初版于 1964 年，1971 年重印，1978 年出版通俗本）

Detailed Annotated Translation of Arabic in the Quran, 1989, translated by Shan Mu Shi, Tong Daozhang (translated from the English version), published by Yilin Publishing House in 1989（《古兰经中阿文对照详注译本》（美）闪目氏·仝道章（自英文版译注）译林出版社，1989 年）

Ding Hong, 1996, "Xidaotang Model – Social Practice of a Religious Faction and Reflections on It", *Journal of Central University for Nationalities*, Issue 5, pp. 49–53.（丁宏，"西道堂模式——一个宗教派别的社会实践及带给我们的思考"，《中央民族大学学报》，1996 年第 5 期，49—53 页）

Ding Jun, 2002, *A Survey of Islamic culture*, Gansu Ethnic Publishing House.（丁俊，《伊斯兰文化巡礼》，甘肃民族出版社，2002 年）

Ding Ke Jia, 2000, "Reconstruction, Dialogue, Cultural Enlightenment – Historical Types and Ideal Pursuits of Chinese Muslim Intellectuals", *Hui Studies*, Issue 3.（丁克家，"重构·对话·文化启蒙--中国回族穆斯林知识分子的历史类型与理想追求"，《回族研究》，2000 年第 3 期）

Ding Shiren,2013, Chinese Islamic Jingtangjiaoyu (mosque education), Gansu People's Publishing House.（丁士仁，《中国伊斯兰经堂教育》，甘肃人民出版社，2013 年）

Donald Daniel Leslie, 1981, *Islamic Literature in Chinese Late Ming and Early Qing: Books, Authors, and Associates*, Canberra College of Advanced Education.

Dong Fangxiao (Editor),1999, *Islam and the World after the Cold War*, China Social Science Literature Press, pp. 309. （东方晓主编，《伊斯兰与冷战后的世界》，中国社会科学文献出版社，1999年, 309 页）

Dru C. Gladney, 1990, *Muslim Chinese: Ethnic Nationalism in The People's Republic*, Harvard University Press.

Editorial staff, 1939, "Trend and Development of Various Peoples in Manchuria", *The Islamic World*, Vol.1, No.4, pp. 1–16. （編集部 "満蒙に於ける諸民族の動向 "《回教世界》第 1 券第 4 号，1939 年, 1-6 页）

Eiichiro Ishida, 1943, "Some Considerations on the Dungan People", *Islamic Area Studies*, Vol.7, No.4, pp. 9–30. （石田栄一郎 "東干にたいする若干の考察" 《回教圏》，第 7 巻第 4 号 ，1943 年, 9-30 页）

Endo Sasaki, 1911, "On China's Muslims", *The Oriental Library*, Vol.1, No.3, pp. 417–421. （遠藤佐々喜 "支那の回回教に就て"《東洋学報》第 1 巻第 3 号，1911 年, 417−421 页）

Fan Ruolan, 2009, *Islam and the Modernization Process of Southeast Asia* , China Social Sciences Press, pp. 458. （范若兰，《伊斯兰教与东南亚现代化进程》，中国社会科学出版社，2009 年, 458 页）

Feng Jinyuan, 1984, "Analysis of 'Lai Fu Ming'", *Journal of World Religious Studies*, Vol. 4，pp. 55–77. （冯今源， " '来复铭' 析"，《世界宗教研究》，1984 年第 4 期，55‐77 页）

Feng Jinyuan, 1984, "Preliminary Exploration of the Islamic Jiaofang System in China" , *World Religious Studies*, Issue 1. （冯今源， "中国伊斯兰教教坊制度初探"，《世界宗教研究》，1984 年第 1 期）

Feng Jinyuan, 1991, "*Islam in China*", Ningxia People's Publishing House. （冯今源，《中国的伊斯兰教》，宁夏人民出版社, 1991 年）

Fildochi Sadi (Iran), 2001, *Persian Classic Library*, translated by Yuan Wenqi, Hunan Literature and Art Publishing House.

(（伊朗）菲尔多西·萨迪 著 元文琪 译,《波斯经典文库》,湖南文艺出版社,2001 年)

Fujio Komura, 1988, *History of Islam in Japan*, Japan Islamic Friendship Federation, pp. 554. (小村不二男《日本イスラーム史》,日本イスラーム友好連盟, 1988 年, 554 頁)

Gan Minyan, 1994, "Investigation of the History and Current Situation of the Islamic Xidaotang in Gansu Province – Focusing on How Islam Adapts to Social Development", *Northwest Ethnic Studies*, Issue 21, pp. 42–47. (甘敏岩, "甘肃伊斯兰教西道堂历史与现状调查—以伊斯兰教如何与社会发展相适应为主",《西北民族研究》, 1994 年 2 期, 42—47 页)

Gao Zhanfu, 2002, "Review and Commentary on the Study of the Western Islamic Church in China", *World Religious Studies*, December. (高占福, "中国伊斯兰教西道堂研究的回顾与评述",《世界宗教研究》, 2002 年 12 月)

Gao zhanfu, 1991, *"Research on the social problems of Muslims in Northwest China"*, Ganzhen nationality press.

Ge Zhi, 1992, "Islam and Traditional Chinese Culture", *Exploration and Contention*, Issue 3. (葛状, "伊斯兰教和中国传统文化",《探索与争鸣》, 1992 年第 3 期)

Habaoyu, 2010, "Islamic Studies in China", *West Asia and Africa*, Issue 4, pp. 50–52. (哈宝玉, "中国的伊斯兰研究",《西亚非洲》, 2010 年第 4 期, 50-52 页)

Habaoyu, 2007, "Academic Research and Characteristics of Islamic Law in China", *Hui Studies*, Issue 4, pp. 113–120. (哈宝玉, "中国伊斯兰教法的学术研究及其特点",《回族研究》, 2007 年第 4 期, 113-120 页)

Han Zhongyi and Zhu Liang, 2012, "Investigation on the Printing and Publication of Chinese Muslim Classics Literature – Taking the Xiaojing 'Kaidani' as an Example", *Journal of Northern University for Nationalities (Philosophy and Social Sciences Edition)*, Issue 4, pp. 118–125. (韩中义,朱亮, "关于中国穆斯林经学文献印行的考察—以小经《开达尼》为例", 《北方民族大学学报（哲学社会科学版）》, 2012 年第 4 期, 118-125 页)

Han Zhongyi, 2005, "Research on the Relationship between Xiaojing Scriptures and Islamic Issues", *World Religious Studies*, Issue 3, pp. 35–40. (韩中义， "小经文献与伊斯兰教相关问题研究"，《世界宗教研究》，2005 年第 3 期，35－40 页)

Han Zhongyi, 2007, "A Preliminary Study on the Related Issues of Xiaojing Literature and Linguistics", *Northwest Ethnic Studies*, Issue 1, pp. 164–175. (韩中义， "小经文献与语言学相关问题初探"，《西北民族研究》，2007 年第 1 期，164－175 页)

Henri Masse (France),1978, *A Brief History of Islam*, translated by Wang Huaide and Zhou Zhenxiang, Commercial Press. ((法国) 昂里・马塞 著，王怀德和周祯祥 译,《伊斯兰教简史》,商务印书馆，1978 年)

Hirofumi Tanada, Research Results and Evaluation of Islamic Studies in Japan during the War Period—An Analysis of the Waseda University ＜Islamic Bunko＞(Research Report, 2003–2004, Grants-in-Aid for Scientific Research KAKENHI C, Number 15530347), 2005, p. 123.

Hirondo Tomizu, 1906, "Muslims among the Beijing Zhangjiakou", *Diplomacy Times*, Vol.6, pp. 14–15. (戸水寛人 "北京張家口間の回々教徒 "《外交時報》第 61 号，1906 年，14－15 页。)

Hiroshi Osawa, 2004, "Islamic Studies in the Early Showa Period-Kaikyoken-Kenkyujo (Institute of Islamic Area Studies) and Okubo Koji", *Journal of Religious Studies*, Vol. 78, No.2, pp. 493–516. (大澤広嗣， "昭和前期におけるイスラーム研究ー回教圈研究所と大久保幸次 "《宗教研究》第 78 卷第 2 号，2004 年，493-516 页。)

Hu Long, 2007, "Also Talking about 'Xiaojing' and Opening the Yidane", *Hui Studies*, Issue 1, pp. 119–123.(虎隆， "也谈 '小经' 开以达尼"，《回族研究》，2007 年第 1 期，119－123 页)

Hu Zuli (Egypt), 1950, *History of Islamic Law*, translated by Pang Shiqian published by Yuehua Cultural Service. ((埃及) 胡祖利著,庞士谦译《回教法学史》,月华文化服务社，1950 年)

Interpretation of Weigaye's Shariah – Introduction to Islamic Shariah,1993, Sai Shengfa translated, Ningxia People's

BIBLIOGRAPHY 229

Publishing House. (赛生发 译《伟嘎业教法经解—伊斯兰教法概论》, 宁夏人民出版社, 1993 年)

Interpretation of the Quran in Mandarin, 1958, published by the Council of the Institute of Islamic Studies of the Chinese Academy of Sciences, Shi Zizhou (translated and annotated from the English version), pp. 908. (《古兰经国语译解》, 時子周（自英文版译注）中华学术院回教研究所理事会出版, 1958, 908 页)

Iwamura Shinobu, 1964, *The Structure of the Chinese Islamic Society*, Japanese review publishing. (岩村忍 《中国回教社会の構造》（上・下）日本評論社版, 1964 年)

J Edkins, 1869, "Notes on Mahommedanism in Peking", *Chinese Recorder and Missionary Journal*, Vol.1, No.1.

Jin Jitang, 1935, "*Research on the History of Chinese Islam*", published by Chengda Normal Publishing Department. (金吉堂, 《中国回教史研究》, 成达师范出版部出版, 1935 年)

Jin Yiji (Editor in Chief), 1995, *Contemporary Islam*, Eastern Publishing House, pp. 401. (金宜久 主编, 《当代伊斯兰教》, 东方出版社, 1995 年, 401 页)

Jin Yijiu (edited), 1997, *Islamic dictionary*, Shanghai Dictionary Publishing House. (金宜久, 《伊斯兰教辞典》, 上海辞书出版社, 1997 年)

Jin Yijiu (edited), 2001, *Little dictionary of Islam*, Shanghai Dictionary Publishing House. (金宜久, 《伊斯兰教小辞典》, 上海辞书出版社, 2001 年)

Jin Yijiu and Wu Yungui (Editor), 2008, *Contemporary Religion and Extremism*, China Social Sciences Press. (金宜久主编, 吴云贵副主编, 《当代宗教与极端主义》, 中国社会科学出版社, 2008 年)

Jin Yijiu and Wu Yungui co-authored, 2001, *Islam and International Hotspots*, Eastern Publishing House. (金宜久 吴云贵 合著, 《伊斯兰与国际热点》, 东方出版社, 2001 年, 650 页)

Jin Yijiu, 1987, *Introduction to Islam*, Qinghai People's Publishing House. (金宜久, 《伊斯兰教概论》, 青海人民出版社, 1987 年)

Jin Yijiu, 1996, *Islam and World Politics*, China Social Science Literature Press. (金宜久，《伊斯兰教与世界政治》，中国社会科学文献出版社，1996 年）

Jin Yijiu, 1998, *History of Islam*, Chinese Academy of Social Sciences Press. (金宜久，《伊斯兰教史》，中国社会科学院出版社，1998 年）

Jin Yijiu, 2008, *Research on Wang Daiyu's Thought*, Ethnic Publishing House. (金宜久，《王岱舆思想研究》，民族出版社，2008 年，448 页）

Jin Yijiu, Wu Yungui, 2000, "Islam in International Politics in the 1990s" (research report), the research group of "Research on Islam and International Political Relations" of the Institute of World Religions, Chinese Academy of Social Sciences, and the "Ninth Five Year Plan" key project of the National Social Science Foundation, completed in 2000. (金宜久，吴云贵，《20 世纪 90 年代国际政治中的伊斯兰》（研究报告），中国社会科学院世界宗教研究所《伊斯兰教与国际政治关系研究》课题组，国家社会科学基金"95"重点项目，2000 年完稿)

Jin Yijiu, 1999, *Exploring Islam in China: A Study of Liu Zhi*, Renmin University of China Press. (金宜久，《中国伊斯兰探秘—刘智研究》，中国人民大学出版社，1999 年，349 页）

Jonathan N. Lipman, 1997, *Familiar Strangers: A History of Muslims in Northwest China*, University of Washington Press.

June Teufel Dreyer, 1976, *China's Forty Millions: Minority Nationalities and National Integration in the People's Republic of China*, Harvard University Press.

K. A. Totah (Syria), 1946, *History of Muslim Education*, translated by Ma Jian, editor of Islamic culture Society, Commercial Press. ((叙利亚）托太哈，《回教教育史》，马坚译，伊斯兰文化学会编辑，商务印书馆，1946 年）

Kazutada Kataoka, 1980, "A Brief History of Chinese Islamic Studies in Japan", *Memoirs of Osaka Kyoiku University II*, vol. 29, No. 1, pp. 21–42. (片冈一忠 "日本における中国イスラーム研究小史 "《大阪教育大学紀要》第 2 部門第 29 卷第 1 号 ，1980 年，21-42 页。)

BIBLIOGRAPHY

Kazuyuki Omura, 1922, *Problems of Chinese Muslims*, Qingdao Defense Forces Staff, pp. 90. (大村一之《支那の回教問題》青島守備軍三謀部, 1922 年, 90 頁)

Kodo Tazaka, 1964, *Islam in China: Its Introduction and Development*, The Oriental Library. (田坂興道《中国における回教の伝来とその弘通》（上・下）東洋文庫, 1964 年)

Kodo Tazaka, 1942, "On the Daido Kiyozane Temple's 'Mikotonori Ken Kiyozane Temple Monument Records'", *Islamic Area Studies*, Vol.6, No.2, pp. 22–32. (田坂興道 "大同清真寺の "勅建清真寺碑記 "に就いて "《回教圏》第 6 巻第 2 号, 1942 年, 22-33 頁)

Li Chen, 2000, *Modern Arab Literature and mysticism*, Social Science Literature Press. (李琛,《阿拉伯现代文学与神秘主义》, 社会科学文献出版社, 2000 年)

Li Fuquan, 2009, "Commentary on the Study of Islamic Shia in China over the Past Three Decades", *Journal of Jiangnan Social College*, Issue 1, No. 4, pp. 35–39. (李福泉, "30 年来国内伊斯兰教什叶派研究述评, 《江南社会学院学报》, 2009 年第 11 期第 4 号, 35-39 页)

Li Kuan, *"Other's Vision and Self elaboration – A History of Islamic Research on Xidaotang"*, 2012 Master's Thesis from Central University for Nationalities. (李寬,《他者眼光与自我阐述——伊斯兰教西道堂研究史》2012 年中央民族大学修士学位論文)

Li Lin, 2011, "Issues and Reflections on Contemporary Islamic Studies in China", *Chinese Muslims*, Issue 3, pp. 18–21. (李林, "当代中国伊斯兰教义学研究的问题和反思", 《中国穆斯林》, 2011 年第 3 期, 18-21 页)

Li Lin, 2011, "Analysis of Contemporary Islamic Philosophy in China: Issues and Mainlines of Ideological Research", *World Religious Studies*, Issue 5, pp. 142–148. (李林, "试析当代中国伊斯兰哲学-思想研究的问题与主线", 《世界宗教研究》, 2011 年第 5 期, 142-148 页)

Li Lin, 2013, "Research on Islam in China: sorting out and preceding the academic history", *China Social Science Daily*.

（李林，"中国伊斯兰教研究：学术史梳理与前"，《中国社会科学报》，2013 年 2 月）

Li Xinghua, Ma Jinyuan (edited), 1985, *Selected references to the history of Islam in China (1911–1949)*, Ningxia people's publishing house, 2 books. (李兴华，马今源编，《中国伊斯兰教史参考文选编（1911-1949）》，1985 年）

Li Xinghua, 1997, religious studies in Chinese Translation of Islam, *Journal of Qinghai University for Nationalities*, Issue 3, pp. 1–8. (李兴华，"汉文伊斯兰教译著的宗教学"，《青海民族大学学报》，1997 年第 3 期，1-8 页）

Lin Song, 1983, "On the decisive role of Islam in the formation of the Hui ethnic group in China", *Social Science Front*, Issue 3, pp. 200–210. (林松，"试论伊斯兰教对形成中国回族所起的决定性作用"，《社会科学战线》，1983 年第 3 期，200－210 页）

Liu Jinghua and Zhang Xiaodong (co-authored), 2000, *Modern Politics and Islam*, China Social Science Literature Press. (刘靖华　张晓东　合著，《现代政治与伊斯兰教》，中国社会科学文献出版社，2000 年，348 页）

Liu Jinghua, 1989, "Revival and Transcendence of Islamic Traditional Values", *West Asia and Africa*, Issue 4. (刘靖华，"伊斯兰传统价值的复兴与超越"，《西亚非洲》，1989 年第 4 期）

Liu Yihong, 2006, *Dialogue between Hui and Confucianism – The Classic of Heaven and the Way of Confucius and Mencius*, Religious Culture Press. (刘一虹，《回儒对话－天方之经与孔孟之道》，宗教文化出版社，2006 年，246 页）

Liu Yingsheng, 2001, "Several Issues on the 'Xiaojing' script commonly used among some Muslim ethnic groups in China", *Hui Studies*, Issue 4, pp. 20–26. (刘迎胜，"关于中国部分穆斯林民族中通行的 '小经' 文字的几个问题"，《回族研究》，2001 年第 4 期，20－26 页）

Liu Zhiping, 1985, *Chinese Islamic Architecture*, Xinjiang People's Publishing House. (刘致平，《中国伊斯兰教建筑》，新疆人民出版社，1985 年）

BIBLIOGRAPHY   233

Lu Jinxian and Lu Juxian, 1994, "Chinese Islamic Xidaotang", *Arab World*, Issue 2, pp. 48–50. (陆进贤, 陆聚贤, "中国伊斯兰教西道堂", 《阿拉伯世界》, 1994 年第 2 期, 48－50 页)

Lu Peiyong, 1989, "Islamic culture and Its Relationship with Civilization", *The Arab World*, Issue 1. (陆培勇, "伊斯兰文化及与文明关系", 《阿拉伯世界》, 1989 年第 1 期)

Ludmilla Panskaya and Donald Daniel Leslie, 1977, "Introduction to Palladii's Chinese Literature of the Muslims", Faculty of Asian Studies, Australian National University Press (Oriental Monographs Series No.20).

M. Rafiq Khan, 1963, *Islam in China*, Delhi: National Academy.

Ma Baoguang (compiled), 1994, "*Chinese Hui Classics Series*", (internal data). (马宝光主编, 《中国回族典籍丛书》, 以内部资料出版, 1994 年)

Ma Deliang and Yu Qian, 1995, "Analysis of the Influence of Liu Zhi's Thought on Xidaotang", *World Religious Studies*, Issue 1. (马德良, 于谦, "刘智思想对西道堂影响浅析", 《世界宗教研究》, 1995 年第 1 期)。

Ma Fuchun, 1983, "The Impact of Mr. Liu Jielian's Religious Translation on the Future Islamic Sects", *Arab World*, Issue 1, pp. 93–98. (马富春, "刘介廉先生的宗教译著对以后伊斯兰教派的影响", 《阿拉伯世界》, 1983 年第 1 期, 93－98 页)

Ma Fude, 2006, *The Pioneer of the Modern Islamic Revival Movement – A Study of Wahab and His Thoughts*, China Social Sciences Press. (马福德, 《近代伊斯兰复兴运动的先驱—瓦哈卜及其思想研究》, 中国社会科学出版社, 2006 年, 218 页)

Ma Liangjun, 1949, *Textual Research on the History of Islam*, Xinjiang Shiyin Publishing House; the full text of the fifth issue of *Xinjiang Religious Research Materials*, published by the Religious Research Institute of the Xinjiang Academy of Social Sciences, published in 1981; Xinjiang People's Publishing House, republished in 1994. (马良俊, 《考证回教历史》, 新疆石印出版社, 1949 年出版; 新疆社会科学院宗教研究所《新疆宗教研究资料》第 5 辑中全文刊印, 1981 年; 新疆人民出版社, 1994 年再出版, 244 页)

Ma Mingliang, 2001, "*A Brief History of Islam*", Economic Daily Press. (马明良,《简明伊斯兰教史》, 经济日报出版社, 2001 年)

Ma Mingliang, 2006, *Collection of Frontier Studies on Islamic culture*, China Social Sciences Press. (马明良,《伊斯兰文化前沿研究论集》, 中国社会科学出版社, 2006 年)

Ma Mingliang, 2006, *The Exchange Course and Prospects of Islamic Civilization and Chinese Civilization*, China Social Sciences Press. (马明良,《伊斯兰文明与中华文明的交流历程和前景》, 中国社会科学出版社, 2006 年, 311 页)

Ma Mingliang, 2006, The Exchange Course and Prospects of Islamic Civilization and Chinese Civilization, China Social Sciences Press. (马明良,《伊斯兰文明与中华文明的交流历程和前景》, 中国社会科学出版社, 2006 年)

Ma Ping, 1997, "The 'Pueblo' of the Hui People in China – A Study of the Xidaotang nailaitidafangzi Lintan Gannan , *Hui Studies*, Issue 2, pp. 1–19. (马平, "中国回族的"普埃布洛"—甘南临潭西道堂尕路提大房子研究",《回族研究》, 1997 年第 2 期, 1—19 页)

Ma Ping, Lai Cunli, 1995, *Chinese Muslim residential culture*, Ningxia People's Publishing House. (马平, 赖存理,《中国穆斯林民居文化》, 宁夏人民出版社, 1995 年)

Ma Ping, 2000, "On the Ethnic Emotions and Rationality of the Hui Ethnic Group", *Hui Studies*, Issue 3. (马平, "论回族的民族情感与民族理性",《回族研究》, 2000 年第 3 期)

Ma Qicheng, 1992, "On the Attribute of Islamic Culture in China", *Journal of the Central Institute for Nationalities*, Issue 6. (马启成, "论中国伊斯兰大文化属性",《中央民族学院学报》, 1992 年第 6 期)

Ma Ruling, 1984, "Further Discussion on the Relationship between Islam and the Formation of the Hui Ethnic Group", *Journal of Ningxia University*, Issue 3, pp. 32–37. (马汝领," 再论伊斯兰教与回回民族形成的关系",《宁夏大学学报》, 1984年第 3 期, 32—37 页)

BIBLIOGRAPHY

Ma Tong, 1983, *A Brief History of Chinese Islamic Sect Menhuan System*, Ningxia People's Publishing House. (马通,《中国伊斯兰教派门宦制度史略》, 宁夏人民出版社, 1983 年)

Ma Tong, 1983, "*A Brief History of Chinese Islamic Sects and Menhuan System*", Ningxia People's Publishing House. (马通, 《中国伊斯兰教派与门宦制度史略》, 宁夏人民出版社, 1983 年)

Ma Tong, 1986, *Tracing the Origin of Chinese Islamic Sect Menhuan*, Ningxia People's Publishing House. (马通,《中国伊斯兰教派门宦溯源》, 宁夏人民出版社, 1986 年)

Ma Tong, 1987, "Review and Perspective on the Research of Islam in the Five Northwestern Provinces", *Ethno-National Studies in Gansu*, Vol. 2, pp. 1–5. (马通,"对西北 5 省(区)伊斯兰教研究的回顾与展望",《甘肃民族研究》, 1987 年第 2 期, 1-5 页)

Ma Tong, 2000, *Muslim Culture on the Silk Road*, Ningxia People's Publishing House. (马通,《丝绸之路上的穆斯林文化》, 宁夏人民出版社, 2000 年, 227 页)

Ma Yiyu, 1941, *A History of Chinese Islam*, Changsha Commercial Press, first edition; Shanghai Commercial Press, revised edition, 1948. (马以愚,《中国回教史鉴》, 长沙商务印书馆, 1941 年初版; 上海商务印书馆, 1948 年修订本)

Maris Boyd Gillette, 2000, *Between Mecca and Beijing: Modernization and Consumption Among Urban Chinese Muslims*, Stanford: Stanford University Press.

Marshall Broomhall, 1987, *Islam in China: a Neglected Problem*, London: DARF Publishers Limited.

Marshall Broomhall, 1911, "The Mohammedan Population of China", *The Moslem world*, Vol.1, p. 32.

Masayoshi Nomura, 1943, "Records of 23 Islamic Narratives Regarding the Moukyu", *Islamic Area Studies*, Vol.7, No.4, pp. 58–62. (野村正良 "蒙疆に於いて採録せる 23 の回教説話"《回教圏》第 7 券第 4 号, 1943, 58-62 页)

Matususaburo Dazai, 1924, *Mantetsu Chosa Shiryo (South Manchuria Railway Research Documents) Volume 26 – Research on Chinese Muslims*, Minamimanzu Railway Co.,

Ltd., General Affairs Department Research Division. （太宰松三郎《満鉄調査資料第 26 篇－－支那回教徒の研究》，南満洲鉄道株式会社　庶務部調査課，1924 年）

Mi Shoujiang, 2000, "A Brief History of Islam in China", Religious Culture Press.（米寿江，《中国伊斯兰教简史》，宗教文化出版社，2000 年）

Mian Weilin, 1997, *Introduction to the Islamic Religious System of the Hui People in China*, Ningxia People's Publishing House. （ 勉维霖，《中国回族伊斯兰宗教制度概论》，宁夏人民出版社，1997）

Michael Dillon, 1996, *China's Muslims* (Images of Asia), New York: Oxford University Press.

Mikinosuk Ishida, 1940, "Arabian Records on China", *The Islamic World*, Vol.2, No.8, pp. 47–56.（石田幹之助　"支那にかんするアラビアの記録 "《回教世界》大日本回教協会発行，第 2 巻第 8 号，47-56 頁）

Muhammad Abdul, 1934, *Islamic Philosophy*, Translated by Ma Jian, Published and distributed by the Commercial Press. （埃及）穆罕默德·阿布笃　著，马坚 译，《回教哲学》，商务印书馆出版发行，1934 年）

Muhammat Imin, 2007, *Arab - History of Islamic culture*, translated by Nazhong, Commercial Press. （（埃及）穆罕默德·艾敏 著，纳忠等 译，《阿拉伯——伊斯兰文化史》，商务印书馆，2007 年，共 8 册本）

Nan Wenyuan, 1991, "On the Leading Role of Islamic culture in the Formation of the Hui Nationality", *Hui Studies*, Issue 3, pp. 31–38.（南文渊，"论伊斯兰文化在回族形成中的主导作用"，《回族研究》，1991 年地 3 期，31－38 页）

Nazhong, Zhu Kai, 1993, *Tradition and Blending: Arab Culture*, People's Publishing House.（纳忠 朱凯 合著，《传统与交融：阿拉伯文化》，浙江人民出版社，1993 年）

Ningxia minority ancient books sorting and publishing plan, 2000, *Chinese Hui ancient books series*.（宁夏少数民族古籍整理出版规划小组，《中国回族古籍丛书》，2000 年）

BIBLIOGRAPHY

237

Ningxia minority ancient prose collation and publication plan, 1998, *The compilation of ancient books of Hui and Chinese Islam,* Tianjin Ancient Books Publishing. (宁夏少数民族古籍整理出版规划小组办公室，《回族和中国伊斯兰教古籍资料汇编》，1998 年)

Noboru Niida, 1944, "Muslim Merchants of Beijing and Friendly Relations", *Islamic Area Studies,* Vol.8, No.6, pp. 2–27. (仁井田陞 "北京の回教徒商工人とその仲間的結合"，《回教圈》第 8 卷第 6 号，1944 年，2-27 頁)

Norio Suzuki, 2004, "Review and Reflection on the Study of Islam in Japan" (Translation by Gao Mingjie), *The Journal of International Studies,* Quaternary Period, pp. 68–75.

Notes to the Koran by Ibn Kesir, 2005, written by Kong Dejun, China Social Sciences Press. (《伊本・凯西尔《古兰经》注》孔德军訳着，中国社会科学出版社，2005 年)

Philip Khuri Hitti (America), 1979, *General History of Arabia,* translated by Ma Jian, Commercial Press. ((美国) 菲利普・胡里・希提 著，马坚 译，《阿拉伯通史》，商务印书馆，1979 年)

Qin Huibin (editor), 1999, *Series of World Civilizations: Islamic Civilization,* China Social Sciences Press. (秦惠彬主编，《世界文明大系：伊斯兰文明》，中国社会科学出版社，1999 年, 436 页)

Qin Huibin, 1989, "The Development of Islam during the Five Dynasties Period", *World Religious Studies,* Issue 1. (秦惠彬，"伊斯兰教在 5 代时期的发展"，《世界宗教研究》，1989 年第 1 期)

Qin Huibin, 1995, *Islam and Traditional Culture in China,* China Social Sciences Press. (秦惠彬，《中国伊斯兰教与传统文化》，中国社会科学出版社，1995 年，136 页)

Qin Huibin, 1997, *"Islam in China",* Commercial Press. (秦惠彬，《中国的伊斯兰教》，商务印书馆，1997 年)

Qu Hong, 2001, *Contemporary Political Islam in the Middle East: Observations and Reflections,* China Social Sciences Press. (曲

洪，《当代中东政治伊斯兰：观察与思考》，中国社会科学出版社，2001 年，382 页）

Quran,1998, translated by Ma Jiang, China Social Science Publishing. (《古兰经》馬堅　訳本, 中国社会科学出版社，1981 年，493 頁）

Raphael Israeli, 1979, *Muslims in China: A Study in Cultural Confrontation*, London: Curzon Press.

Ren Yuji (edited), 1998, *religious dictionary*, Shanghai dictionary press. (任继愈 (主编)，《宗教大辞典》，上海辞书出版社, 1998 年)

Richard V. Weekes, 1978, *Muslim Peoples: A World Ethnographic Survey*, Greenwood Press: Westport, Connecticut.

Rokuro Kuwata, 1925, "Minmatsu Shinsho no Kaiju (Chinese Muslim scholars from the End of the Ming Period to the Early Qing Period)", Haku Doctor 60th Anniversary Memorial Oriental Paper, pp. 377–386. (桑田六郎　"明末清初の回儒"《白博士還暦記念東洋論冊》1925 年，377‐386 页）

Rudolf Loewenthal,1957, "Russian Materials on Islam in China: A Preliminary Bibliography", *Monumenta Serica Journal of Oriental Studies*, Vol.16, No.1/2, pp. 449–479.

Sha Zongping, 2004, *Arab-Islamic Studies in China*, Beijing University Publishing. (沙宗平，《中国的天方学》，北京大学出版社，2004 年）

Sha Zongping, 2002, "Maximizing the Cycle, Ending the End, and Returning to the Beginning: A Preliminary Exploration of the Philosophical Outlook of Liu Zhi, a Hui Thinker in the Early Qing Dynasty", *Hui Studies*, Issue 2, pp. 78–87. (沙宗平，"大化循环，尽终返始--清初回族思想家刘智哲学观初探"，《回族研究》，2002 年第 2 期，78-87 页）

Shuijingjun, 2002, "*History of Chinese Muslim Women's Temples*", Sanlian Bookstore (水镜君，《中国清真女寺史》，三聯书店,2002 年）

Shuizi Li, 1923, *A Brief History of World Islam*, Beiping Niujie Halal Book Newspaper, Reprinted in 1930. (水子立，《世界回教史略》，北平牛街清真书报社，1923 年，1930 年再版）

BIBLIOGRAPHY   239

Shumei Okawa, 1942, *Introduction to Islam*, Keio Library. (大川周明《回教概論》, 慶應書房, 1942 年, 167 頁)

Sun Zhenyu, 2006, *Critical biography of Wang Daiyu and Liu Zhi*, Nanjing University Press. (孙振玉,《王岱舆 刘智评传》, 南京大学出版社, 2006 年, 506 页)

The History of Ming Dynasty: Biography of the Western Regions (《明史 西域传》)

The Islamic Research Office of the World Religion Research Institute of the Chinese Academy of Social Sciences, 1991, *Aspects of Islamic Culture*, Qilu Press. (中国社会科学院世界宗教研究所伊斯兰教研究室合编,《伊斯兰教文化面面观》, 齐鲁出版社, 1991 年, 325 页)

The Quran (Annotations to the Quran), 2004, translated and introduced by Li Jingyuan, published by World Chinese Publishing House. (《古兰经注释》, 李静远（自英文版译介, 其子张承迁继其遗志）, 世界华人出版社, 2004 年)

The Toa Kenkyujo, 1943, *Reports of Research Projects on East Asian Peoples for the Years 1941 and 1942*, Center for East Asian Studies publish. (東亜研究所《昭和十六・七年度東亜諸民族調査事業報告》東亜研究所, 1943 年)

The translation of the Koran, 1946, translated by Wang Jingzhi, Shanghai Shuixiang Printing Library, reprinted by Dongfang Publishing House. (《古兰经译解》, 王静斋 訳本, 上海水祥印書館, 1946 年, 再版東方出版社, 2005 年, 872 頁)

Usuki Akira, 2002, "*A Legacy of Wartime Islamic Studies: As a Prototype of Islamic Area Studies in Post-war Japan*", Shiso, Vol. 941, pp. 191–204. (臼杵陽 "戦時下回教研究の遺産－戦後日本のイスラーム地域研究のプロトタイプとして "《思想》第941 号, 191－204 頁, 2002 年。)

Vasilij Pavlovich Vasil've, 1960, *Islam in China*, translated from the Russian by Rudolf Loewenthal, Central Asian Collectanea, No.3, Published by Washington, D.C, pp. 37.

Wan Yaobin, 2000, "Reflections on the Study of Islam in China in the New Century", *World Religious Studies*. (宛耀宾 等， "对新世纪中国伊斯兰教研究的思考"，《世界宗教研究》，2000 年)

Wang Fuping, 2007, "Hai Sifu's Contribution to Chinese Jingtangjiaoyu", *Hui Studies*, Issue 4, pp. 101–103. (王伏平， "海思福对中国经堂教育的贡献"《回族研究》，2007 年第 4 期，101－103 页)

Wang Huaide and Guo Baohua (co-authored), 1992, *History of Islam*, Ningxia People's Publishing House. (王怀德，郭宝华合著，《伊斯兰教史》，宁夏人民出版社，1992 年)

Wang Jiaying, 2003, *History of Islamic Religious Philosophy*, Ethnic Publishing House. (王家瑛，《伊斯兰宗教哲学史》，民族出版社，2003 年，1061 页)

Wang Junrong, 2006, *Unity of Heaven and Man, Truthfulness of Things and Me: A Preliminary Exploration of Ibn Arabi's Existentialism*, Religious Culture Press. (王俊荣，《天人合一，物我还真—伊本·阿拉比存在论初探》，宗教文化出版社，2006 年)

Wang Yizhou, 2002, *Tracing the Origin of Terrorism*, Social Science Literature Press, pp. 296. (王逸舟，《恐怖主义溯源》，社会科学文献出版社，2002 年，296 页)

Wang Yujie, 2006, *Religion and the State: A Study of Contemporary Islamic Shia*, Social Science Literature Press, pp. 335. (王宇洁，《宗教与国家：当代伊斯兰教什叶派研究》，社会科学文献出版社，2006 年，335 页)

Wang Yujie, 2006, *Islamic History of Iran*, Ningxia People's Publishing House. (王宇洁，《伊朗伊斯兰教史》，宁夏人民出版社，2006 年)

Wang Yujie, 2001, "The Trend of Political Islam in the 21st Century", *Research on World Religions*, Issue 1, pp. 19–25. (王宇潔， "21 世纪政治伊斯兰的走向"，《世界宗教研究》，2001 年第 1 期，19-25 页.)

Wu Bingbing, 2004, *The Rise of Shi'ite Modern Islamism*, China Social Sciences Press, pp. 370. (吴冰冰，《什叶派现代伊斯兰主义的兴起》，中国社会科学出版社，2004 年，370 页)

Wu Yandong, 2004, Commentary on Chinese Hui Thinkers, Religious Culture Press, pp. 214. (吴艳冬，《中国回族思想家评述》，宗教文化出版社，2004 年，214 页)

Wu Yiye (Edited), 1999, *Historical Manuscripts of the Hui and Islam in Nanjing*, Islamic Association of Nanjing. (伍贻业主编，《南京回族，伊斯兰教史稿》，南京市伊斯兰教协会，1999 年)

Wu Yiye, 1991, "Enlightenment and Reflection on Wang Daiyu to Liu Zhi: Islamic Thought in 17th Century China", *Research on the Hui Ethnic Group in China*, Issue 1. (吴贻业，"王岱舆到刘智的启示和反思—17世纪中国伊斯兰教思潮"，《中国回族研究》，1991 年第 1 期)

Wu Yungui and Zhou Xiefan (Co-authored), 2001, "*Islamic Thought and Movement in Modern Times*", Social Science Literature Press. (吴云贵，周燮藩合著，《近现代伊斯兰教思潮与运动》，社会科学文献出版社，2001 年)

Wu Yungui and Zhou Xiefan (co-authored), 2000, *Modern Islamic Thought and Movement*, Social Science Literature Press, pp. 391. (吴云贵，周燮藩合著《近代伊斯兰教思潮和运动》，社会科学文献出版社，2000 年，391 页)

Wu Yungui, 1994, *The Awakening of the Muslim Nation: Modern Islamic Movement*, China Social Sciences Press. (吴云贵，《穆斯林民族的觉醒：近代伊斯兰运动》，中国社会科学出版社，1994 年，118 页)

Wu Yungui, 1995, *Islamic Doctrine*, China Social Sciences Press. (吴云贵，《伊斯兰教教义学》，中国社会科学出版社，1995 年，138 页)

Wu Yungui, 1995, "*Islamic doctrine*", China Social Sciences Press. (吳雲貴，《伊斯兰教义学》，中国社会科学出版社, 1995)

Wu Yungui, 2003, *Contemporary Islamic Shariah*, China Social Sciences Press. (吴云贵，《当代伊斯兰教法》，中国社会科学出版社，2003 年)

Wu Yungui, 1993, *Dharma of Allah – Islamic Shariah*, China Social Sciences Press. (吴云贵，《真主的法度—伊斯兰教法》，中国社会科学出版社，1993 年)

Wu Yungui, Zhou Xiefan, Qin Huibin (editor), 1994, *Islamic culture Series* (12 sets), China Social Sciences Press.（吴云贵，周燮藩，秦惠彬 主编，《伊斯兰文化小丛书》（12 本套装），中国社会科学出版社，1994 年）

Wu Yungui,1996, "The Generality and Individuality of Islamic culture", *World Religious Culture*, Issue 5.（吴云贵， "伊斯兰文化的共性与个性"，《世界宗教文化》，1996 年第 5 期）

Xiao Xian and Gao Zhanfu, 2000, "Summary of Islamic Studies in China in the 20th Century", *Northwest Ethnic Studies*, Issue 2, pp. 26–32.（高占福， "中国 20 世纪伊斯兰教研究综述"，《西北民族研究》，2000 年第 2 期，26-32 页）

Xiao Xian, 1994, The Return of Tradition: Contemporary Islamic Revival Movement, China Social Sciences Press.（肖宪，《传统的回归：当代伊斯兰复兴运动》，中国社会科学出版社，1994 年，128 页）

Xiao Xian, 1997, *Contemporary International Islamic Tide*, World Knowledge Press.（肖宪，《当代国际伊斯兰潮》，世界知识出版社，1997 年）

Yang Guiping and Ma Xiaoying (co-authored), 2007, *Islam Changming*, Religious Culture Press.（杨桂萍，马晓英合著，《清真长明》，宗教文化出版社，2007 年）

Yang Guiping, 2004, *Research on Ma Dexin's Thought*, Religious Culture Press.（杨桂萍，《马德新思想研究》，宗教文化出版社，2004 年，pp. 225）

Yang Haocheng, Zhu Kerou, 2000, *Historical Exploration of Contemporary Middle East Hot Issues: Religion and Secularity*, People's Publishing House.（杨灏城，朱克柔 主编《当代中东热点问题的历史探索——宗教与世俗》，人民出版社，2000 年， 457 页）

Yang Huaizhong and Yu Zhengui (co-authored), 1995, *Islam and Chinese Culture*, Ningxia People's Publishing House.（杨怀中，余振贵（合著），《伊斯兰与中国文化》，宁夏人民出版社，1995年，633 页）

Yang Wenjiong, 2002, "Women's Education: The Expansion of Jingtangjiaoyu and the Shift of the Center of Gravity in

Cultural Communication", *Hui Studies*, Issue 1, pp. 25–33. (杨文炯, "女学：经堂教育的拓展与文化传播承角色的重心位移", 《回族研究》, 2002 年第 1 期, 25－33 页)

Yoshinobu Nakata, 1970, "Literature on the Hui People" ,in the Institute of *Asian Economic Affairs* "A Comprehensive Study of Modern Islam", Showa 44 Interim Report (II). (中田吉信 "回回民族に関する文献 " (アジア経済研究所所内資料《現代イスラームの総合研究》〔昭和 44 年度中間報告（II）〕所收, 1970 年。)

"*Yu Gong*" Journal, including two dedicated issues, "Islamic and Hui Special Account" (Volume 5, Issue 11, 1936) and the "Islamic Special Account" (Volume 7, Issue 4, 1937), which published over 40 papers.

Yu Zhengui, 1996, "*Chinese Political Power and Islam in Past Dynasties*", Ningxia People's Publishing House, (余振贵, 《中国历代政权与伊斯兰教》, 宁夏人民出版社, 1996 年)

Yu Zhengui, Yang Jinzhong,1993, *Summary of translation Chinese Islamic Literature*, Ningxia People's Publishing House. (余振贵, 杨怀中, 《中国伊斯兰教文献译著大要》, 寧夏人民出版社, 1993 年)

Yu Zhengui, Yang Yizhong, 1993, *Abstracts on the writing and translation of Chinese Islamic Literature*, Ningxia People's publishing house. (余振贵, 杨怀中, 《中国伊斯兰文献著译提要》, 1993 年)

Ze Masaki, 2012, "The Study of Chinese Muslims in Japan-Focusing on the Study of Hui Nationality after 1980" (Translated by Wang Rui), Religious Anthropology (Series III). Beijing: Social Science Literature Press, pp. 286–302.

Zhang Bingmin (edited)，2002 年, *Islamic Philosophy of Law*, Ningxia People's Publishing House, 2002. (张秉民 主编《伊斯兰教法哲学》, 宁夏人民出版社, 389 页)

Zhang Bingmin, 2007, *A Concise History of Islamic Philosophy*, Ningxia People's Publishing House. (张秉民主编, 《简明伊斯兰哲学史》, 宁夏人民出版社, 2007 年, 363 页)

Zhang Juling, 2000, "Commentary and Review on Islamic Studies of the Hui Ethnic Group in China in the Early 20th Century", *Hui Studies*. (张巨龄，"20 世纪初中国回族伊斯兰研究述补及评"，《回族研究》，2000 年 2 月)

Zhang Ming, 1999, *Islamic Revival Movement in the Perspective of Modernization*, Chinese Social Science Press. (张铭，《现代化视野中的伊斯兰复兴运动》，中国社会科学出版，1999 年，315 页)

Zhang Wende, 2002, *History of Sufism in Central Asia*, China Social Sciences Press. (张文德，《中亚苏菲主义史》，中国社会科学出版社，2002 年)

Zhang Xueqiang, 2002, *History of Northwest Hui Education*, Gansu Education Press, (张学强，《西北回族教育史》，甘肃教育出版社，2002 年)

Zhao Can, 1989, *Genealogy of Classics Department*, People's Publishing House, Qinghai ((清) 赵灿，《经学系传谱》，青海人民出版社，1989 年)

Zhou Chuanbin, 2005, "Stones from Other Mountains: A Review of Western Studies on Chinese Hui Islam", *Northwest Ethnic Studies*, Issue 1, pp. 97–118. (周传斌，"他山之石—西方学界对中国回族伊斯兰教的研究述评"，《西北民族研究》，2005 年第 1 期，97-118 页)

Zhou Xiefan and Li Lin, 2011, "Islamic studies" ,recorded in Zhuo Xinping (edit), *Research on Contemporary Religion in China*, China Social Sciences Press. (周燮藩 李林，"伊斯兰教研究"，载入卓新平主编《当代中国宗教学研究》，中国社会科学出版社，2011 年)

Zhou Xiefan and Li Lin, 2008, "Islamic studies", recorded in Zhuo Xinping, *Thirty Years of Religion in China Studies (1978–2008)*, China Social Sciences Press. (周燮藩 李林，"伊斯兰教研究"，载入卓新平主编《中国宗教学 30 年（1978-2008）》，中国社会科学出版社，2008 年)

Zhou Xiefan, 2012, *The Way of Sufei: A Study of Islamic Mysticism*, China Social Sciences Press. (周燮藩，《苏非之道：伊斯兰教神秘主义研究》，中国社会科学出版社, 2012 年, 472 页)

Zhou xiefan, 2006, "Preface to the halal ceremony", *research on world religions*, Vol.2, pp. 147–148. (周燮藩，"清真大典前言"，《世界宗教研究》，2006 年第 2 期，147-148 页)

"Qingzhen Dadian", 2006, was recorded in *"the Integration of Chinese religious history documents"*, Huangshan publishing house. (《清真大典》，隶属于《中国宗教历史文献集成》，黄山书社，2006 年）

Milton Keynes UK
Ingram Content Group UK Ltd.
UKHW051258200624
444506UK00007B/65